THE REASONABLY COMPLETE SYSTEMIC SUPERVISOR RESOURCE GUIDE

Cheryl L. Storm, Editor
Pacific Lutheran University

Thomas C. Todd, Editor
Adler School of Professional Psychology

D1157546

Authors Choice Press
New York   Lincoln   Shanghai

The Reasonably Complete Systemic Supervisor Resource Guide

Authors Choice Press
an imprint of iUniverse, Inc.

For information address:
iUniverse
2021 Pine Lake Road, Suite 100
Lincoln, NE 68512
www.iuniverse.com

Originally published by Allyn and Bacon

ISBN: 0-595-26137-X

Printed in the United States of America

Table of Contents

INTRODUCTION

Our Dream: A User Friendly Guide

I. CONTEXT: MULTIPLE PERSPECTIVES

II. PHILOSOPHY: PREFERRED IDEAS, VALUES, & BELIEFS

IV. PRAGMATICS: METHODS & INTERVENTIONS

V. TRAINING SUPERVISORS: TEACHING & SUPERVISING

INTRODUCTION

Our Dream: A User Friendly Guide

From the initial inception of *The Complete Systemic Supervisor: Context, Philosophy, & Pragmatics*, we always imagined a resource guide to accompany it. We knew many supervisors conducted supervision outside of academic institutions, making usual academic resources difficult to obtain. Like the chapter authors, we often thought of additional materials which were too specific to include in the chapters but which could be of great practical value to supervisors.

We wanted the additional material in the resource guide to be much more inviting than a dry collection of appendices. To this end Cheryl (with amazingly extensive assistance from her husband John) has sought to give the selections eye appeal and consistently interesting layout. Hundreds of hours later we hope you will agree that we have achieved this objective!

The sections of the resource guide have been laid out to be parallel to the corresponding parts of the book. Material selected was chosen to represent a wide variety of supervisory orientations and to present a stimulating collection of diverse offerings. We have prodded chapter authors and supervisors we know, asking them to provide brief materials which can be immediately useful to supervisors. These can include training exercises, handouts, supervision forms and instruments, research highlights, and condensed reprints of supervision articles.

Supervisory Challenges

Throughout the book we have introduced sections with brief "supervisory challenges". In each area we have sought to identify unanswered questions to stretch the reader to grapple with issues which have no easy answers. You are challenged to find your own answers and to discuss them with fellow supervisors.

Pointers

In the table of contents we have included "pointers" to tell you how you can use the material to enhance your work as a supervisor. For example, the first pointer, "Knowing the Guidelines" under the section *Practicing Ethically Sensitive Supervision*, tells you that the two contributions will help you be knowledgeable about ethical guidelines.

Icons

Icons (see below) are inserted throughout the resource guide to help you find certain types of material at a glance -- exercises for you to do or to use with your supervisees, forms that can enhance your supervision practice, instruments that can be used for various types of assessment, or available readings and tapes.

The clipboard of forms highlights written documents you can use to enhance your practice. You can freely adapt and reproduce the material for your supervisory use.

The exerciser indicates an activity that you can do by yourself or with your supervisees to gain understanding of a specific topic via experiential learning.

Reading lists related to the section topics are identified by the book icon. The reading list is not intended to be comprehensive, but rather to include diverse readings that we have found very helpful on the topic.

The cup of pens and pencils indicates an instrument that you can use to assess some aspect of supervision.

This tape icon highlights audio- and videotapes that are available on the topic. You can obtain the tapes by calling the source noted in the resource lists. Their numbers are: Resource Link (800) 241-7785, the American Association for Marriage and Family Therapy (202) 223-2329, or the Milton H. Erickson Foundation, Inc. (602) 956-6196.

CONTRIBUTORS

Brent J. Atkinson, PhD, Associate Professor, Marriage & Family Therapy (MFT) Program, Northern Illinois University, DeKalb, IL.

Lois Dennett, BA, Masters Student, MFT Program, Pacific Lutheran University, Tacoma, WA.

Patricia M. Dwyer, DMin, Adjunct Faculty, LaSalle University, Philadelphia, PA.

Steve Engleberg, JD, Senior Vice-president, Monsanto Company, Washington, DC.

Mona DeKoven Fishbane, PhD, Faculty, Chicago Center for Family Health, Chicago, IL.

Marshall Fine, EdD, Associate Professor, MFT Program, University of Guelph, Ontario, Canada.

Karen Gautney, MS, Deputy Executive Director, Washington, DC.

Kenneth V. Hardy, PhD, Professor, MFT Program, Syracuse University, Syracuse, NY.

Ingeborg E. Haug, DMin, Assistant Professor, MFT Program, Fairfield University, Fairfeild, CT.

Susan H. Horwitz, MS, Assistant Professor, Division of Family Programs, University of Rochester, Rochester, NY.

David Ivey, PhD, Assistent Professor, MFT Program, Texas Tech University, Lubbock, TX.

Bruce Kahl, PhD, Private Practice, Merrick, NY.

Jay Lappin, MSW, Director, CENTRA, Philadelphia, PA.

Tracey Laszloffy, Doctoral Student, MFT Program, Syracuse University, Syracuse, NY.

John Lawless, MS, Doctoral Student, MFT Program, University of Georgia, Athens, GA.

Pieter le Roux, DLitt et Phil, Clinical Associate Professor, Family Medicine & Pediatrics, University of Rochester, Rochester, NY.

Janie Long, PhD, Assistant Professor, MFT Program, University of Georgia, Athens, GA.

Susan H. McDaniel, PhD, Professor, Division of Family Programs, University of Rochester, Rochester, NY.

Teresa McDowell, MA, Clinical Faculty Supervisor, MFT Program, Pacific Lutheran University, Tacoma, WA.

Fred P. Piercy, PhD, Professor, MFT Program, Purdue University, West Lafayette, IN.

Carla Pond, MA, Private Practice, Millford, CT.

Layne Prest, PhD, Assistant Professor, Department of Family Medicine, University of Nebraska Medical Center, Omaha, NE.

Anne Hearon Rambo, PhD, Associate Professor, MFT Program, Nova Southeastern University, Fort Lauderdale, FL.

Debby L. Schwarz Hirschhorn, MS, Doctoral Student, MFT Program, Nova Southeastern University, Fort Lauderdale, FL.

Sandra Rigazio-DiGilio, PhD, Associate Professor, MFT Program, University of Connecticut, Storrs, CT.

Jane Hill Riley, PhD, Acting Director, Annie Tran Center, Prosser, WA.

Lee Shilts, PhD, Associate Professor, MFT Program, Nova Southeastern University, Fort Lauderdale, FL.

Keith Schrag, MDiv, Private Practice, Ames, IA.

Douglas H. Sprenkle, PhD, Professor, MFT Program, Purdue University, West Lafayette, IN.

Carol Stanley, MA, Executive Director, Valley Counseling Associates, Renton, WA.

Betsy Sullivan, BA, Masters student. Pacific Lutheran University, Tacoma, WA.

Jean Turner, PhD, Assistant Professor, MFT Program, University of Guelph, Ontario, Canada.

Fred Wegener, MDiv, MS, Therapist & Director of Training, Northwest Pastoral Counseling, Tacoma, WA.

Lee Williams, PhD, Assistant Professor, Marriage, Child, & Family Counseling Program, University of San Diego, San Diego, CA.

Arnold Woodruff, MA, Director, Juvenile Mental Health Services, Alexandria, VA.

Charles D. York, PhD, Associate Professor, MFT Program, Pacific Lutheran University, Tacoma, WA.

Toni Schindler Zimmerman, PhD, Assistant Professor, MFT Program, Colorado State University, Fort Collins, CO.

D. Blake Woodside, MD, Director of the Eating Disorder Inpatient Unit, Toronto Hospital, Toronto, Canada.

I. CONTEXT: MULTIPLE PERSPECTIVES

Supervisory Challenge 1:
Practicing Ethically Sensitive Supervision

How confident are you that your colleagues, whether experienced or beginners, behave ethically? Do you believe that other therapists, either in agencies or private practice, are tempted to cut ethical corners?

Taking on the role of supervisor introduces new ethical challenges, as the chapter on ethics illustrates. Acting as a supervisor introduces another level of complexity that is rarely discussed: By virtue of being at the top of a supervisory pyramid, supervisors often hear a great deal about the therapeutic and supervisory practices of other colleagues not present in the supervisory hour, as well as a variety of agency policies and practices as they impact on clinical cases of supervisees.

At one extreme, supervisors may be quick to believe a colleague may have engaged in questionable or outright unethical practices. Such supervisors may need to remind themselves that they have not observed this behavior first-hand and have often obtained such "data" filtered through the lenses of a comparatively inexperienced supervisee. Ethical standards of all the mental health professions caution a professional to proceed cautiously and to check out information directly rather than presuming guilt.

It can also be tempting to go to the opposite extreme: Instead of taking action, the supervisor rationalizes that a senior colleague could not really be guilty of unethical practice. Supervisees get the message that their perceptions must be naive and inaccurate, or they are left to deal with what they view as questionable practices with little support or direction from the supervisor.

While none of us would like to believe that we overreact or underreact to unethical behavior, to which extreme are you more likely to gravitate? Are there particular "hot button" issues where your ethical judgment would be less objective? Do you have a clear and systematic plan of action when you hear of possible unethical behavior on the part of another helping professional?

Supervisory Ethics and Standards of Practice

Ingeborg E. Haug

Matt Stiller and Kathy Lopez are both part-time employees at a Family Service Agency. Matt has a masters of social work degree and just graduated from a post-degree program in marriage and family therapy, and Kathy is a pastoral counselor. Both maintain a small private practice. They make a joint appointment with you to arrange for supervision of their private cases. In your first meeting you explore Matt and Kathy's professional training and experience as well as their expectations for supervision. You find out that Matt hopes to accumulate supervision hours toward his social work license as well as toward membership in the American Association for Marriage and Family Therapy. Kathy is working toward fellow status in the American Association for Pastoral Counselors, an advanced membership level.

As you reflect on Kathy and Matt's different needs, you realize that you, like many supervisors, are not clear on the various mental health professions' standards and ethics guiding supervisory practices. What credentials are required of you as a supervisor to provide supervision acceptable to the various professional groups? What standards are applicable concerning fulfillment of your threefold supervisory responsibilities, namely to protect clients' welfare, to mentor supervisees in their professional development, and to protect the interests of the profession and the public at large? Where are the resources you might consult for information?

Mental health service providers and supervisors are accountable to the codes of ethics adopted and published by their respective professional organizations, namely (in alphabetical order according to the organizations' acronyms): The American Association for Marriage and Family Therapy (AAMFT), The American Association for Pastoral Counseling (AAPC), The American Counseling Association (ACA), The American Psychological Association (APA), and the National Association of Social Workers (NASW). In addition to their ethics codes, AAMFT, ACA through its founding division, the Association for Counselor Education and Supervision (ACES), and NASW publish separate documents

2

explicitly detailing standards of clinical and/or supervisory practices. All of these documents are periodically reviewed and revised to incorporate new insights or emphasis and to reflect the accumulated wisdom of the respective disciplines. Ethically informed supervisors are expected to stay informed of these changes in codes and supervisory guidelines.

While not the focus of this chapter, supervisors need to be equally aware that ethical and professional standards of supervisory practice are also determined by legal regulations in those states which license or certify mental health providers. State regulations might differ not only from organizations' codes but also vary from state to state. Some states, for instance, do not permit supervisees to directly reimburse their supervisors for supervision toward licensure. Supervisors' knowledge of these and other requirements is crucial for the integrity of the supervision process. In preparation for Matt's supervision, you will therefore want to review your state's stipulations for social work licensure.

Membership and Continuing Education Supervision Requirements

Supervision occurs during graduate training, and post–degree in order to fulfill entry–level and/or advanced level membership requirements of the various professional organizations, to maintain clinical competence, and to satisfy continuing education or licensing stipulations. AAMFT and AAPC are the only professional organizations which base entry level full membership on the fulfillment of specific post degree clinical and supervision requirements rather than solely on the acquisition of a qualifying degree. Some mental health organizations require further clinical hours and supervision for advanced credentials such as, for example, "Diplomate" standing in AAPC or NASW. None of the mental health disciplines require ongoing supervision of its members, although all recommend it in various degrees of specificity.

Supervisor Credentials and Supervisory Activity

Since Matt and Kathy want to accumulate supervision hours to satisfy requirements in their respective professions, you as their supervisor need to meet specific criteria and conduct supervision in prescribed ways. While the various professions differ in who they deem to be qualified supervisors, there is considerable agreement in how supervisory roles and activities are defined.

SUPERVISOR'S CREDENTIALS & ACTIVITY GRID

Organization	Supervisor Credentials	Supervisory Role & Activity
AAMFT	Most specific	Very well defined
AAPC	Very specific	Not specifically addressed
ACA/ACES	Less specific	Very well defined
APA	Doctoral degree + state license	Minimally defined
NASW	More specific	Very well defined for Clinical Social Workers

AAMFT is the only discipline with a supervisory designation distinct from clinical membership levels (i.e., AAMFT Approved Supervisor). AAMFT requires supervisors to complete specific, rigorous didactic and clinical supervision training and to submit to a review process of their competencies. Supervisor status must be renewed. AAPC is the only other mental health profession requiring specific supervisory experience which members have to document in order to reach the diplomate level of membership and be able to supervise independently.

AAMFT, ACA/ACES, and NASW all are very explicit in defining supervisory roles and activity, including differentiating between supervision and consultation (ACES, APA, NASW) and between supervision and training

4

(NASW), delineating the context, setting, and frequency of supervision, its focus (AAMFT: "raw data"; NASW: "priority is client care"), and its conduct (NASW: "interactive process" and establishing "learning plans"). In addition, NASW also specifically addresses accountability and liability issues while AAMFT clarifies its definition of individual supervision and group supervision.

AAPC and ACA are the only professional organizations which credit supervision received from interdisciplinary sources toward the fulfillment of membership requirements. AAMFT has established policies for the rare exceptions when it will grant alternate supervisor status to supervisors from other disciplines. Since you are an AAMFT Approved Supervisor but not a social worker, Matt would therefore not be able to count the supervisory hours toward the advanced NASW credentials.

NASW provides the most explicit guidelines for record keeping. To protect all parties involved, supervisors and supervisees should document the dates of contact, issues and recommendations discussed, and progress toward agreed upon learning goals. Client records need to reflect "the client's knowledge that supervision is taking place, the nature of information that is being shared, (and) verification that the client has the name, address, and phone number of the supervisor" (NASW, 1994, p. 10).

Responsibility to Clients

Supervisors often wonder about the level of responsibility they incur with regard to the client services their supervisees render. Particularly in live supervision, supervisors are continually faced with choosing responses which balance the needs of their supervisees' clients and those of supervisees' professional development. AAMFT, ACES, and NASW clearly advise that the major emphasis of supervision ought to be on the quality of client services, including protecting clients' autonomy and confidentiality. "In a reciprocal dialogue, the supervisor provides oversight, guidance, and direction in assessing, diagnosing, and treating clients" (NASW, 1994, p. 2) and identifies "practices posing a danger to the health and welfare of the supervisee's clients or to the public" (NASW, 1994, p. 14). AAMFT's legal counsel reminds supervisors that they carry legal responsibility for their supervisees' clients as well (Brown, personal conversation, May 1996).

SUPERVISOR'S RESPONSIBILITY TO CLIENTS

Organization	Client Care	Client Informed Consent	Client Confidentiality
AAMFT	Major focus of supervision	Not specifically addressed	Not specifically addressed
AAPC	Not specifically addressed	Not specifically addressed	Only client's first name used in supervision
ACA/ACES	Major focus of supervision	Clients informed + give specific permission for information to be used in supervision	Clients informed re limits of confidentiality due to supervision, protection of records
APA	Not specifically addressed	Clients informed fully including name of supervisor	No identification of clients without their consent
NASW	Major focus of supervision	Clients informed of supervisor's name & phone number	Clients informed re supervision & nature of information shared

NASW is the most specific of all professions in stipulating that supervisors address boundary issues which may arise between supervisees and clients and "provide special assistance in dealing with all feelings, including sexual feelings" that may occur in the client-therapist relationship (NASW, 1994, p.12).

The most controversial issue will most likely be the degree of specificity of information regarding supervision to which clients are entitled. While AAMFT and AAPC do not specifically address this, the grid on the previous page summarizes the information the other organizations require. The stipulation by NASW that your supervisees give their clients your name and telephone number makes you understandably reluctant to accept Matt and Kathy as supervisees. What if all twelve of their private clients were to contact you with emergencies, complaints, and so on?

Responsibility to Supervisees

In order to maximize clarity and minimize confusion, most professions advise supervisors to form explicit, even written, agreements with supervisees concerning the policies and procedures governing their professional relationship. (See "Supervisee Informed Consent" column in the grid on the next page regarding the degree the various professional organizations address agreements.) To refresh your memory, you review NASW's and AAMFT's guidelines of the topics to be included in a supervision contract: supervisory context, format and schedule, learning plan, supervisor responsibilities, accountability, evaluation measures, documentation and reporting, conflict resolution, compensation, client notification, and duration and termination (NASW, 1994). AAMFT advises that contracts also include policies regarding clinical emergencies. In addition, NASW and APA admonish supervisors to "treat the supervisee with respect and regard" (National Association of Social Workers, 1989 p.13) and to "avoid engaging in conduct that is personally demeaning to...supervisees" (American Psychological Association, 1992, Code 6.03).

Responsibility to the Profession and Public at Large

In order to maintain quality control, AAMFT, ACA/ACES, and NASW require that supervisors screen potential supervisees' qualifying degree, knowledge base, and skill level prior to accepting them. ACA/ACES and NASW address supervisees' incompetence, impairment, or unethical conduct and advise supervisors to take action through appropriate channels and to assist supervisees' remediation. Continuing education for supervisors is required by AAMFT, recommended by ACA/ACES and NASW, but not specifically addressed by AAPC

RESPONSIBILITY TO SUPERVISEES GRID

Organization	Supervisee Informed Consent	Supervisee Confidentiality	Supervisee Competence	Supervisee Evaluations & Endorsements
AAMFT	Explicit, detailed supervision agreements	Clearly articulated limits to confidentiality	Do not permit supervisee to function outside level of competence	Periodic reviews, concerns shared with supervisee in writing
AAPC	Not specifically addressed	Not specifically addressed	Do not permit unsubstantiated claims of competence	Not specifically addressed
ACA (ACES)	Explicit, detailed supervision agreements	Less explicit, inform supervisee of ramifications of self-disclosure	Not specifically addressed	Ongoing verbal and written feedback, no endorsements if not qualified
APA	Less explicit, informed about services beforehand	Not specifically addressed	Do not permit supervisee to function outside level of competence	Establish process of feedback and evaluations
NASW	Explicit, detailed supervision agreements	Clarify limits to confidentiality	Not specifically addressed	Fair evaluations, based on objective criteria shared with supervisee

or APA. AAMFT recommends that supervisors offer pro bono services and states that supervisory standing does not constitute advanced clinical status. ACA/ACES stipulates that supervisors not recruit supervisees from places of employment or promote products or training events to supervisees.

Conclusion

To inform yourself in more detail about the various professions' standards of ethical and professional supervisory practice and to request the pertinant documents, you can consult the professional associations on the next page.

American Association for Marriage and Family Therapy (AAMFT) (1991). *AAMFT code of ethics*. Washington, DC: Author.

AAMFT (1993). *AAMFT Approved Supervisor designation: Standards and responsibilities*. Washington, DC: Author.

American Association of Pastoral Counselors (1994). *Code of ethics*. Fairfax, VA: Author.

American Counseling Association (1995). *Code of ethics and standards of practice*. Alexandria, VA: Author.

Association for Counselor Education and Supervision (1993). *Ethical guidelines for counseling supervisors*. Alexandria, VA: Author.

American Psychological Association (1992). *Ethical principles of psychologists and code of conduct*. Washington, DC: Author.

National Association of Social Workers (NASW) (1993). *Code of ethics of the NASW*. Washington, DC: Author.

NASW (1989). *NASW standards for the practice of clinical social work*. Washington, DC: Author.

NASW (1994). *Guidelines for clinical social work supervision*. Washington, DC: Author.

ping Abreast of Standards of Supervision Practice

org E. Haug

American Association for Marriage & Family Therapy (AAMFT)

> *AAMFT Code of Ethics*

> *AAMFT Approved Supervisor Designation: Standards & Responsibilities*

AAMFT at 1133 15th Street, NW, Suite 300; Washington, DC 20005
Phone number: (202) 452–0109; fax number: (202) 223–2329

American Association of Pastoral Counselors   (AAPC)

> *Code of Ethics*

> *Bylaws*

AAPC at 9504 A Lee Highway, Fairfax, VA 22031
Phone number: (703) 385–6967; fax number: (703) 352–7725

**American Counseling Association (ACA) &
Association for Counselor Education & Supervision (ACES)**

> *American Counseling Association Code of Ethics & Standards of Practice*

> *Ethical Guidelines for Counseling Supervisors*

ACA at 5999 Stevenson Avenue, Alexandria, VA 22304
Phone number: (703) 823–9800; fax number: (703) 823–0252

American Psychological Association (APA)

> *Ethical Principles of Psychologists and Code of Conduct*

APA at 750 First Street, NE; Washington, DC 20002
Phone number: (202) 336–5500; fax number: (202) 336–5907

National Association of Social Work (NASW)

> *Code of Ethics of the NASW*

> *NASW Standards for the Practice of Clinical Social Work*

> *NASW Guidelines for Clinical Social Work Supervision*

NASW at 750 First Street, NE, Suite 700, Washington, DC 20002
Phone number: (202) 408–8600 or (800) 638–8799; fax number: (202) 336–8310

Informed Consent Form

Brent J. Atkinson

Different family therapy supervisors often have vastly different expectations of therapists in supervision. Therapists-in-training also vary widely in their expectations of supervisors. I believe that the task of matching the right supervisors with the right therapists is one that is often not given enough consideration. Frequently, therapists and supervisors do not fully realize that they have different expectations of each other before beginning supervision. Sometimes this works out all right -- expectations are negotiated as they go along. Sometimes, however, this lack of clarity results in considerable wasted time at best and feelings of disappointment, betrayal, or exploitation at worst. Supervision which involves a focus on the person of the therapist can be especially complex and confusing. I believe that the issues involved in such supervision should be discussed carefully before supervision begins. Supervisors can begin by stating their preferences and assumptions at the outset.[1] During the past six years, I have attempted to initiate meaningful discussion about expectations in supervision through an informed consent document. This document has evolved continuously over the years -- below is the latest revision. Feel free to use any sections that you feel might apply well to your own supervision.[2]

Notes

[1] I also believe that therapists have the responsibility to state their preferences and expectations to clients in therapy (see: Atkinson, 1992; Atkinson & Heath, 1990).

[2] If you intend to publish any material that you use from this informed consent, please reference appropriately.

Atkinson, B. (1992). Aesthetics and pragmatics of family therapy revisited. *Journal of Marital and Family Therapy, 18*, 389-393.

Atkinson, B., & Heath, A. (1990). Further thoughts on second-order family therapy (This time it's personal). *Family Process, 29*, 145-155.

INFORMED CONSENT FOR SUPERVISION

Assumptions about Supervision

I believe that supervision is most useful when the focus of supervision moves back and forth between the professional and personal functioning of the therapist. Professional aspects include learning how to apply theory and technique to the practice of assessment, interviewing, case planning, and so on. It involves knowing what to do next, where and how to direct therapy, what to give attention to, and what to ignore.

The personal functioning of the therapist is much more complex, involving automatic internal and interpersonal processes that are not always under the therapist's conscious control. Indeed, therapists' reactions to clients are often so automatic that therapists may not even be aware of them. I have come to believe that the effectiveness of each therapist is determined largely by the extent to which they are successful in becoming aware of these reactions, listening to them, learning from them, and helping them change when change is needed.

As a supervisor, I observe therapists interacting with clients and help them identify automatic interpersonal and internal reactions that occur regularly. As therapists refine awareness of reactions set in motion during therapy sessions, they also generally choose to explore them during supervision. Often, this involves accessing and attending to these reactions directly during the supervision hour. Thus, a portion of supervision becomes a context for practicing the art of listening to, accepting, receiving suggestions from, and eliciting cooperation from aspects of oneself that sometimes operate at a tacit level. As supervision progresses, therapists generally experience greater sensitivity to the nuances of their reactions to clients, a greater ability to use this information effectively in therapy, and a greater sense of internal harmony as they become more skilled in exploring and calming uncomfortable aspects of their experience with clients. Sometimes therapists are interested in discussing aspects of their personal histories or present circumstances in supervision, particularly if it occurs to them that some of the reactions they are having with clients parallel the ones they are having (or have had) in their own lives. Therapists are never pressured to discuss such information, but often choose to do so as they seek to give attention to automatic processes that operate in their relationships with clients.[1]

While supervision that focuses on the personal functioning of the therapist is sometimes therapeutic, it is not therapy, and should not substitute for therapy when therapy is needed. When is therapy needed? Each therapist in training must decide this for him/herself. However, when distress in a therapist's personal life is impairing the therapist's clinical work, I will strongly encourage the therapist to seek therapy. Unlike personal therapy, the primary concern of person-of-the-therapist supervision is improvement of one's performance as a therapist. Even when therapists experience profound changes during supervision, the ultimate goal is not complete until these changes are used as resources for their work with clients.

To better understand my approach as a supervisor, I encourage students to read about Aponte's "person/practice" model of supervision (Aponte, 1994). I share many of Aponte's assumptions about supervision. It is often helpful for therapists to know that I prefer to keep relationships with therapists limited to the professional context. Finally, I want therapists to know that I treat information that arises during supervision, as well as information about the supervisory process, as confidential, with the normal exceptions (information regarding potential harm, court-ordered information), and one additional exception: Family Center supervisors sometimes consult with each other regarding the supervision of Family Center therapists. Formal written evaluations are also treated as confidential, with some possible exceptions (see Evaluation section).

Risks of "Person-of-the-Therapist" Supervision

In the first few weeks of supervision, we will discuss your level of comfort with person-of-the-therapist aspects of supervision. It is common to feel some apprehension about working with a supervisor on one's internal process. One of the reasons often has to do with the fact that part of a supervisor's responsibility is to evaluate you at various points during supervision. There is sometimes a natural reluctance to disclose one's internal experience with someone who has organizational authority over you.[2] There is a possibility that your supervisor could become biased and/or use personal information against you in an evaluation. Conversely, you may feel that your supervisor's evaluation was biased by personal information, even if the supervisor made every effort to be honest and objective. There is also a risk of psychological distress if you disclose aspects of your internal experience with your supervisor, then feel judged, rejected, disapproved of, or betrayed by this person who you have come to trust and respect.

Several considerations often help ease this apprehension. First, supervisor bias and reactivity are possible in any type of supervision. I believe that the risks are most minimal with supervisors who place a high priority on maintaining awareness of their reactions to therapists during supervision, and attending to these reactions when they arise rather than letting them simmer beneath the surface. The risks are higher with supervisors who are less attentive to their internal reactions during supervision. As a supervisor, I consider awareness of my reactions to be the most important aspect of my work. However, I don't expect therapists to take my word for it. The person-of-the-therapist portion of supervision is entirely optional, and I will do only the amount of it that therapists feel comfortable with. I encourage therapists to wait to work on person-of-the-therapist issues until they are confident that (a) I have a strong committment to maintaining awareness of my own reactions during supervision, and would be able to recognize and be willing to acknowledge any reactions that were more extreme than a situation warranted, (b) I really care about their well-being and have their best interest at heart, and (c) I would be receptive if they expressed discomfort with anything that I said or did in supervision.

Second, I never push therapists to explore aspects of their experience that (a) they don't think are important to explore, or (b) they don't feel ready to explore. I encourage therapists to operate according to their own sense of what is right for them, not my sense. Finally, I have an open policy regarding inviting in a third party to supervision meetings. If a therapist should ever feel too uncomfortable to talk with me about an issue one-on-one, or feel unsuccessful in attempting to do so, I would encourage the therapist to bring another person with him/her -- someone with whom the therapist could feel safe. This could be another supervisor, a colleague, or whoever the therapist would like.

Evaluation

For the sake of saving space, I have omitted this section, which contains specific information regarding the avenues and specific criteria for evaluation, as well as information regarding how written evaluations will be used, where they will be stored, and who may have access to them. Please contact me if you would like a copy of this section.

Choice of Supervision

Although I believe that any therapist-in-training could benefit from the kind of supervision outlined in this paper, I don't assume that every therapist will feel comfortable enough with the supervisory process described here to begin. In fact, one of the purposes of this paper is to help therapists assess their level of comfort with the process I have proposed. If you are hesitant to begin supervision as described in the first section of this paper, let's talk it over and see if we can come to an agreement about what might work. For example, you might be comfortable using supervision as a context for identifying automatic internal and interpersonal reactions to clients, but uncomfortable with accessing and working directly with these reactions during supervision. I am flexible about supervision (within a certain range), and am optimistic that we can work something out. If we simply cannot come to an agreement, we will meet with the other clinical supervisors, discuss the situation, and decide what to do from there.

___ I understand the assumptions and policies outlined in this paper, and I am
    interested in beginning supervision with my supervisor as described here.

___ I understand the assumptions and policies outlined in this paper, and I am
    interested in beginning supervision with as described here, with the following
    modifications:
_____

___ I would like to discuss a substantially different supervision contract.

_____
 Signature / Date

Notes
1 See Aponte (1994), Kantor & Mitchell (1992), Storm (1993), and Tomm (1993) for discussion on the relation between personal therapy and person-of-the-therapist supervision.

2 This is true of any relationship which can be described as hierarchical (see: Atkinson, 1993).

Aponte, H. (1994). How personal can training get? *Journal of Marital and Family Therapy, 20,* 3-15.

Atkinson, B. (1993). Hierarchy: The imbalance of risk. *Family Process, 32,* 167-170.

Kantor, D., & Mitchell, E. (1992). Letter to the editor. *Supervision Bulletin, 2,* 4 & 7.

Storm, C. (1991). Changing the line: An interview with Edwin Friedman. *Supervision Bulletin, 7,* 1 & 2.

Tomm, K. (1993). Defining supervision and therapy: A fuzzy boundary? *Supervision Bulletin, 6,* 2.

A Packet of Supervision Forms

Patricia M. Dwyer

"The supervisor's responsibility [is] to keep such records or documents which could be used to explain in a systematic manner the intentions and events of a supervisory relationship" (Bridge & Bascue, 1990, p. 81). The following forms are offered as examples of ways you can fulfill these responsibilities. They have been designed to be printed on supervisors' or agencies' stationary. It is important that names, addresses, phone numbers, and professional association affiliations of supervisors are clearly stated on each form. Forms can easily be adapted to practicum or agency needs.

[1]The **SUPERVISION RECORD** and the **SUPERVISION OF SUPERVISION RECORD** forms are the documentation of supervisors' systematic manner of crediting the work or spotting the problems of supervisees and of supervisors-in-training.

The **SUPERVISION LOG** is a form that can be attached to the back of the front file folder. This information makes it easier for supervisors to keep an accurate record of the percentage of report and raw data supervision hours. It also makes it easier for supervisors to complete supervision report forms.

The **CLINICAL REPORT FORM** is to help supervisees keep track of all the supervision they receive during their training. This form can be redesigned to summarize and validate the total number of clinical and supervision hours for end of semesters, practica, or training. It was designed after a colleague's supervisor died suddenly. My colleague's only proof of the number of supervision sessions he had were his canceled checks. I have also known supervisors who moved out of the area or to another state leaving supervisees floundering for documentation of their supervision. Smart supervisors may want to keep a copy for their records.

The **SUPERVISEE'S AGREEMENT OF CONFIDENTIALITY** and the **SUPERVISOR-IN-TRAINING AGREEMENT OF CONFIDENTIALITY** is designed to draw both supervisors' and supervisees' attention to the importance of confidentiality. You may find this form helpful in training programs and agencies where supervisees and supervisors-in-training need to become more conscious of the boundaries of confidentiality.

And finally, the **PERMISSION TO TAPE AND PRESENT IN SUPERVISION** is designed to inform clients and supervisees of their rights, the limits of the use of their tapes and information, and to raise supervisees' awareness of the importance of confidentiality. This form can easily be altered to permit the presentation of supervision sessions in training programs and in supervision courses.

When these forms or a version of these forms are used, supervisees and supervisors have a written record of their supervision. If problems arise, there is a "paper trail" that will enhance the fair treatment of clients, therapists, supervisors, and supervisors of supervisors.

Note

[1] This form was first designed by Bridge and Bascue (1990) and later expanded by Bridge and Dwyer.

Bridge, P., & Bascue, L. (1990). Documentation of psychotherapy supervision. *Psychotherapy in private practice, 8,* 79-86.

ANOTHER SOURCE OF USEFUL FORMS

FORMS BOOK

Professional Forms for Marriage and Family Therapists

American Association for Marriage and Family Therapy

Call (202) 452-0109 for More Information

SUPERVISION RECORD

Name _____ Session # _____ Date:_____

Liability: Dangerous clients of supervisee: _____

_____ to themselves _____ to others	
_____ family warned	_____ Date
_____ authorities warned	_____ Date
_____ hospitalization	_____ Date
_____ Critical Incident Report filed	_____ Date
_____ Agency supervisor informed __ Phone __ In person	_____ Date

Action(s) taken by supervisee:_____

_____

_____

Case # _____ ___ Open ___ Cont ___ Closed ___ Permission ___Genogram
                                                      on File   on File

Supervisee's concern(s)

_____

_____

Supervisee's Activity	*Supervisor's Activity*
1. Supporting documentation	1. Actions mandated by supervisor:
a. Audio/visual	_____
b. Live	_____
c. Report	_____
2. Presenting issues of the client:	2. Date completed by supervisee:
_____	_____
_____	3. Observation of therapeutic
_____	interventions:
_____	_____
3. Actions of the therapists:	_____
_____	_____
_____	_____
_____	_____
_____	_____
4. Self awareness of therapist:	4. Comments and Training
_____	recommendations:
_____	_____
_____	_____
_____	_____
_____	_____

_____
Supervisor's Signature

Developed by P. Dwyer.

SUPERVISION-OF-SUPERVISION RECORD

Supervisor-in-training Name _____ Session # _____ Date: _____

Liability: Dangerous clients of supervisee
_____ To themselves:
_____ To others:
_____ Family members warned:
_____ Authorities notified:
_____ Critical Incident Report filed

Liability: Dangerous clients of supervisor
_____ To themselves:
_____ To others:
_____ Family members warned:
_____ Authorities notified:
_____ Critical Incident Report filed

Action(s) taken by supervisee:
_____
_____

Action(s) taken by supervisor-in-training:
_____
_____

Case # _____ _____ Open _____ Cont _____ Close _____ Permission _____ Permission
                                                    of client on file   of supervisee
                                                                          on file

Supervisor's-in-training concern(s):
_____
_____

Supervisor's-in-training Activity
1. Supporting documents
    a. Audiovisual
    b. Live
    2. Therapists issues:
_____
_____
_____
_____

3. Supervisor's interventions:
_____
_____
_____
_____
_____

4. Supervisor's-in-training self awareness:
_____
_____

Supervisor's Activity
1. Activity(s) mandated by supervisor:
_____
2. Date action completed by supervisor
   designate:
_____
3. Date action completed by supervisee:
_____
4. Observation of supervisory intervention:
_____
_____
_____
_____

5. Recommendations:
_____
_____
_____

Supervisor's Signature

Developed by P. Bridge, L. Bascue, & P. Dwyer.
Copyright © 1997 by Allyn and Bacon

19

SUPERVISION LOG

Supervisee: _____

Date Began: _____   Date Ended:_____

Number Hours Case Presentaation: ____
Number Hours Audio/Video/Live: ____

Number Hours Individual Therapy: ____
Number Hours Couples Therapy: ____
Number Hours Family Therapy: ____

Date of Payment	Report	Audio/ Video/ Live	Group	Individual/ Pair	Evaluation

_____   _____
Signature Supervisor   Date

CLINICAL REPORT FORM

Clinical Hours

Month:_____

Agency:_____

Number of Clients
_____ Individuals
_____ Families
_____ Couples

_____
Signature of Administrative Supervisor

Supervision Hours

INDIVIDUAL SUPERVISOR:_____

Hours This Month _____

_____
Signature of Supervisor

_____
_____

GROUP SUPERVISOR _____

Hours This Month:_____

_____
Signature of Supervisor

Developed by P. Dwyer.

SUPERVISEE'S AGREEMENT OF CONFIDENTIALITY

I, _____, hereby agree to maintain the confidentiality of my clients and the clients of my fellow supervisees.

My fellow supervisees are as follows:

Name of Supervisee	Agency	Agency's Phone Number

I will not reveal identifying data when presenting cases in supervision.

I will transport notes in the following manner:
1. Genograms with no identifying data.
2. Minimal information needed for supervision.
3. I WILL NOT TAKE CASE NOTES FROM THE CLINIC SITE.

I will transport audio/video tapes in the following manner:
1. Only my name and the client's file number will appear on the tapes.
2. Tapes will be in my possession at all times.
3. I will tape over, erase, or destroy the tapes following supervision.

I will not discuss any case with anyone unless I have a signed Permission to Tape and Present in Supervision form. I will not discuss cases with anyone except my supervisor, my supervision group, my site supervisor(s), or persons so designated on my agency's confidentiality form. This restriction includes my family, friends, colleagues, supervisors, faculty, referral sources, administrators, or students.

I understand that if I breach this Code of Confidentiality it may result in the undersigned supervisor terminating the supervision contract and reporting this brreach to the agency and Ethics Committee of any and all professional organizations to which I belong.

This agreement is valid from this date of execution to the termination of supervision with the undersigned supervisor.

Date:_____

_____
Signature of Supervisee

_____
Signature of Supervisor

Developed by P. Dwyer.

SUPERVISOR-IN-TRAINING AGREEMENT
OF CONFIDENTIALITY

I, _____, agree to maintain the confidentiality of my supervisees and the supervisees of my supervision-of-supervision partner.

Name of supervision-of-supervision partner: _____

I will not reveal identifying data when presenting cases in supervision-of-supervision.

I will transport case notes in the following manner:

      1. Only my name and the supervisee's file number will appear on the tapes.
      2. Tapes will be in my possession at all times.
      3. I will tape over, erase or destroy the tapes following supervision-of-supervision.

I will not discuss any case with anyone unless I have a signed Permission to Present in Supervision-of-Supervision form with the last name of my supervisee(s) blotted out.

I will not discuss my supervisees or their clients with anyone except my supervisor-of-supervision, my supervision-of-supervision partner, my site supervisor(s), or persons so designated on the confidentiality forms of the agencies I am employed at or are in placement with. This restriction includes my family, friends, colleagues, supervisors, faculty, referral sources, administrators, or students.

I understand that if I breach this code of confidentiality it may result in the undersigned supervisor terminating the supervision-of-supervision contract and reporting this breach to the agency and Ethics Committee of any and all professional organizations to which I belong.

This agreement is valid from this date of execution to the termination of supervision-of-supervision with the undersigned supervisor.

Date:_____

_____
Signature of Supervisor-in-training

_____
Signature of Supervisor-of-Supervision

Developed by P. Dwyer.
Copyright © 1997 by Allyn and Bacon

23

PERMISSION TO TAPE AND PRESENT IN SUPERVISION

I, _____, give permission to _____ to audio/video tape and present my case material for the purpose of supervision from this date _____ to _____.

I understand that any information given regarding my case be limited to my therapist, his/her supervision group, and/or his/her supervisor.

I understand that those parties who may have my case material presented to them or will hear or view tapes of my sessions have signed an Agreement of Confidentality and are bound by that agreement with the undersigned supervisor. Any breach of that confidentiality may necessitate their immediate dismissal from supervision and the notification of the agency and the Ethics Committee of any and all professional organizations to which they belong.

I understand that the original copy of this permission form will remain in the agency's file and my therapist will present a copy of this permission form to his/her supervisor with my last name blotted out.

I agree to the stipulations as they are stated in this agreement:

_____

_____

_____
Signature of Client

I agree to the stipulations as they are stated in this agreement with the following exceptions or additions:

_____

_____

_____
Signature of Client

_____
Signature of Therapist

_____
Signature of Supervisor

Date _____

Developed by P. Dwyer.

Resources For Practicing Ethically Sensitive Supervision

American Association for Marriage and Family Therapy (AAMFT) (1996). *AAMFT code of ethics*. Washington, DC: Author.

AAMFT (1993). *AAMFT Approved Supervisor designation: Standards and responsibilities*. Washington, DC: Author.

> ***In a survey about the practices of marriage and family therapists, over half of the respondents reported never providing therapy to a supervisee, another one-fourth said they did so rarely, while the remainder did so at least sometimes.***

Brock, G., & Coufal, J. (1994). A national survey of the ethical practices and attitudes of marriage and family therapists. In G. Brock (Ed.), *Ethics casebook* (pp. 27-48). Washington DC: American Association for Marriage and Family Therapy.

Cormier, L., & Bernard, J. (1982). Ethical and legal responsibilities of clinical supervisors. *Personnel and Guidance Journal, 60*, 486-490.

Douglas, M., & Rave, E. (1990). Ethics of feminist supervision of psychotherapy. In H. Lerman, & N. Porter, (Eds.), *Feminist ethics in psychotherapy* (pp. 137-146). New York: Springer.

Engelberg, S., & Heath, A. (1990). Legal liability in supervision. *Supervision Bulletin, 3*, 2- 4.

Engleberg, S., & Storm, C. (1990). Supervising defensively: Advice from legal counsel. *Supervision Bulletin, 3*, 2 & 4.

Heath, A. (1989). Let's provide pro bono supervision. *Family Therapy News, 20*, 5.

Huber, C., & Baruth, L. (1987). *Ethical, legal, and professional issues in the practice of marriage and family therapy*. New York: Merrill.

Kaiser, T. L. (1992). The supervisory relationship: An identification of the primary elements in the relationship and an application of two theories of ethical relationships. *Journal of Marital and Family Therapy, 18*, 283-296.

Kapp, M. (1984). Supervising professional trainees: Legal implications for mental health institutions and practitioners. *Hospital and Community Psychiatry, 35*, 143-147.

Minnes, P. (1987). Ethical issues in supervision. *Canadian Psychology, 28,* 285-290.

Munson, C. (1984). Uses and abuses of family-of-origin material in family therapy supervision. In C. Munson (Ed.), *Family-of-origin applications in clinical supervision* (pp. 61-70). New York: Haworth Press.

Ratliff, N. (1994). Responsibility to students, employees, and supervisees. In G. Brock (Ed.), *Ethics casebook* (pp. 79-84). Washington DC: AAMFT.

Slovenko, R. (1980). Legal issues in psychotherapy supervision. In A. Hess (Eds.), *Psychotherapy supervision* (pp. 453-473). New York: John Wiley & Sons.

Stewart, K., & Amundson, J. (1995). The ethical postmodernist: Or not everything is relative all at once. *Journal of Systemic Therapies, 14,* 70-78.

Tanenbaum, R., & Berman, M. (1990). Ethical and legal issues in psychotherapy supervision. *Psychotherapy in Private Practice, 8,* 65-77.

Upchurch, D. (1985). Ethical standards and the supervisory process. *Counselor Education and Supervision, 25,* 90-98.

Vesper, J., & Brock, G. (1991). *Ethics, legalities, professional practice issues in marriage and family therapy.* Boston: Allyn & Bacon.

Panel. *Where to draw the line?* (Video #534). Washington, DC: AAMFT.

Panel. *Dual relationships in supervision.* (Video #565). Washington, DC: AAMFT.

Dwyer, P., & Bridge, P. *Document supervision: Contracts, progress, & evaluation.* (Audio #703-334). Norcross, VA: The Resource Link.

Huber, C., & Peterson, C. *MFT supervision: Evaluating & managing criticsl issues.* (Audio #705-318). Norcross, VA: The Resource Link.

Peterson, C. *MFT supervision: Evaluating & managing dual relationships.* (Audio # 706-615). Norcross, VA: The Resource Link.

Supervisory Challenge 2:
Practicing Contextually Sensitive Supervision

One supervisor, whose community was slowly changing from an affluent, homogeneous Caucasian population to a multicultural and diverse socioeconomic one, was stunned when an upper-class, Caucasian supervisee said "I can't work with these new families in our community. They dress funny and they smell." A supervisor described her struggles in refraining from sugar coating her responses to her male supervisees. Another supervisor described a situation where a minority supervisee was not being asked by his peers to be a cotherapist or participant on therapy teams even though he consistently volunteered to do so. Because his training setting emphasized these experiences as critical to learning family therapy, the supervisee believed he had the right to have the same educational opportunities as his peers. Still another supervisor recounted a supervision session where a well intentioned supervisee delivered a directive that instructed a female client to relinquish her access to the financial resources of the family in exchange for more love from her husband.

Many of the situations uncovered emotional reactions from the supervisors as well as their supervisees. What were your reactions? Did you identify with the supervisor or even the supervisee? Did you become angry at the supervisee and want to boot him/her out of the profession? Did you immediately know what to do? Or, were you unsure of your response?

In order to exhibit sensitivity to all supervisory participants, a supervisor would clearly need to respond to each of these situations. However, supervisors often have difficulty deciding what the appropriate supervisory response should be. What would your response be if you were facing these situations? How would you check your own contextual sensitivity? Finally, how would you meet your responsibility of helping your supervisees become more contextually sensitive? You may want to review the suggestions made by authors in the Context section of the text before formulating your answers.

Fostering Respect for Differences

Both sets of exercises which follow are ideally suited for marriage and family therapy (MFT) classes in preparation for supervised practice. While they can be adapted for supervision, especially group supervision, they are most stimulating when conducted and processed in a group setting. These are detailed examples of the practices to promote sensitivity to context described in chapter 10.

The first exercise is intended to give supervisees the experience of having a familiar story, such as a fairy tale, shift dramatically when retold from a different perspective or with a different connotation. Particular exercises can be chosen to highlight a specific issue, such as the impact of the medical model, or comparing gender perspectives. By implication, supervisees can understand the narrowness of viewing their clinical cases from one perspective. If a more explicit bridge to clinical cases seems desirable, similar story transforming exercises can be created.

The second exercise can provide a rich cultural experience when used with a large group of clinical supervisees. The hypothetical families that have been incorporated were intended to represent some of the myriad of possibilities in South Florida. Particular characteristics should be changed to be representative of ethnic/cultural diversity in the areas where supervisees will be practicing.

Much of the value of the exercises derives from the experience of being immersed in the day to day reality of a family from a radically different background, such as actually looking for a dwelling or finding a suitable grocery store. If these issues are merely discussed, rather than experienced, supervisees typically minimize differences and express the belief that they are "culturally sensitive." While the value of comparing cultural notes is lost outside a group setting, it is possible for you to use similar cross cultural "homework" to increase a supervisee's understanding of a particular culture.

1. Story Transforming Exercise

Anne Hearon Rambo & Lee Shilts

First,
- Retell the Cinderella story, or any familiar fairy tale, to someone else, and make your telling interesting and original enough to hold that person's attention for at least ten minutes.

Then,
- Find someone else and retell the story again, this time from the stepmother's or someone else's point of view.

- Write up Cinderella's story as a case history, using medical Terminology and a DSM-IVR diagnosis.

- Find someone else and retell the story again, this time from the perspective of the village as a whole. How does it feel to be governed by someone who selects his future consort on the basis of her shoe size? What implications does this have for the larger context? What cultural assumptions may we infer?

Now, retell the story with a shift in connotation.
- Tell the story from the perspective of the "wicked" stepmother. What if the whole thing is a historical frame job? What if it's the stepmother who was the wronged innocent? Who wrote this fairy tale anyway?

- Tell the story from the perspective of the prince. How does it feel to be a plot device? Did he live happily ever after, too? How come downtrodden young boys, as opposed to girls, never get rescued by fairy godmothers?

Finally, retell the story from a different point in time.
- Tell the story as a prequel, that is before the problem occurred. What was the situation like ten years before the fairy godmother arrived on the scene, when Cinderella was a young child first welcoming her new stepmother?

- Tell the story as a sequel, that is after the problem has been resolved. Imagine life for Cinderella and her prince ten years after the wedding; the stepmother is long gone, there are three princelets, the glass slippers don't fit anymore...

- Tell the story as if it is occurring in the 1990's.

- Tell the story as if it is occurring in prehistoric times. Cinderella and her prince are cave people.

29

2. Shadow Family Exercise

Anne Hearon Rambo & Lee Shilts

Following are descriptions of five hypothetical families, representative of a cross section of South Florida life. These families are NOT designed to reflect prevailing stereotypes, nor to counter them, and they cannot provide a complete cross section of the wealth of ethnic/cultural diversity in South Florida. The families were simply drawn from the supervisors' clinical experiences, and designed to illustrate an interesting variety of life situations. The names and specific identifying details are fictitious, but not unlikely; the salaries for each occupation were verified by a phone survey and current classified advertising in this area. You can ask supervisees to select a family group as different from their own background as possible. Because the exercise can be done with one to five supervisees per group, you can use this exercise in small or large group supervision formats. Once having selected a family group, the supervisees should complete the following exercises over time, recording and discussing their experiences.

Each family group should locate a dwelling, either to rent or own. Determine the price of this dwelling (do not neglect security deposit, and so on) and your family budget (including food, utilities, and so on), and the location of the dwelling. Include a snapshot of the dwelling as well. In addition, the group should have the name of a grocery store, which carries the following items:

- for the Morgans: fresh (not frozen) bagels,
- for the Avilas: vino secor para cocinar, and plantains,
- for the Desvarieux: yucca and plantains,
- for the Manns: a kosher food section, and
- for the Taylors: RC cola and moon pies.

Include a photo of the grocery store. How much does a gallon of milk cost in the grocery store you located? Would you predict that grocery store prices are more or less expensive in affluent areas? Why? (Note: it often comes as a surprise to supervisees that grocery prices are more expensive in low income areas, where consumers have fewer options and less mobility to price shop).

THE FAMILIES

The Morgan Family

Janet and Bob Morgan have recently moved to South Florida from New York City. The move was prompted by Bob's promotion to a higher position within his company. Janet is a legal secretary, and was able to find a commensurate position. Janet earns $26,000 a year, and Bob earns $65,000 a year. Both have college degrees. Bob also has an M.B.A. Both are of African American descent. Bob was active in the civil rights movement and feels strongly that the family should not allow their newfound affluence to disconnect them from their heritage; Janet, however, is looking forward to the ability affluence brings to live someplace safe with good schools, and is less concerned with the possibility that they may move into a neighborhood in which their ethnic heritage will make them a minority. They attend the Methodist Church. Bob is 40 and Janet is 36. They expect their first child in October.

The Avila Family

Lourdes and Andres Avila emigrated to the United States from Cuba three years ago. At that time, they were able to obtain immediate citizenship. Andres is employed as a security guard. In his native country, he was a high school teacher, and he attends school during the day to obtain his teaching certificate for this country. Lourdes baby-sits the children of neighbors, and does sewing at home. Her income brings in enough to cover Andres' tuition and books, but they rely primarily on his salary of $7 an hour. Most weeks he is able to work 40 to 50 hours. Both have high school degrees from their native country, and Andres has a university degree. Both speak Spanish and English, but Lourdes' English is at present quite limited. They are practicing Catholics. Lourdes is 19 and Andres is 29. They expect their first child in October.

The Desvarieux Family

Marie and Jeanbart Desvarieux emigrated to the U.S. from Haiti six months ago. They have not yet been able to obtain legal citizenship status. Marie and Jeanbart work together in their home and office cleaning business. They work as many hours as they can, six to seven days a week, and are thus able to average an income of $250 a week. They are both fluent in Creole and English. Their formal education was limited, owing to wartime conditions in Haiti. Jeanbart suffers from recurring nightmares about his torture at the hands of military police in Port au Prince. Marie and Jeanbart are practicing Catholics. They are both 22. They expect their first child in October.

The Mann Family

Judy and David Mann retired to South Florida from Long Island, New York, 10 years ago. They have been living in a condominium complex for those 55 and older. (Judy is 55, and David 60.) Now, however, their family has expanded. Jennifer, their 30 year old daughter, has moved back in with them. Jennifer is a computer programmer who earns $25,000 a year. She has a B.S. in computer science. The Manns have a total retirement income of about $25,000 a year. Jennifer has never been married. She is expecting her first child in October, and refuses to discuss the father of her child with her parents. She has told her parents she wants to keep and raise her child as a single mother, and her parents, though shocked and troubled, have agreed to help her. The Manns are Jewish, and are members of a Conservative synagogue. They are of European American descent.

The Taylor Family

Ruby and Jonah Taylor were both born and raised in South Florida. Ruby is a waitress at a local pancake restaurant; Jonah is a skilled cabinetmaker. Ruby earns approximately $15,000 a year, including tips; Jonah earns $7.50 an hour and works a 40 hour week. Ruby is 21 and Jonah is 19. They both graduated from high school. They are of European American descent. They attend a charismatic Pentecostal church at which there is occasional speaking in tongues. Jonah is an elder (or deacon) in this church. They expect their first child in October.

CONGRATULATIONS! For the purposes of this exercise, we will assume that Ellen Morgan, Lourdes Avila, and Marie Desvarieux give birth to healthy baby girls, and Jennifer Mann and Ruby Taylor give birth to healthy baby boys. Each family group should choose a name for their newborn child, and explain this decision to the larger supervision group. Consider both ethnic/cultural tradition, and pressure towards assimilation. Once the name is chosen, each family group will hold a naming ceremony. Be prepared to describe this ceremony to the larger group, and attend a similar ceremony in real life if possible. The Morgans will have their baby baptized in the Methodist Church; the Avilas and the Desvarieux will have their babies christened in the Catholic church; the Manns will hold a bris; and the Taylors will consult the pastor of their Pentecostal church to learn their position on infant baptism and their church's preferred ritual.

Next, each group should come in prepared to discuss child care arrangements for the new baby. This decision should include a revised budget. If seeking care outside the home, price your options and visit them. The day care center or family day home chosen should be photographed.

Quicker than you may realize, your babies are babies no more, and it is time to consider their education. Visit your neighborhood elementary school, and evaluate its services. Price the alternative private and/or parochial schools. Choose a school, and be prepared to discuss this. A photo of your child's school should be included.

Your family group's child has now come of age. Come prepared to describe the coming of age ceremony you arrange for your child. The Morgans arrange a formal debut through an African American sorority; the Avilas hold a quinceanara; the Desvarieux have a party for their child's First Communion; the Manns have a bar mitzvah; and the Taylors' child becomes born again at a church revival. Explain and describe these ceremonies, and arrange to attend a similar ceremony in real life.

The Cultural Genogram: An Application

Kenneth V. Hardy & Tracey Laszloffy

How do I help my supervisees, especially non-minorities, talk about cultural issues in supervision and therapy? How important is it for supervisees to explore their cultural identities before they can deal effectively with cultural issues with their clients? And, how do I assist my supervisees in transferring the exploration of cultural issues in supervision to their work as therapists? Questions such as these are recurring queries for many supervisors as they struggle with finding concrete ways to facilitate the integration of cultural issues into clinical supervision.

The cultural genogram is a tool that you can use to explore culture in the context of supervision and ultimately therapy. The cultural genogram process promotes cultural awareness and sensitivity by helping supervisees to understand their cultural identities. Through this process supervisees gain greater insight into, and appreciation for, the ways in which culture impacts their personal and professional lives, as well as the lives of their clients. Due to limitations of space, we discuss the cultural genogram within the context of team supervision only.

The cultural genogram process is divided into three stages: 1.) preparation and construction, 2.) presentation and interpretation, and 3.) synthesis. For a detailed discussion of the stages and steps of the cultural genogram process, the reader is referred to Hardy & Laszloffy (1995).

Stage One: Preparation and Construction

During this stage, supervisees are required/encouraged to research their culture-of-origin and prepare a cultural genogram that will be presented in supervision. A copy of "How to Prepare a Cultural Genogram" (Figure 1) should be available to supervisees to help facilitate completion of this stage. This document outlines each step in stage one, and defines all essential terminology.

HOW TO PREPARE A CULTURAL GENOGRAM

Culture-Of-Origin:
We define culture-of-origin as the group(s) from which an individual has descended over several generations.

Identify the groups that comprise your culture-of-origin. Research each group you have identified as part of your culture-of-origin. Your research should culminate in the creation of a Cultural Framework Chart(s).

Cultural Framework Chart (CFC):
A CFC is comprised of organizing principles, pride/shame issues, and pride/shame symbols.

Create one chart for each group that comprises your culture-of-origin.
Each chart should consist of the following:

Organizing Principles:
These are fundamental constructs which shape perceptions, beliefs, and behaviors of members of a group. These should be listed in the chart.

Pride/Shame Issues:
These originate and derive their meaning from organizing principles. They are aspects of a culture that are sanctioned as distinctly positive or negative. These should be listed on the chart.

Symbols:
These are used to visually depict each pride/shame issue. They should be placed directly on the chart beside each corresponding pride/shame issue.

Genogram:
The genogram is a graphic depiction of one's family-of-origin. Through the use of colors and the placement of pride/shame symbols, the genogram reveals the cultural identities of each individual, as well as occurrence of specific pride/shame issues throughout the family system.

Construct at least a three generation genogram of your family-of-origin.
The following should appear on the genogram:

Colors:
Select a color to represent each group in your culture-of-origin. Next, color-code the circles and squares on the genogram accordingly to depict the cultural identities of each individual.

Pride/Shame Symbols:
Place the symbols on the genogram to identify where various pride/shame issues are manifest.

Stage Two: Presentation and Interpretation

This stage involves the presentation of the cultural genogram. During the presentation, the supervisee begins by presenting the Cultural Framework Chart(s) (CFC) s/he has constructed for her/his culture-of-origin. Specifically, the supervisee briefly introduces and explains each of the organizing principles and pride/shame issues on her/his chart(s). When referring to each pride/shame issue, the supervisee should make corresponding references to the genogram as a way of demonstrating where each of the issues is manifest in her/his family. Thus the CFC(s) and the genogram are presented in a complementary and integrated manner.

Following the presentation, the supervisee should have the opportunity to respond to observations or questions that might have been generated for the supervisor and/or members of the supervision team. The purpose here is to identify significant culturally-based patterns, themes, or dynamics that might emerge for the supervisee, and for members of the supervision team as well.

It is helpful to have a designated facilitator during the actual presentation. Depending upon your theoretical orientation, you may prefer to assume the role of facilitator, assign it to another supervisee, or encourage the team to select one. Regardless of the methodology employed for selecting a facilitator, you are ultimately responsible for the supervision session. However, the individual(s) functioning as the facilitator actually directs the cultural genogram process.

The role of facilitator during the presentation process involves guiding the interaction between the presenting supervisee and the team. In this way, the facilitator remains "meta" to the process and helps to facilitate in a way that challenges and supports all members' exploration of their culturally-based beliefs, suppositions, and assumptions. In other words, this is not a linear process whereby only the presenting supervisee is challenged to think and learn about her/himself culturally. Rather, the process is intended to be interactive and systemic such that all members of the group are encouraged to identify and explore their culturally-based beliefs, suppositions, and assumptions.

The presenting supervisee, Alan, began by defining his culture-of-origin as German. He presented his CFC for German culture and explained each organizing principle. Next Alan described each German pride issue and referred to his genogram to demonstrate where each of these were manifest in his family system. However, with regard to German shame issues, Alan had drawn a picture of a grayish "blob" which he said depicted a generalized but unidentifiable kind of shame that's "just sort of all around but it can't be linked to anything in particular."

Members of the observing team asked Alan what his theory was about, why he was so adept at defining pride issues and yet was so inept at identifying shame issues? Alan suspected it was because he had not devoted enough time to preparing his genogram. However, one supervisee, Elana, explained to Alan that she believed the Holocaust constituted a significant German shame issue, and as a Jew, she felt offended that he had failed to acknowledge this. Alan became sullen and said, "But what do you want me to do about that? I often feel like you want something from me but I don't know what. It makes it really hard for me to be around you." Elana answered by saying, "For starters what I want from you is for you to own the shameful parts of who you are....I often feel this sense of anger toward you that I've never understood, but now I realize it's because I've always seen you as trying to show how perfect you are and you never own the ugly parts of yourself...and culturally-speaking, that really threatens me."

In this example, the cultural genogram process was a catalyst for promoting an exchange between two supervisees who were struggling with culturally-based issues. Alan, with regard to his German ancestry, was struggling with his shame, and Elana, in relation to her Jewish identity, was struggling with her fear and anger regarding the Holocaust. The cultural legacies of Germans and Jews in relation to the Holocaust linked and yet divided both individuals; although it had been between them for months, it had never been acknowledged. The facilitator used this interaction to help the two supervisees consider the implications their cultural legacies had in supervision and on their work as therapists.

The most critical dimension of this stage of the process involves helping supervisees make connections between their cultural legacies and identities, and their roles as members of the supervision team and as therapists. Thus, they shouldbe encouraged to consider the ways in which their cultural selves shape how they interact in supervision and therapy.

Critical Tasks for Facilitators

There are several critical tasks for the facilitator to consider during the cultural genogram process. In situations where you assume the role of the facilitator, you therefore incur direct responsibility for attending to these tasks. When another member of the team assumes the role of the facilitator, you incur indirect responsibility for these tasks in the sense that you observe, and/or if deemed necessary, assist the facilitator.

First, it is important for you to be alert to helping supervisees distinguish between their family-of-origin and culture-of-origin. It is common for supervisees to blur the two, however, since the purpose of the exercise is to focus on cultural issues, it is important to keep family-of-origin and culture-of-origin clearly differentiated. Second, it is useful for you to attend to shame issues closely. Supervisees often struggle with identifying, and discussing shame issues because of the pain and discomfort this typically generates. Moreover, how supervisees respond to and communicate shame issues also may have cultural underpinnings. Relatedly, it is helpful for you to be sensitive to culturally-based reasons for the differences in how supervisees respond to and participate in the process. While differences may be attributable to family-of-origin variables, there also may be cultural explanations for particular differences.

It is further recommended that you manage your anxiety and reactivity. The degree to which you have explored your culturally-based pride/shame issues will enhance your ability to manage your anxiety and reactivity effectively with supervisees. Moreover, it is critical that you help supervisees to stay with the emotional intensity that often is generated during a cultural genogram presentation. Supervisors who have dealt with their cultural selves are better positioned to help supervisees work through their cultural issues.

Stage Three: Synthesis

In the third and final stage of the cultural genogram process, the presenting supervisee synthesizes what s/he has learned about her/himself culturally. Specific emphasis should be placed upon requiring the supervisee to explore the implications for their role as therapist. It is ultimately your responsibility to help supervisees make critical connections between what they discover during the cultural genogram process and therapy.

Summary

The preparation, presentation, and synthesis of a cultural genogram can be quite useful in helping supervisees and supervisors negotiate the cultural dimensions of supervision and ultimately therapy. When used effectively in supervision, the cultural genogram process can give direction to all those pragmatic, "how to" questions that often are asked regarding the integration and exploration of culture in supervision and therapy.

Hardy, K., & Laszloffy, T. (1995). The cultural genogram: A key to training culturally competent family therapists. *Journal of Marital and Family Therapy, 21*, 227-237.

Beginning Reading List on Sexual Orientation:
One Supervisor's Favorites

Janie Long

Blumfield, W. (Ed.). (1992). *Homophobia: How we all pay the price.* Boston: Beacon Press.

Dworkin, S., & Gutierrez, F. (Eds.). (1992). *Counseling gay men and lesbians: Journey to the end of the rainbow.* Alexandria, VA: American Counseling Association.

Greene, B., & Herek, G. (1994). *Lesbian and gay psychology: Theory, research, and clinical applications.* Thousand Oaks, CA: Sage.

Klein, K. (1993). *The bisexual option.* (2nd ed.). New York: Hayworth Press.

Weston, K. (1991). *Families we choose: Lesbians, gays, and kinship.* New York: Columbia University Press.

These references are only a starting point. The Gay/Lesbian/Bisexual Caucus of the American Association for Marriage and Family Therapy maintains an extensive reading list of books often used by therapists working with gays, lesbians, or bisexual individuals, couples, and families. For further information contact: Gene Ritter, Gainesville Family Institute, 1031 NW 6th St.-Building.C, Gainesville, FL 32601, (904) 376-5543.

Professional Groups and Organizations

The Gay/Lesbian/Bisexual Caucus
of the American Association for Marriage & Family Therapy

Committee on Lesbian and Gay Concerns
of the American Psychological Association

P-FLAG -- A support group for parents & friends
of sexual minorities with local chapters across the country

Straight But Not Narrow
Heterosexuals who support sexual minorities & their issues

What If They Ask Me If I'm Married?
A Supervisee's View

Karen Gautney

I remember the first day of our marriage and family therapy (MFT) practicum. It was finally time to practice and we were pretty nervous. My classmates asked one of those practical questions every therapist thinks about at some point, "What if they ask me if I'm married?" For her and many other students, it was a matter of credibility. "Will they respect me if they think I'm too young or if I don't have children?"

For me, the question of whether I was married held a different meaning. As a lesbian, I had thought extensively about how to answer the question from friends, colleagues, anyone. Now, I could expect to hear it from a client. Technically, I could not be legally married to my life partner. But a flat out "no" did not acknowledge that I was in a long term relationship like many of my married clients. If I completely acknowledged m y relational status, how would clients react? Would this self-disclosure inflict my own agenda on clients? On the other hand, if I did not disclose that I was in a lesbian relationship, would my silence give the message that homosexuality is something to hide and be ashamed of?

As I began to see clients, I confronted several other challenging situations around the issue of sexual orientation. As I had expected, I

Disclosing Homosexuality:
A Supervisor's View

Keith Schrag

As an openly gay supervisor, I believe it is important that I disclose my sexual orientation to my supervisees. Although some people consider this a "private" matter, I wholeheartedly disagree. It is not a personal statement as much as it is a professional and political statement.

In our culture heterosexuality is the accepted and approved way of life. It is supported by religions, common practice, and society's laws. Homosexuality is outlawed in many states/provinces and is railed against by most religions. Most of us gay/lesbian/bisexual persons still suffer ongoing emotional and spiritual abuse from homophobic and heterosexist persons. Many of us experience withdrawal of basic human rights -- firings, evictions from property, non-promotions -- merely because of our orientation. Too many of us across the land are still physically assaulted, even killed, often without full access to police protection.

Although 1973 (when homosexuality was no longer considered a mental disorder by the American Psychiatric Association) is two decades past, many trained therapists are not personally or professionally ready to go to work with gay/lesbian/ bisexual clients in a constructive manner. Their religious, personal, or other biases often interfere with their giving homosexuals proper

41

found that many of my clients did not have a positive image of gays/lesbians. One client, as we were constructing a genogram, announced in a matter of fact voice that his brother was a "faggot." A female, accused by her husband of having an affair with a woman, defended herself by proclaiming that she could never do something so gross. A father expressed his fear that his wife was turning their son into a "queer" by making him do household chores. Should I confront these prejudices? Then, there were the times when I suspected that a client was gay or lesbian. Should I bring it up?

I am sure any supervisor reading this article could provide helpful answers, or at least entertain a discussion, about the questions I had as a trainee. Unfortunately, my supervisors did not know I had questions about how to address my sexual orientation with clients or clients' views about homosexuality-- unless they guessed -- and nothing they said in supervision led me to believe they did. Oh, I was "out" to the faculty and my fellow students; that wasn't the problem. The problem, in retrospect, was their attempts to demonstrate that my homosexuality was not an issue led us into a conspiracy of silence.

My motivation to remain silent was very real to me then, although I now wish I had trusted my supervisors more. I had many people ask why a lesbian would want to be a marriage and family therapist, and I wondered if I would be welcome in the field. There was

therapeutic services. In my opinion, marriage and family therapists must be both willing to 1.) understand gay/lesbian/bisexual clients and their families and their experiences, AND 2.) be willing to work for broader societal understanding and healing. Therefore, as a supervisor, I believe it is my duty to inform my supervisees of my orientation. Through my own disclosure and their reactions to it, I help them prepare to deal with the personal and professional issues that such a disclosure by their clients raises. They do not have to agree with me or my beliefs. But they must be prepared to provide the services our Code of Ethics indicates-- specifically, not allowing their own biases to interfere with providing services clients need. As a supervisor, I am responsible to assure that my supervisees meet this, as well as all the other ethical requirements.

My disclosure can serve as a rich training ground in itself. It calls for an ethical and appropriate response from supervisees. By self-disclosing to my supervisees I can provide a model of openness and self-acceptance for them which is vital in our heterosexist culture.

Those supervisees who are gay/lesbian/bisexual themselves have access to a good resource for further dealing with their unique issues as therapists and supervisors-in-training. The silence referred to in Karen Gautney's piece does not occur, as the questions she raised are central to the supervision I provide. I can offer an opportunity for all my little in the MFT publications to indicate there were many others like me and I felt a responsibility to be a positive example. I was determined to be open about my sexuality, and equally determined to prove that it was not a problem for me and it would not be a problem for my clients. I was afraid that, if I raised these issues, it would be seen as a weakness. As a student, my primary objective was to be seen as competent.

My supervisors had a different reason for not anticipating or discussing my questions. I was the first openly lesbian student in the program, and they wanted me to feel comfortable. They did not want to use me as a guinea pig for their learning, and did not want to presume that my sexuality would present problems. They also did not want it to appear that *they* had a problem with it, so they waited for me to bring it up. I didn't.

In the profession, we seem to have given ourselves permission to discuss some differences (racial and gender in particular) at length in supervision. I sense, and this is confirmed by my discussions with others, that sexual orientation is still rarely talked about. Sexual orientation is one of those "invisible" differences, or at least some people think it is. Most homosexuals are attuned to the signals others give about their sexual orientation such as talk of children (not by itself definitive), photos on the desk,

(Continued in next column)

supervisees to deal with their own sexuality issues -- be they of gender, sexual orientation, or other diversity concerns.

Furthermore, my openness models a method of moving from shame to self-empowerment, from abuse to compassion, and from secrecy to taking care of myself. These are pivotal skills for all therapists to acquire. Because of my own journey, I offer modeling and professional resources for my colleagues-in-training with me. This is a powerful and empowering privilege both for them and for me.

wedding rings, references to "him" or "her," and so on. Homosexuals see these "blatant" signals, yet we learn
to be careful about when and how we send our own. We learn to consider not only our own comfort level in any revelation, but the comfort of others as well. Heterosexuals, trying to be "politically correct" and also respect others' privacy, are all too willing to avoid the topic.

The advice I am about to give is strictly from the perspective of a lesbian supervisee to supervisors: Bring it up. Talk about it. Whether your supervisee or her clients are heterosexual or homosexual, sexual orientation is a relevant issue that may be avoided unless you attend to it. Take the responsibility, because you probably have less to risk than your supervisees. And if your supervisees are gay or lesbian, believe me, they are already thinking about it.

Self-Assessment of Gender Practices: FFTS

You and your supervisees can complete the scale below to gain a quick assessment to what degree your ideas about gender, clients, and therapy reflect feminist beliefs (Black & Piercy, 1991). If done with an individual or supervision group, this exercise can lead to a rich discussion regarding values and assumptions.

The Feminist Family Therapy Scale

The following statements describe different ways therapists might conceptualize gender, clients and the process of therapy. Please put the number which best describes your opinion about these issues after each statement.

Strongly Agree	Agree	Have Mixed Feelings	Strongly Disagree	Disagree
1	2	3	4	5

Example:	Family therapists should only see individuals.	5

1. Traditional approaches to family therapy validate the uniqueness of women's experiences.
2. In the family system, women have equal power to men.
3. The traditional nuclear family does not provide men with the experience of being emotionally responsive.
4. Special attention should be directed to what is unique about the problems of women.
5. Notions about masculine and feminine roles are major determinants of family rules.
6. The traditional nuclear family supports women's psychological health.
7. If therapists do not challenge traditional relationships, clients will perceive this as approval of these relationships.
8. Most women enter therapy with power equal to that of men.
9. The traditional nuclear family supports women's productive creative selves.
10. Family therapist should not influence the distribution of power in intimate relationships.
11. Families are structured by generational and gender hierarchies.
12. Therapists reinforce traditional sex roles by not addressing them.
13. The traditional nuclear family views the role of peripheral male as normal.
14. Interactional patterns within the family reflect our patriarchal social system.
15. In dual-career families, women often have the primary responsibility for the emotional and psychological well-being of both their children and spouse.
16. Patriarchal values are not inherent in our socio-political system.
17. The traditional nuclear family conditions women to an inferior status.

Black, L., & Piercy, F. (1991). A feminist family therapy scale. *Journal of Marital and Family Therapy, 17*, 111-120.

Two Thumbs Up: A Supervisor's Guide to the Use of Films

Jay Lappin

The Lion's story will never be known if the hunter is the one who tells it.
African Proverb

Supervising in couple and family therapy requires building supervisees' capacity to hold multiple -- and sometimes contradictory -- viewpoints. They must "get" that social realities are constructions -- a melange of perspectives. The natural tendency to see things "one" way can reduce a supervisee's tolerance for complexity and ambiguity. The bottom line is that introducing and nurturing diverse perspectives is hard work for *all* parties -- supervisor and supervisee alike.

 "Using movies diversifies the learning experience."

Supervisors model the point that there are many ways to make a point. By way of metaphoric affinity and as a respite from the dusty pages of academic and professional journals, movies can greatly reduce the anxiety of learning something new. Supervisors have found that movies can help supervisees "see" systemically because watching the "whole" becomes an experiential reframe that gives supervisees a broader and deeper base from which to learn. For example, by discussing Malle's (1981) *My Dinner with Andre*, a film about two men exchanging their views on life, one can open the supervisee's world to non-clinical differences. They begin to understand that story and context are inseparable companions.

Other differences such as culture, class, gender, power, sexual orientation, and so on can also be explored through film. For example, renting one of the films listed or another contextual-based movie can be one way supervisees (or even supervisors) approximate an experience of difference.

45

Here are some key questions you can use to open up the movie-learning process:

- What issues does the film bring up for supervisees? What parts made them uncomfortable?

- How did the character's contextual experience frame his/her personal perspective?

- What does your cultural/sexual orientation/gender group say about the group depicted in the movie?

- What was your family of origin's beliefs about your own cultural group and others? Could you talk to your family about where these ideas came from? What would their response be? Why? How might these beliefs affect how you conduct therapy?

- How could you use what is learned from the film and the discussion when working with different populations, including your own, or in everyday life?

Other ways to highlight the learning experience: Change an aspect of the movie's plot or its characters and discuss how those changes might effect the outcome or the experience of the characters. Show a brief clip and ask several supervisees to write their version of what is "really" happening, compare the different versions, then show the rest of the clip. Ask supervisees to list their top five "firsts and worst" films and then compare their likes and dislikes. Rather than have culture and difference simply be a one-shot appearance, have an on-going assignment of having supervisees contribute films for use by others. The more supervisees participate in their own systemic insights, the more likely they will be to appreciate and discover difference in others and themselves.

One cautionary note. At the precise moment of printing, any list of great films (like the one on the next pages) becomes immediately outdated. At best it will be looked upon as incomplete and at worst, seen as "quaint." The limits of space and subjectivity further limited the choices. Despite the appeal of new films, there will always be "classics" that will serve as rich and historical source material -- even the discussion of why a particular film is a classic will surface diversity of opinion. The reader is urged to return to these new and old classics for just those reasons. But better still, develop your own lists of "Top Tens" as you expand upon the suggestions here. Enjoy and save me a seat on the aisle!

Malle, L. (1981). My dinner with Andre. New Yorker.

SUGGESTED MOVIES

Movie Title	Year	Director	Studio
Culture			
Annie Hall	1977	Woody Allen	United Artists
Avalon	1988	John J. Anderson	Rapid Eye Movement
Boyz in the Hood	1991	John Singleton	Columbia Studios
The Grapes of Wrath	1940	John A. Ford	20th Century Fox
The Color of Fear	1994	Lee Mun Wah	Stir Fry Productions
Roots	1977	Marvin J. Chomsky	Wolper Productions
Schindler's List	1993	Steven Spielberg	Universal Studios
Straight Out of Brooklyn	1991	Matty Rich	Samuel Goldwyn Company
To Sleep with Anger	1990	Charles Burnett	Samuel Goldwyn Company
The West	1996	Steven Ives & Ken Burns	PBS
Immigration			
Alamo Bay	1985	Louis Malle	Tristar
The Joy Luck Club	1993	Wayne Wang	Buena Vista
The Perex Family	1995	Mira Nair	Samuel Goldwyn Company
The Killing Fields	1984	Roland Joffe	Warner Brothers

There are several commercial services available to access a wealth of movie information. CD ROM resources include Microsoft's *Cinemania 96* software (around $30, but only compatible with Windows 95 or Windows NT version 3.5 or later) and Corel's *All Movie Guide* (for non Windows 95 users). Each program includes monthly Internet Website updates.

MORE MOVIES

Movie Title	Year	Director	Studio
Women			
All About Eve	1950	Joseph Maniewicz	20th Century Fox
Crimes of the Heart	1986	Bruce Beresford	DEG
Steel Magnolias	1989	Herbert Ross	Tristar
Shirley Valentine	1989	Lewis Gilbert	Paramount
The Trip to Bountiful	1985	Peter Masterson	Island Pictures
The Women	1939	George Cukor	MGM
Thelma & Louise	1991	Ridley Scott	MGM-Pathe
Waiting to Exhale	1995	Forest Whitaker	20th Century Fox
Men			
Beautiful Girls	1996	Ted Demme	Miramax Films
Circle of Recovery	1991	Tom Casciato	Mystic Fire Video
East of Eden	1954	Elia Kazan	Warner Brothers
From Here to Eternity	1953	Fred Zinneman	Columbia Studios
Full Metal Jacket	1987	Stanley Kubrick	Warner Brothers
I Never Sang for My Father	1970	Gilbert Gates, Jr.	Columbia Studios
The Great Santini	1980	Lewis John Carlino	Orion/Warner Brothers
Nothing in Common	1986	Garry Marshall	Tristar

MORE MOVIES

Movie Title	Year	Director	Studio
Sexual Orientation			
Adventures of Priscilla: Queen of the Desert	1994	Stephen Elliot	Gramercy Pictures
And the Band Played On	1993	Roger Spottiswoode	Home Box Office
Birdcage	1996	Mike Nichols	United Artists
Celuloid Closet	1995	Robert Epstein	Home Box Office
Desert Hearts	1986	Donna Deitch	Samuel Goldwyn Company
Philadelphia	1993	Jonathan Demme	Tristar
Go Fish	1994	Rose Troche	Samuel Goldwyn Company
The Wedding Banquet	1993	Ang Lee	Central Motion Pictures
Torch Song Trilogy	1988	Paul Bogart	New Line Cinema
Class			
Educating Rita	1983	Michael Cheyko	Columbia Studios
Flirting with Disaster	1996	David Russell	Miramax Films
The Milagro Beanfield War	1988	Robert Refdord	Universal Studios
Officer & a Gentleman	1982	Taylor Hackford	Paramount
Ruby in Paradise	1993	Victor Nunez	October Films
Silkwood	1983	Michael Hausman	20th Century Fox
Stanley & Iris	1990	Martin Ritt	MGM

MORE MOVIES

Movie Title	Year	Director	Studio
Disability			
Awakenings	1990	Penny Marshall	Columbia Studios
Bright Victory	1951	Mark Robson	UI
Best Boy	1979	Ira Wohl	International Film Exchange
Bill	1981	Anthony Page	Alan Landsburg Productions
Miracle Worker	1989	Jim Sheridan	United Artists
My Left Foot	1962	Arthur Penn	Miramax Films
Rain Man	1988	Barry Levison	MGM/United Artists
Power			
Citizan Kane	1941	Orson Welles	Mercury
Gandhi	1982	Lord Richard Attenborough	Columbia Studios
Giant	1956	George Stevens	Warner Brothers
Man of Marble	1976	Andrzej Wajda	New Yorker
Roger & Me	1989	Michael Moore	Warner Brothers
Wall Street	1987	Oliver Stone	20th Century Fox
Meet John Doe	1941	Frank Capra	Warner Brothers

Contributors to this list include: Jay Lappin, Janie Long, Jo Ellen Patterson, George Sargeant, and Howard Stevens. Some movies were taken from Janine Roberts suggestions from the 1993 *American Family Therapy Academy Resource Packet: Honoring and Working with Diversity.* Special thanks to Frank Pittman, III, for his contributions and critiquing of the proposed list, and to Bruno Oriti for his suggestions.

Contextually Sensitive Contracting

There are two ways you can use a formal contracting process with an accompanying written document to structure supervision that is sensitive to women and minorities. First, contracting can minimize the inherent hierarchy in the supervision relationship, because contracts typically stipulate shared responsibility for learning (Wheeler et al, 1989). Many female supervisees report that it is helpful to know the parameters of the supervisory relationship in determining when it is appropriate for them to assert themselves about their supervision needs, desires, and dissatisfactions. Second, if during the contracting process you acknowledge your supervisees' backgrounds and experiences with others who are participants of different groups and your own background and such experiences, you a.) destroy the "myth of sameness," b.) facilitate understanding in the supervisory relationship, and c.) create permission for supervisees to address contextual variables in therapy and supervision.

Wheeler, D., Avis, J., Miller, L., & Chaney, S. (1989). Rethinking family therapy training and supervision: A feminist model. In M. McGoldrick, C. Anderson, & F. Walsh (Eds.), *Women in families: A framework for family therapy* (pp. 135- 151). New York: W. W. Norton.

Cross Gender Cotherapy Teams

When you encourage cotherapy teams, you create opportunities for supervisees to experience gender influences on patterns of interaction in their professional relationships with each other as well as with clients in therapy. When stereotypical gendered interactions occur between therapists within and/or outside therapy, you can intervene and create an opportunity for both sexes to experience their professional roles differently. For example, we occasionally find ourselves proactively intervening when a female supervisee tends to defer to the ideas of her male partner and he assumes she has fewer ideas. Our intervention can range from a simple comment regarding our observation to a directive which has our male supervisees seeking input from our female supervisee's on their area expertise.

Reviewing Tapes for Contextual Influences

Cheryl L. Storm

Because many supervisees tended to only acknowledge contextual influences (e.g., gender, race, culture, socioeconomic status, sexual orientation, religion, and so on) when there was an "issue" brought up by clients, I created the following exercise to help them understand the continual, ever-present effect of these influences on their interaction with their clients. Supervisees are asked to bring a videotape (could be done with audio tapes) in which one of the clients in the therapy session is of the opposite gender and where the clients are different from them in some other contextual way. At first, supervisees often groan about the difficulty of finding just such a session, but a cursory review of their caseload usually results in finding a number of cases that fit the bill. During group or individual supervision, we randomly select a short segment to review with the questions below in mind. Reviewing a therapy tape and discussing these questions promotes awareness of supervisees' values, assumptions, reactions, and responses to contextual influences while also underscoring those of clients.

- How do contextual influences shape how therapist and clients respond to one another? Their language? The interaction between family members?

- How do contextual influences shape the presenting problem? The content expressed? Is the problem considered normal if viewed from the clients' context? Or, are the clients masking problems by offering a contextual explanation of the problem?

- How are the therapist's and clients' values of gender, class, and so on expressed?

- If a therapist working with this case felt it was important to intervene in a manner that also contributed to change in the larger sociopolitical, economic, and historical context of gender; how could he or she do so?

- If you were of the other sex or another race how might you imagine this therapy session to be different?

- What do you notice is different/similar about the therapist and the client's context?

- How have the similarities/differences in the contextual experiences of the therapist and clients influenced the therapy process? In what ways have they enhanced therapy? In what ways have they created challenges for both in therapy?

How Inclusive Are We in Supervision?

Roberts (1991) recommends coding the process of therapy, individual supervision, or group supervision sessions as a way to discover the gendered ways participants may communicate with one another. You or someone designated by you codes the number of times, the amount of talk, who talks after whom, who responds to whom, body language, and whether content is relational or instrumental. When Cheryl coded a supervision group comprised of four females and two male supervisees, she was amazed to find that the males filled the majority of the air time. After discussing this finding, the group was able to balance the involvement of all members more equally. When supervision groupings are comprised of majority and minority members, you can use this exercise to determine to what degree all participants are being included in the group process. The exercise can create a non confrontational, safe environment for discussion about steps supervisors and supervisees can take to eliminate any marginalization of group members that is occurring resulting in a more inclusive process.

OBSERVING & GENDER

Time observing _____
Place _____

Name	Number of times talks (code with tallies)	Amount of times talks (code in minutes)	Talk after whom (code in initials)	Who responds to their talk (code in initial & A-affirmation B-disqualification C-neutral)	Body language what to whom (code with brief notes)	Content is more relational (R) or instrumental (I) (code in R or I & brief notes)

Roberts, J. (1991). Sugar and spice, toads and mice: Gender issues in family therapy training. *Journal of Marital and Family Therapy, 13,* 157-165.

Supervisee Self-analysis: Using the FFBC

You can critique therapy interaction from a feminist lens via the Feminist Family Therapy Behavioral Checklist (FFBC) (Chaney & Piercy, 1988) to underscore the many opportunities for intervention in gendered interaction. Two of Cheryl's recent supervisees volunteered to review one of their therapy sessions using the FFBC. Here is their response to the exercise:

A Reaffirming Experience

When someone asks me if I am a feminist, I always consider the question and the questioner before I respond. Different people mean different things when they use the term "feminist." Although I consider myself a feminist, I realize that some feminists might not include me in their ranks, because I am not militant or angry enough. So, I was not sure what to expect.

I was pleased to see that the values expressed on the checklist were consistent with mine about how men and women relate in our society. Furthermore, I recognized many of the behaviors that I regularly use in therapy on the list. In my session, many of the behaviors were present, even ones that I had not remembered using. Other behaviors that were not present, I knew I had used in prior sessions.

Using the FFBC underscored the extent of influence feminist thinking has on my work. It is so much a part of who I am that I do not always recognize its presence. It also validated the expression of these values as being beneficial to my clients. I believe that sex-role socialization is oppressive to men and women. As a therapist, I have the opportunity to allay some of that oppression by the way I guide the conversation.

Lois Dennett

An Unsettling Experience

When I first began this exercise, I was only supposed to watch fifteen minutes of a videotaped session. What I ended up doing, however, was watching the entire hour-long session because I found as I was not addressing as many of the areas listed in the exercise that I thought I had. I kept thinking to myself as I watched the video, "I know I had to have talked about gender differences more in this session than I am." In the end, after discussing the assignment with my former supervisor and colleague, I realized that I was not commenting on gender differences and inequities in my clients' relationships as much as I thought I was. As a direct result of this experience, I have regularly begun to address more gender differences and inequities (such as those listed in the exercise) with my clients and how these differences may have an impact on their relationships. I found this exercise helpful in that it showed me that I needed to actually do more of what I thought I was doing when working with my clients.

Betsy Sullivan

54

FEMINIST FAMILY THERAPIST BEHAVIOR CHECKLIST

Directions: Rate the therapist regarding whether each item was present or not in the therapy session.

	Not Present	*Present*	*The therapist...*

A. Sex-Role Analysis

1. _____ _____ Educates clients regarding the inequality of status and power between the sexes.
2. _____ _____ Redefines males' abusive behavior (e.g., incest or battering) as conforming to society's promotion of male violence.
3. _____ _____ Raises sex-role issues whether or not the clients bring them up.
4. _____ _____ Introduces sex-role issues when dealing with family-of-origin problems.
5. _____ _____ Discusses the differential impact of divorce on men and women.
6. _____ _____ *Reframes* clients' definition of the problem to include the impact of socialization.
7. _____ _____ *Challenges* clients' definition of the problem to include the impact of socialization.
8. _____ _____ Reeducates clients about roles which are oppressive to both men and women.

B. Shifts Balance of Power Between Male and Female Clients

9. _____ _____ Challenges clients to develop more egalitarian relationships.
10. _____ _____ Suggests alternative sex-role behaviors to clients.
11. _____ _____ Negotiates a more equal distribution of child rearing tasks.
12. _____ _____ Negotiates a more equal distribution of household tasks.
13. _____ _____ Indicates that individual well-being will not be sacrificed to preserve the marital relationship.
14. _____ _____ Offers a nonsexist hypotheses to explain family problems.
15. _____ _____ Holds male and female clients equally responsible for change.
16. _____ _____ Challenges both male and female clients to incorporate other instrumental and expressive behaviors into their response.
17. _____ _____ Directs female clients to become involved in status related activities outside the family.
18. _____ _____ Supports freedom from assigned sex-roles among children in the family.
19. _____ _____ Helps the family develop network supports that will be encouraging of anticipated sex-role changes.
20. _____ _____ Supports clients' moves to expand beyond traditional sex-role behavior.

	Not Present	Present	The therapist...

C. Therapist Empowers Female Clients

21.	_____	_____	Enhances self-esteem of female clients by focusing on their unique and positive contributions to the family.
22.	_____	_____	Underlines female client's competence.
23.	_____	_____	Supports female client's decision-making abilities.
24.	_____	_____	Encourages female clients to be more assertive.
25.	_____	_____	Encourages female client to develop her own social support network rather than relying on male partner for support.
26.	_____	_____	Helps female client identify and deal with her patterns of dependency.
27.	_____	_____	Supports *competence* in women in both traditional and non traditional roles.
28.	_____	_____	Helps female client negotiate for her own personal area in or outside the home.
29.	_____	_____	Helps female client negotiate for her own personal time.

D. Skill Training

30.	_____	_____	Educates female client about assertive and functional ways of expressing anger.
31.	_____	_____	Uses role play to help clients integrate new sex-role behaviors.
32.	_____	_____	Teaches female client to become more distant from the needs of her husband and children.
33.	_____	_____	Teaches female client to assess and meet her own needs.
34.	_____	_____	Teaches male client to recognize and express his feelings.
35.	_____	_____	Teaches male client to better meet the emotional and nurturing need of the family.

E. Therapist Minimizes Hierarchy Between Therapist and Client

36.	_____	_____	Models both instrumental and expressive behaviors.
37.	_____	_____	Clearly communicates her/his own sex-role values.
38.	_____	_____	Assumes a collaborative role with the family.
39.	_____	_____	Encourages clients to assess their own change and growth.

Developed by S. Chaney & F. Piercy.

Reprinted with permission by Brunner/Mazel from the article Chaney, S., & Piercy, F. (1988). A feminist family therapist behavioral checklist. *American Journal of Family Therapy, 16*, 305-318. Copyright 1988.

Resources For Practicing Contextually Sensitive Supervision

American Family Therapy Association (AFTA). (1993). *AFTA resource packet: Honoring and working with diversity in family therapy.* Washington, DC: Author.

Aponte, H. (1991). Training the person of the therapist for work with the poor and minorities. *Journal of Independent Social Work, 5,* 23-39.

Ault-Riche, M. (1987). Teaching an integrated model of family therapy: Women as students, women as supervisors. *Journal of Psychotherapy and the Family, 3,* 175-192.

Avis, J. (1987). Deepening awareness: A private study guide to feminism and family therapy. *Journal of Psychotherapy & the Family, 3,* 15-46.

Berstein, B. (1993). Promoting gender equity in counselor supervision: Challenges and opportunities. *Counselor Education and Supervision, 32,* 198-202.

A study of Approved Supervisors of the American Association for Marriage and Family Therapy found a significant increase in the numbers of female supervisors and of supervisors under the age of 45 during the last decade.

Nichols, W., Nichols, D., & Hardy, K. (1990). Supervision in family therapy: A decade review. *Journal of Marital and Family Therapy, 16,* 275-285.

Buhrke, R. (1989). Lesbian-related issues in counseling supervision. In E. Rothblum, & E. Cole (Eds.), *Loving boldly: Issues facing lesbians* (pp. 195-206). New York: Harrington.

Caust, B., Libow, J., & Raskin, P. (1981). Challenges and promises of training women as family systems therapists. *Family Process, 20,* 439-447.

Chaney, S., & Piercy, F. (1988). A feminist family therapist behvioral checklist. *American Journal of Family Therapy, 16,* 305-318.

Falicov, C. (1988). Learning to think culturally. In H. Liddle, D. Breunlin, & R. Schwartz (Eds.), *Handbook of family therapy training and supervision* (pp. 335-357). New York: Guilford Press.

Goodyear, R. (1990). Gender configurations in supervisory dyads: Their relationship to supervisee influence strategies and skill evaluations of the supervisee. *Clinical Supervisor, 8,* 67-79.

Hardy, K., & Laszlofly, T. (1992). Training racially sensitive family therapists: Context, content, and contact. *Families in Society, 73,* 364-370.

Hunt, P. (1987). Black clients: Implications for supervision of trainees. *Psychotherapy, 24,* 114-119.

Leighton, J. (1991). Gender stereotyping in supervisory styles. *Psychanalytic Review, 78,* 347-363.

Libow, J. (1985). Training family therapists as feminists. In M. Ault-Riche (Ed.), *Women and family therapy* (pp. 16-24). Rockville, MD: Aspen Systems Corporation.

Long, J. (1996). Working with gay, lesbian, and bisexuals: Addressing heterosexism in supervision. *Family Process, 35,* 377-388.

Long, J. (1994). MFT supervision of gay, lesbian, and bisexual clients: Are supervisors still in the dark? *Supervision Bulletin, 7,* 1 & 6.

Nelson, T. (1991). Gender in family therapy supervision. *Contemporary Family Therapy: An International Journal, 13,* 357-369.

Peterson, F. (1991). Issues of race and ethnicity: Emphasizing who you are, not what you know. *Clinical Supervisor, 9,* 15-31.

Piercy, F., Hovestadt, A., Fennell, D., Franklin, G., & McKeon, D. (1982). A comprehensive training model for family therapists serving rural populations. *Family Therapy, 9,* 239-249.

Reid, E., McDaniel, S., Donaldson, C., & Tollers, M. (1987). Taking it personally: Issues of personal authority and competence for the female in family therapy training. *Journal of Marital and Family Therapy, 13,* 157-165.

Roberts, J. (1991). Sugar and spice, toads and mice: Gender issues in family therapy training. *Journal of Marital and Family Therapy, 13,* 157-165.

Wheeler, D., Avis, J., Miller, L., & Chaney, S. (1989). Rethinking family therapy training and supervision: A feminist model. In M. McGoldrick, C. Anderson, & F. Walsh (Eds.), *Women in families: A framework for family therapy* (pp. 135-151). New York: W. W. Norton.

Bacigalupe, G., Green, S., & Shilts, L. *When approved is not enough: Revisioning supervision.* (Audio #706-221). Norcross, VA: The Resource Link.

Panel. *Gender & cultural issues in MFT supervision and training.* (Audio #705-118). Norcross, VA: The Resource Link.

Long, J., Lindsey, E., Manders, J., & Dotson, D. *Training MFTs to work with gay & lesbian couples and families.* (Audio #703-533). Norcross, VA: The Resource Link.

Walters, M., Cunningham, D., Letich, L., Levener, L., & Scrafford, D. *The process of contextual supervision.* (Video #563) Washington, DC: American Association for Marriage and Family Therapy.

Supervisory Challenge 3:
Supervising in Universities & Institutes

When you provide supervision within an educational institution--whether a university or an institute setting -- typically you will find the terms of the supervision contract relatively well defined. The institution sets the framework for supervision. It determines the way in which supervision is conducted, when it occurs, and how long it lasts. The institution further defines the supervisor's job responsibilities.

The institution tells supervisees what to expect from a supervisor and what is expected of them by the institution prior to entering into supervision. In this type of context, supervisees complete requirements as specified in a syllabus, obtain satisfactory evaluations, and complete the specified hours of supervision and therapy hours to graduate from the program.

Supervisors are under an institutional umbrella in which there are procedures for evaluating supervisors' performance, procedures for processing complaints, and opportunities to discuss supervision issues. If supervisors do not hold up their part of the contract, supervisees can complain and the educational institution takes action ranging from mediating the disagreement to firing supervisors. If supervisors have held up their end of the supervision agreement, but supervisees have not complied with their part of the agreement or progressed satisfactorily, supervisors can receive the backing they need to stand their ground and require remedial work or counsel supervisees out of the profession.

Although some contracting still occurs directly with supervisees, the primary contract is between the supervisee and the educational institution, and the supervisor and the educational institution. As a result, supervisors negotiate the majority of the supervision contract with the institution rather than with supervisees.

Supervisors working in these settings have less freedom to implement their philosophy of supervision. If you supervise in this setting, how will you meet institutional requirements while honoring your own philosophy of supervision?

Practica Syllabi: Essentially A Supervision Contract

Cheryl L. Storm & Charles D. York

We found approaching the internship requirement as a class has distinct advantages. The academic community is more likely to view our supervisory time as a legitimate teaching endeavor. This results in internships being viewed as important learning experiences and supervision gaining credibility. We have even found it easier for us to receive credit for the supervision we do.

Like in all of our classes, we develop syllabi for our internship courses to guide the learning process. We approach the syllabi as a "supervision contract by another name." Institutional expectations for supervisors and supervisees are spelled out. At the same time, we allow room for individualizing the contract for the specific supervisors and supervisees involved.

The areas cited in the chart below receive special attention in our syllabi. Logistics are highlighted because supervisees must fulfill certain requirements to pass the course and ultimately graduate. Many of the specific requirements, such

---

SPECIFIC ASPECTS RECEIVING SPECIAL ATTENTION

- **Logistics (e.g., When, How Much, Use of Raw Data)**
- **Clarification of Supervisory Relationships**
- **Evaluation Procedures**
- **Clarification of Roles of Multiple Supervisors**

---

as frequency of supervision are predetermined by accrediting bodies. Supervisees are usually assigned, rather than allowed to choose their supervisors, leading to a greater need for clarification of the supervisory relationship with particular attention to supervisors' and supervisees' prefered ideas, methods, and styles. Evaluation procedures are highlighted because academic contexts emphasize clear, set procedures at specified points in time (usually midway and at the end of the term). Because in most programs supervisees have an individual and a group supervisor, addressing the relationship between supervisors reduces supervisee (and supervisor!) confusion.

60

A Limited Contract: Common Practice in Institute Settings

In institute settings, supervisors commonly agree to supervise a specified number of clinical cases on the condition that supervisees practice the marriage and family therapy (MFT) they are learning during their institute training. Therapists continue to practice with their other cases as they normally would, frequently from a nonMFT perspective. Supervisors assume they are not liable for those cases not in the original agreement. If you are supervising in this situation, you will be interested in the excerpt below from an interview with Steve Engelberg, an attorney knowledgeable about MFT practice, regarding the risks involved and the steps you can take to be sure you are supervising responsibly.

STORM: *Is this an erroneous assumption?*

ENGLEBERG: This is an uncharted legal area. Assume that one of your supervisees was sued on a case that was outside your agreement. The client was a depressed man who committed suicide and there were obvious warning signs the therapist did not heed. Your attorney argues that this case is not from a MFT point of view. This particular case was treated from an individual point of view outside your expertise. This argument is plausible because it is not that you didn't want to help the supervisee, but that you did not have the expertise to do so. Some judges may accept this argument. However, the attorney on the other side could very well counter by asking: Do marriage and family therapists treat depression? Of course, they do. Does the standard of care for marriage and family therapists require action if a client is in danger? Again, the answer is yes. Essentially, the legal issues in handling the suicidal case are the same regardless of the model of therapy used. Thus, it is prudent to go through a drill regarding risky situations on supervisees' entire caseloads. The idea is to force the supervisee to reveal information about serious cases and for the supervisor to attempt to spot problems and take responsible action. Remember legal issues do not usually arise around bad therapy. Rather, they arise in regard to whether the therapist provided therapy consistent with the standard of care in the field or acted unethically. In the above case, all well trained therapists should react in a similar way in a crunch...Clearly, the best course of action is to talk in general ways about your supervisee's caseload to make sure there is not a problem lurking somewhere. Exceeding the standard of care is always the safest course of action. Additionally, since you are hired to help the supervisee, I believe, supervisors should go beyond their technical duty in providing supervision.

STORM: *Some have proposed that a formal written contract may help a supervisor practice "defensively." Do contracts, in fact, protect supervisors?*

ENGELBERG: Contracts can be useful and it certainly doesn't hurt. If a problem arose, a written contract could strengthen the supervisor's case if the contract limited supervision in a legitimate way. But, a written contract does not neccessarily shield a supervisor from legal liability. A principle of law is that you cannot limit certain types of liability by a contract. Another reason to develop written formal contracts with supervisees quite apart from liability is because it makes good business sense to clarify the supervisor-supervisee relationship.[1]

In addition to highlighing the emergency procdures for high risk clients, the most useful contracts pay special attention to the areas cited in the chart below.

SPECIFIC ASPECTS RECEIVING SPECIAL ATTENTION

- **Emergency Procedures for High Risk Clients**
- **Logistics**
- **Notification of Clients**
- **Clarification of Supervisory Relationship**
- **Supervisory Methods**

Because supervisees usually practice in a location other than the institute, suervisors must outline the logistics of supervision (e.g., when, where, how, and so on). As chapter 8 notes, institute supervisees are usually seasoned professionals, fully credentialed in another mental health discipline; so they may be unaware of the ramifications of obtaining supervision at this point in their careers. Clarifying the role of a supervisor, including the accompanying legal responsibility, helps both parties to fully understand the supervisory relationship. In addition, supervisees must inform clients that a supervisor (and other supervisees if supervision occurs in dyads or groups) is privy to their therapy. Because supervision frequently occurs in a different site than therapy, supervisors and supervisees face working out ways for supervisors to directly access supervisees' work either through audio- or videotapes, and/or live supervision; and for supervisors to access clinical records. Supervisees must inform clients and obtain their consent to the use of audio- and videotapes for supervision or to participate in live supervision. Supervisees must take steps to ensure client confidentiality especially regarding the transportation of tapes and/or case records to and from supervision. The ease or difficulty in reaching these agreements depends on the context in which supervisees practice, and the setting's degree of endorsement of supervision.

[1]This is an excerpt from the article Engleberg, S., & Storm, C. (1990). "Supervising defensively: Advice from legal counsel" from Volume (4), Number 3, of the *Supervision Bulletin*, Copyright 1991, American Association for the Marrriage and Family Therapy. Reprinted with permission.

Learning the Biz: An Alternate Contract

Carol Stanley

At our marriage and family therapy institute, it is our belief that many excellent therapists do not succeed in independent practice -- whether solo or group -- because they were never trained in how to operate a small business. We endeavor to teach these business skills as well as model the skills through the way we operate and transact business within our organization. Thus, we provide internships and externships with the express purpose of training people to enter into independent practice, which makes us a bit different from other institute settings where supervisees obtain their supervised clinical practice.

Our Setting

The senior staff at Valley Counseling Associates (VCA) provides therapy to individuals, couples, and families in the local community at prevailing rates. Additionally VCA operates a training program for students completing internships as part of fulfilling master degree requirements as well as a postgraduate extern program for therapists completing requirements for state certification. The interns and externs see clients on a sliding scale, providing therapeutic services for that portion of the population which cannot afford the higher fees. We also have the in between category of resident -- certified therapists who rent space and secretarial services from us and participate in our supervision groups.

All the individuals at VCA, with the exception of myself and my husband, who are the owners, and the clerical staff, are independent contractors providing therapy for the community as private practitioners. A unique situation does present itself at times. Because we are a group of private practice clinicians there does not exist the "employer-employee" relationship at the senior staff level that other agencies experience. When the senior staff act as supervisors for us, our relationship with them parallels our relationships with the interns/externs. They are independent contractors providing a service on our behalf. This necessitates a continual conversation between supervisors and us regarding our expectations for the supervision process and about the progress of interns/externs.

The supervisees in our intern and extern programs are also independent contractors we hire. There are some specific legal requirements for the use of independent contractors, and ethical guidelines for the supervision of interns/externs. These led us, with the help of our attorney, to develop a specific and detailed contract that we have each therapist, including our student supervisees, sign. The purpose of our contract is to make clear the different responsibilities and obligations of both VCA and the therapist as we go about the business of providing therapy, training, and supervision.

Our Business Contract with Supervisees

The business portion of what we offer begins with the review and signing of our twelve month contract by each independent contractor. We have four different contracts that we hold our staff accountable to depending on their relationship with us. Hoping to develop successful therapists, each level of our staff is on a graduated financial arrangement with us. Our hope is that as our interns mature into externs and our externs mature into residents they will experience greater and greater financial success as therapists. At each succeeding layer our financial and supervisory relationship changes. Eventually, as a senior staff member, a true private practice exists and the relationship with VCA is virtually one of landlord and renter. One exception to this landlord/renter relationship occurs in supervision. Because supervision is done by our staff on our request and on our behalf, we retain "supervision of supervision" obligations and responsibilities. Becoming a member of our senior staff, who are the individuals who provide supervision to the interns/externs, is solely at the discretion of ourselves as owners and not an automatic progression. We begin this process with the contract.

Our four contracts have some differences. I will focus on the two contracts we have developed for our intern and extern programs. Although they are similar in many ways, they are different primarily because interns are starting out while externs are midway through the financial transitions to independent practice. Interns need training and supervision while externs need supervision, growing administrative support and guidance regarding their professional development. In addition, the supervision offered at VCA is less "directive" for the extern than the intern.

The contracts are similar in that they both begin by a.) stating the purpose of the contract as defining obligations of each party as we conduct therapy, training, and supervision; b.) defining that all business the interns/externs do will be under our name, and c.) the length of the agreement. Thus, the contract clearly defines the role of the therapist -- whether intern or extern -- in relationship to us. The intern is defined as a "student" while the extern is defined as a "trainee." In both contracts, we specify that our written contract is the only valid agreement between VCA and the intern/extern.

Each contract describes the relationship between VCA and the intern/extern. It is here we establish the independent contractor relationship. The intent of this section is to define our financial relationship (i.e., overhead payment and percentage of fees collected) and professional relationship (i.e., need to follow the laws of the state and the American Association for Marriage and Family Therapy ethical guidelines). There are also limits defined here such as subletting space or binding us to any contracts.

This section is followed by a description of what we provide the intern/extern. This section outlines the supervision we require and provide, and outlines the number of supervision hours required.

One of the areas that is included in the contract and is tied intricately to our purpose of preparing independent contractors is the inclusion of a noncompetition clause. For two years following working with VCA, the extern is not allowed to set up a competitive program within a specified geographic area. We outline the financial penalties that would be imposed if this section was violated. The intent of this section is to protect us. Externs have access to mailing lists, training materials, and computer programs. We want to prevent a group of therapists breaking off and starting a competing program, utilizing our resources and contacts. After two years, our externs are free to work where they wish in the full spectrum of private practice.

We realize that our contracts are long and for some individuals difficult to comprehend. To counteract this we designed general guidelines interns/externs must meet to honor the contract. These guidelines that cover items such as videotaping, continuing education, supervision criteria, and observation of senior staff conducting therapy.

Conclusion

VCA is an exciting and busy place to do an internship/externship and to be supervisees. Clients come as early as 6 am and as late as 9 pm six days a week. There are new interns and externs every year -- sometimes as many as 20. With the mixture of so many personalities, learning styles, degrees of professional maturity coupled with long hours, heightened anxieties regarding learning to be an independent pratitioner, and new experiences some misunderstandings develop. Although I believe these are kept to a minimum, they do occur. The strength and clarity of our contract helps to prevent these misunderstandings.

Our contracts are lengthy (as many as fifteen pages long!) and legally binding. As supervisors and independent business owners, we engage in serious business matters daily. It is our hope that not only does our contract protect VCA, a small business, but that it models the important facets of doing sound business as a therapist and as a therapy center. It would be a shame if we could not continue to offer quality supervision and therapy to the community simply because we or our staff (including our intern/extern supervisees) did not pay attention to important legal, ethical, and financial details. The actions of one often have an impact on the lives of many. Our contract limits the negative impact of those actions. Further, our contract enables the learning therapist to develop those skills necessary to simultaneously enter successfully the business and therapy worlds.

Resources For Supervising in Universities & Institutes

Avis, J., & Sprenkle, D. (1990). A review of outcome research on family therapy training. *Journal of Marital and Family Therapy, 16,* 225-240.

Anderson, S. (1992). Evaluation of an academic family therapy program: Changes in trainees' relationship and intervention skills. *Journal of Marital and Family Therapy, 4,* 365-376.

Bardill, D. & Saunders, B. (1988). Marriage and family therapy and graduate social work education. In H. Liddle, D. Breunlin, & R. Schwartz (Eds.) *Handbook of family therapy training and supervision* (pp. 316-330). New York: Guilford Press.

Berger, M. (1988). Academic psychology and family therapy training. In H. Liddle, D. Breunlin, & R. Schwartz (Eds.) *Handbook of family therapy training and supervision* (pp. 303-315). New York: Guilford Press.

Supervisors across education programs agree that supervisees should experience a variety of supervision experiences during their training.

Henry, P., Sprenkle, D., & Sheehan, R. (1986). Family therapy training: Student & faculty perceptions. *Journal of Marital and Family Therapy, 12,* 249-258.

Berman, E., & Dixon-Murphy, T. (1979). Training in marital and family therapy at free-standing institutes. *Journal of Marital and Family Therapy, 5,* 29-42.

Bloch, D. (1981). Family therapy training: Institutional base. *Family Process, 20,* 133-146.

Cantwell, P., & Holmes, S. (1995). Cumulative process: A collaborative approach to systemic supervision. *Journal of Systemic Therapies, 14,* 35-46.

Cooper, A., Rampage, C., & Soucy, C. (1981). Family therapy training in clinical psychology programs. *Family Process, 20,* 155-156.

Commission on Accreditation for Marriage and Family Therapy Education. (1994). *Manual on accreditation.* Washington, DC: Author.

Everett, C. (1979). The master's degree in marriage and family therapy. *Journal of Marital and Family Therapy, 5,* 7-14.

Garfield, R., & Lord, G. (1982). The Hahnemann master's of family therapy program: A design and its results. *American Journal of Family Therapy, 10,* 75-78.

Henry, P., Sprenkle, D., & Sheehan, D. (1986). Family therapy training: Student and faculty perceptions. *Journal of Marital and Family Therapy, 12,* 249-258.

Herz, F. & Carter, B. (1988). Born free: The life cycle of a free-standing postgraduate training institute. In H. Liddle, D. Breunlin, & R. Schwartz (Eds.) *Handbook of family therapy training and supervision* (pp. 93-109). New York: Guilford Press.

Joanning, H., Morris, J., & Dennis, M. (1985). An overview of family therapy educational settings. *American Journal of Family Therapy, 13,* 3-6.

Keller, J., Huber, J. & Hardy, J. (1988). What constitutes appropriate marriage and family therapy education? *Journal of Marital and Family Therapy, 14,* 297-306.

LaPerriere, K. (1979). Family therapy training at the Ackerman Institute: Thoughts of form and substance. *Journal of Marital and Family Therapy, 5,* 53-58.

Olkin, R., & Gaughen, S. (1991). Evaluation and dismissal of students in master's level clinical programs: Legal parameters and survey results. *Counselor Education and Supervision, 30,* 276-288.

Piercy, F., & Sprenkle, D. (1984). The process of family therapy education. *Journal of Marital and Family Therapy, 10,* 399-408.

Sprenkle, D. (1988). Training and supervision in degree-granting graduate programs in family therapy. In H. Liddle, D. Breunlin, & R. Schwartz (Eds.) *Handbook of family therapy training and supervision* (pp. 233-248). New York: Guilford Press.

Sutton, P. (1985/86). An insider's comparison of a major family therapy doctoral program and a leading nondegree family therapy training center. *Journal of Psychotherapy & the Family, 1,* 41-51.

White, M., & Russell, C. (1995). The essential elements of supervising systems: A modified Delphi study. *Journal of Marital and Family Therapy, 21,* 33-54.

Winkle, C., Piercy, F., & Hovestadt, A. (1981). A curriculum for graduate level marriage and family therapy education. *Journal of Marital and Family Therapy, 7,* 201-210.

Supervisory Challenge 4: Supervising in Agencies

What do you believe is the role of the agency supervisor? Should you stay clear of "organizational politics" and focus as exclusively as possible on the clinical cases of your supervisees? Or, do you see your job as assisting supervisees in becoming valued employees for their organizations even if that means spending time helping them deal with "non-clinical issues" such as the ones described here: 1.) Helping your supervisees cope with difficult work relationships; 2.) Assisting your supervisees to fulfill case management responsibilities including mundane tasks such as completing forms; or, 3.) Helping your supervisees maintain professionalism in their relationships with their colleagues and other professionals outside of the therapy room?

Minuchin (1993), in an interview, expressed the following opinion on this topic:

"As a supervisor, I must enter into the world of organizational politics. I am supervising a director of a psychiatric hospital. To help the therapist change to work with families I must first help the hospital change the way they do intakes. We then realized that we had to change the way the hospital was constructed to arrange for space to interview families. We must create new social structures that are family therapy friendly" (p. 2).

Do you agree or disagree with Minuchin's vision of the supervisory role? Are you a "social engineer" (Minuchin, 1993, p. 1) creating family friendly institutions? Or, is this responsibility, in your opinion, better left to those within the agencies and really none of your business?

Storm, C., & Minuchin, S. (1993). Creating family friendly organizations: An interview with Salvador Minuchin. *Supervision Bulletin, 3,* 1-2.

A Two Pronged Agreement

Although agency supervisors are interested in promoting the professional development of their supervisees, they are unique because their *primary* purpose for supervision is to ensure clients are receiving appropriate and quality services. They frequently supervise as part of their job responsibilities with staff assigned to them, who may or may not be already fully credentialed clinicians, may or may not be interested in being supervised, and may or may not be practitioners who share a common treatment philosophy with them. On occasion their supervision services may be a negotiated employment benefit for new therapists who are still in need of supervision for credentialing or licensing. As Woodruff points out in the article that follows, "the customer of supervision" can be confusing. Is the customer the agency or the supervisee?

This results in the supervision agreement having two prongs. One prong is a formal agreement between the supervisor and the agency. This prong specifies the logistics of supervision (e.g., proportion of time spent in supervision, who one supervises, and so on), the acceptable and typical methods of supervision, procedures for handling clinical issues such as emergencies, and protocol for employee (the supervisee!) evaluations. The other prong is a negotiated agreement with the assigned employees. This prong of the agreement requires special time devoted to the areas highlighted in the chart here.

ASPECTS RECEIVING SPECIAL ATTENTION

- **Creating a Working Relationship**
- **Clarifying Multiple Relationships**
- **Identification of Supervision Goals**

If you join the ranks of agency supervisors, you and your supervisees may find it helpful to spend some extra time learning about your respective preferred ideas, methods, and styles of working in order to create an effective working relationship. This is especially important if you are in a supervision relationship because of your agency positions (perhaps even a long term relationship that will last as long as you both are employed by the organization). Each of you must be able to contribute to the supervisory process *and* make good use of the time taken out of your work day for supervision. Supervisors will find flexibility is a good companion. Few employees will quit their jobs because their clinical supervisor and they do not share the same therapy approach and few agencies require therapists to practice in a certain way.

Your dual role in the agency as supervisor and colleague to your supervisees also requires special attention. This is particularly important in smaller agencies where staff can develop close personal relationships and fulfill several positions at once. If agency protocol requires supervisors to evaluate supervisee's in ways that lead to the determination of pay increases or promotions, clarifying these responsibilities in advance can help all participants keep their work environment a comfortable rather than a dreaded place to face each day. When supervision occurs because of an agency mandate rather than because therapists are requesting it, balancing the goals of the agency while attending to the ways supervision can meet personal, individual goals of participants can remove supervision from a therapist "have to" to a "want to"!

Am I in a dual relationship if I am a therapist's boss in an agency as well as supervising her clinical work?

Yes, technically you are because of the multiple agendas. In your roles as employer, you may be responsible for evaluating the therapist's work for promotions and raises. The clinician, wishing to advance professionally, is encouraged to demonstrate confidence and competence in the job. In your other role, however, you are asking her to define the areas she needs assistance with in supervision. For example, many supervisors ask their supervisees to identify "stuck cases" and growth areas. Thus, there can be tension between these two competing agendas for the therapist and supervisor. Some agencies resolve this dilemma by identifying a separate individual for clinical and administrative supervision. This dual agenda can also be managed by openly addressing the potential tension, spelling out specific evaluation procedures that involve input from both parties, and specifically addressing the responsibilities of each in the initial contract.

Considering the "Customer" in Supervision

Arnold Woodruff

For purposes of this article, the customer is the individual or group who most wants to see change in a problematic situation. This is very often not the client who comes in to "benefit" from the therapist's services. Common examples of customers are judges, probation officers, lawyers, workers in other agencies (social services if you work in mental health and mental health if you work in social services), spouses, and parents. Most of us have devised strategies for dealing with this in therapy, but what impact does customership have on supervision?

I think that customership is more likely a problem in agency settings than in institutes or universities. Presumably, the training context where services are given is known to supervisees and to referral sources. It should be clear to all involved that, while a primary obligation for supervision is to clients, there is also a strong obligation to supervisees' learning by the organization. "Swooping in" to rescue a confused novice therapist is reasonable supervisor behavior in this setting, however embarrassing to the initiate (at least at the beginning).

In an agency, however, such supervisory behavior may lead to a very different outcome. First, of all, therapists may not understand that receiving supervision is a requirement of their position. Many still see being supervised as a sign of internship or traineehood. Family therapy is nearly unique among the professions in the strong advocacy for supervision throughout one's career. Secondly, clients may not understand the value of supervision and may also assume that this marks some defect in their therapists. Third, agency administrators may not understand the cost effectiveness of supervision, particularly the live variety, and may feel they are paying for two hours of professional time that can only be billed once. Finally, if the client sitting in the consulting room is "involuntary," not only is the therapist likewise being compelled but so too is the supervisor.

Each of these "customers" can and must be dealt with by the therapist and supervisor (or possibly the supervisor-of-supervision) if a successful outcome is to be achieved. The systemic understanding we, as family therapists, bring to the work must always be extended to the supervision we provide.

72

The "Butterfly Effect:" Supervising in Non-systems Agencies

Jane Hill Riley

In the best of worlds, we will all find ourselves supervising in a training institute with supervisees totally invested in a well grounded systems perspective. In reality, however, many of you may find yourselves, like I did, in more challenging situations. If you are asked to supervise therapists who have less than sterling backgrounds in marriage and family therapy (MFT), perhaps this model will be of service to you. I believe that with just a few adjustments this approach could easily be adapted to smaller groups and individual supervision.

While supervising the clinical staff of a nonprofit agency, I was asked to develop MFT skills in a diverse group of therapists. I had many reservations concerning the task. I was simultaneously excited by the possibilities and frightened by the potential problems. I could imagine exciting some therapist, who would return to school with the goal of pursuing MFT licensure on one hand, while realizing that I might simply be wasting time on another therapist totally embedded in his or her own perspective. I took on the task with the hope of utilizing the "Butterfly Effect" to make a difference. The "Butterfly Effect" refers to the idea that by making some small impact on therapists' perspectives I would create a small change that would in most cases only be a beginning.

Initially, my supervision group was made up of two certified mental health counselors, one psychiatric nurse, one socialworker, one chemical dependency counselor, one school psychologist, two social work interns, and one therapist in the process of becoming certified as a mental health counselor. Later, a practitioner with a pastoral counseling degree was added to the group. The theoretical backgrounds for this group ranged from no real grounding to Rogerian to psychodynamic. However, most had psychodynamic leanings, including the MFT. Only the psychiatric nurse was fairly well grounded in systems theory, and another therapist had studied the contextual MFT approach ten years earlier. To add to the diversity, the range of experience was from intern level to 17 years. All were seeing families and couples in therapy and, thankfully, all were interested in expanding their strategies for dealing with these clients.

I realized that if I disregarded the seasoned therapists' skills and backgrounds, I would lose their interest and support, as well as waste a golden opportunity to broaden their ability to help their clients and introduce them to a systemic view of treatment. Additionally, if I overloaded the newer therapists with too much theory and information too soon, I would lose them as well. Consequently, I needed to develop a method of broadening their expertise, while respecting their strengths. I began my "Butterfly Effect" approach with an inclusion phase, because my first goal was to broaden their conceptualization of the "client" to a more inclusive model. Although this appears to be a small adjustment to one's thinking, it can have dramatic impact on therapists' perspectives and their ability to work with families. Subsequently, an expansion phase of my approach was developed by first briefly describing and discussing several of the MFT theories to the group, and then encouraging each therapist to identify one h/she might be interested in exploring in more depth.

The Inclusion Phase

In order to accomplish my first goal, I needed to encourage the therapists to recognize their clients' embeddedness in larger systems and help them structure their sessions in a more systemic framework. Consequently, I began by giving the therapists a training session on utilization of the genogram during intake sessions as a way of information gathering. I framed it primarily as a way of gathering a lot of information in a short amount of time. I began this training by giving a case presentation myself using a genogram. The case I presented went back four generations and I was able to show patterns of alcoholism and sexual abuse in each generation. I examined the types of questioning I had utilized to access the information and stressed that the genogram gave me a vehicle with which to visually track the family patterns in front of the family. I encouraged the therapists to ask questions about general patterns of alcohol or drug use, pregnancies, abuse, disease, and so on, as a means of gaining general information. The therapists all responded favorably and began to include this as a standard part of their intake assessments. Some had difficulty in actually drawing the genogram, especially when there were divorces and remarriages. Whenever these problems occurred, we used them as training opportunities by putting them on a chalkboard. It became apparent from the beginning that this simple exercise helped them begin to depathologize their clients and as a result they began to explore what *else* could account for their clients' symptoms.

The Expansion Phase

I was then ready to move to the expansion phase of my approach. I began with a session focused on brief descriptions of several MFT approaches. I gave handouts to the therapists with more information and included a short bibliography of sources on each approach. In the description, I stressed similarities with theory and strategies I knew they were familiar with. I then suggested that each therapist choose a family therapy theory to study. I offered to loan them articles and books on the theory of their choice and I encouraged them to chose one that fit somehow with the theory in which they were already grounded. For those who had no real theory, I suggested problem focused (Mental Research Institute model) or solution focused materials which had several well developed "how to" pieces for them to delve into.

During supervision each week we had two therapists present cases in which they were utilizing their "new" approaches. These sessions became forums for their questions and observations. I encouraged everyone's participation and could consequently see each therapist begin to develop a more processed focused orientation. Furthermore, I remained available to answer questions during the week if problems or questions came up. Because of a weekly rotation, the therapists regularly received an introduction to all the theories chosen. It was gratifying to see these therapists broaden their world views and perceptions of what could be included and achieved in psychotherapy. I began to have questions occur like "Wouldn't it be easier or better if everyone in the family came in instead of just the child?" to which I replied "What a great idea! How could you get them all to come in?" And so we explored possibilities together. Even the seasoned therapists enjoyed the exercise and felt validated by the expansion of their own theories to encompass a more systemic view of clients' problems. I continuously encouraged them to look at alternatives based on theory while meanwhile stressing the validity of each theoretical background. The importance of matching strategy to theory was central and I pointed out that what one therapist used might not fit someone else's approach. Having them present different theories allowed me the opportunity to emphasize the importance of a theoretical underpinning for any strategy and how strategies don't work unless connected by theory. I never indicated that their way of doing therapy was inappropriate or inadequate, rather I simply described ways to add to their knowledge base and increase their confidence in dealing with families and couples.

My overall intention was not to invalidate the therapists' methods of therapy. Instead, I wanted to respectfully shift their perception of clients and their families in small but dramatic ways. It was exciting and fascinating observing these therapists grow and develop and, more importantly, become excited about their growth. As a firm believer in the "Butterfly Effect," I believe this was enough. I saw these therapists begin to challenge their long held reliance on the medical model and its pathology as the only way to look at their clients.

Resources For Supervising in Agencies

Carl, B., & Jurkovic, G. (1983). Agency triangles: Problems in agency-family relationships. *Family Process, 22,* 441-451.

Kaslow, F. (1986). Supervision, consultation and staff training -- Creative teaching/learning processes in the mental health profession. In F. Kaslow (Ed.), *Supervision and training: Models, dilemmas, and challenges* (pp. 1-16). New York: Hawthorne Press.

McDowell, T. (1991). Contracting from the top down. *Supervision Bulletin, 4,* 3-4.

Lindblad-Goldberg, M., Itzkowitz, A., & Fussner, A. *Creating relationships for mastery* (Audio #703-134). Norcross, VA: The Resource Link.

Russell, T., Shuiz, C., & Moline, M. *Plantation to Co-op: Nonhierarchical supervision in a private agency* (Audio #700-731). Norcross, VA: The Resource Link.

Woodruff, A. *Real time supervision: The supervisor in an agency setting.* (Audio #700-731). Norcross, VA: The Resource Link.

Supervisory Challenge 5: Supervising in Private Contracts

Both of us remember when we almost always responded eagerly when approached by someone seeking private supervision. It is quite flattering to have a former student seek you out for further supervision, or to have someone call you for supervision because of your reputation. Yet each of us have independently become more cautious when considering a private supervision contract. Because the field continues to need supervisors willing to enter into privately contracted supervision, we do not wish to dissuade you from doing so, but we want to be sure that you ask yourself the appropriate questions rather than rushing in blindly.

From the supervisor's perspective, electing to enter into a private supervision contract is rarely about money. Most supervisors recognize, however, that the cost of supervision is often significant for a young professional who is not yet licensed. Before you agree to some kind-hearted price for supervision, ask yourself a few questions: How much additional liability am I assuming for the cases I will be supervising? Am I providing enough supervision? For example, Tom realized that he had agreed to provide private supervision to two supervisees who shared 90 minutes per week, each of whom saw about 20 cases weekly. On reflection, it was clear that he would never have agreed to contract for such limited supervision had he not been concerned about the supervisees' pocketbooks.

Will I have adequate information about the cases I supervise, since many of the normal channels for obtaining information are unavailable? Do not underestimate the importance of being able to watch a case live, having brief conversations about cases, looking through case files, and so on. In privately contracted supervision, this information is curtailed or must be specifically sought, often with significant logistical obstacles. Interface issues in privately contracted supervision can be formidable, especially when therapy is being provided in a setting with which the supervisor is unaffiliated. Am I willing to perform all the additional work necessary to minimize interface issues, such as meeting with agency administration and supervisors, familiarizing myself with agency policies, and so on? All of this work is probably not "worth it" just for the money, but is worth it to help new professionals enter the field with adequate supervision.

Striking the Supervision Bargain

When you enter into a private supervision contract with therapists, the contract is determined by you in conversation with supervisees. Although credentialing bodies and regulatory laws may shape the contract and even specify certain components of the contract, the specific contract is the agreement you and your supervisees negotiate. Thus, there is great freedom to individualize the contract as well as little structure to guide the process. The terms of the contract are only as clear as you and your supervisees make them. Over time, we found a written explicit contract is critically important outlining the contract we have struck with our supervisees in our privately contracted supervision. We believe it reduces the margin that exists for misunderstandings and difficulties while increasing the potential for success since we can all evaluate whether the supervision contract is being fulfilled.

Because of the complexities of this context discussed in chapter 10 of the text, several aspects receive special attention in these written contracts. In the arena of logistics, the handling of the fee -- how much, how to handle cancellations, and the fee when supervision is shared -- is focal since supervisors are paid directly by supervisees. Since supervisors and supervisees are not in the same location, supervisees' transporting of audio- and videotapes, and case records are an issue. Supervisees also have to notify clients that another pair of eyes and ears, who are outside supervisees' work context, are involved in their case.

SPECIFIC ASPECTS RECEIVING SPECIAL ATTENTION

- **Logistics Especially Money Matters & Raw Data**
- **Notification of Clients**
- **Responsibilities of All Parties** (e.g., record keeping, ratio of supervision to therapy hours, emergencies)
- **Relationship Between Multiple Supervisors**
- **Resolution of Disagreements**

If supervisees work for an agency, supervisors cover several areas if supervision is to be a beneficial process rather than stressful for supervisors and supervisees. All parties need to understand the responsibilities of the privately contracted supervisor, the agency supervisor, and the supervisee. Tom includes the following clause in his contract regarding the relationship.

"All parties recognize the supervisee has entered into this supervisory relationship voluntarily, in pursuit of (e.g., licensure, Clinical membership of the American Association for Marriage and Family Therapy, and so on), and that the agency incurs no financial responsibility for the supervision. On the other hand, the agency recognizes that the supervisee lacks specialized marriage and family supervision within the agency and welcomes the supervisor's input."

When supervisees work in agencies with procedures for emergencies and internal supervisors, privately contracted supervisors have back-up for high risk clients. On the other hand multiple supervisors can lead to confusion regarding whose supervisory opinion reigns if there is disagreement about a direction supervisees should take. Thus, privately contracted supervisors and agency supervisors can minimize confusion by having solid working relationships. In the private sector, there is no defined way to proceed if difficulties arise within the supervision process. Although the best resolutions are those that occur between supervisors and supervisees, the nature of the contract may make resolution at times difficult. Because supervisors evaluate supervisees and negative evaluations can seriously effect supervisees' careers, supervisees may be reluctant to discuss their concerns with supervisors until late in the process. They may be hesitant to end supervision and seek another supervisor. Similarly, supervisors may be unintentionally less open with constructive or even critical feedback since they can be fired.

In contrast if supervisees are in a private solo or group practice, supervisors' responsibilities loom large. There is no built in back-up -- regarding everything from record keeping to the handling of emergency situations. Supervisors also become responsible for insuring that the solo practitioner or group practice has conducted the business of their practice ethically and within the standard of practice of the field.

Contracting From the Top Down

Teresa McDowell

As marriage and family therapists we pride ourselves in being aware of family systems even when working with individuals. Yet when we contract to provide supervision, how often do we enter the supervisee's work system in a planful way which intentionally enhances the relationships between supervisee, those she works with, and ourselves?

Some time ago I received a call from a therapist at a local mental health agency. She stated that she and several of her colleagues were interested in group supervision. They discussed this with their director and he agreed to have her call me for more information. I found myself responding to her much as I would a child asking to set up an appointment for her family, encouraging her to ask the director to contact me. I wanted to make sure I had "parental" permission.

When the director and I eventually met we discussed the agency's goals, policies, and other relevant information such as the therapist's responsibilities in the area of case management. As we reviewed who should be in the supervision group, I again found myself responding as I would when working with a family, considering how supervision could strengthen and clarify the existing holons in the

"...how often do we enter the supervisee's work system in a planful way which intentionally enhances the relationships between the supervisee, those she works with and ourselves?"

agency. Our meeting allowed me an opportunity to explain the supervision process, clarify any discrepancies in philosophy or theoretical approach, delineate the roles of clinical and agency supervisors, determine the process of evaluation, and specify the procedure for notifying me of emergency situations and ethical issues. By the end of our meeting the director and I were in agreement and I believe he saw me as an ally he could trust with his "family". We set up a time to meet with the unit supervisor. I felt the supervision process was not likely to be undermined or triangulated by the system. If a problem arose, the groundwork had been laid for finding a solution.

Since this experience, I have begun keeping in mind a "supervision" map which includes the supervisee, members of her work system, the client family, and other relevant systems involved with any given case. This map helps direct many of my decisions, including those aimed at encouraging hierarchical congruence and clarity within the work system.

By recognizing supervisees as part of a system we can acknowledge the effect that system has on the supervision process and on the therapist's ability to work with families. We can also acknowledge the effect we as supervisors have on the work system and realize our responsibility for insuring that our impact is beneficial, eventually enhancing the supervisee's success in helping families change.

A Letter of Understanding

Patricia M. Dwyer

The *Agency Supervision Agreement Form* makes the relationship between off–site supervisors, who are privately contracted, and training programs clear. Training programs can expand this form to include specific training or practicum requirements.

AGENCY SUPERVISION AGREEMENT

_____ agrees that

Agency

_____ may present cases for

Intern/Student Therapist

supervision with the undersigned supervisor.

It is agreed that clients of the above named intern, student, or therapist have signed a permission form for off-site supervision. The above named intern, student, or therapist has agreed not to remove documents or records from the agency's premises, to present all materials for supervision in a confidential manner, and to keep his/her administrative supervisor informed regarding clients presented in supervision.

The agency administrative supervisor, training program supervisor, and the undersigned supervisor have agreed to inform each other if the therapist fails to act in an ethical manner regarding the safety of clients, safety of others in the client's context, client confidentiality, third party fraud, or sex with clients. The undersigned supervisor agrees to inform the agency administrative supervisor of problems and concerns regarding the therapist's professional behavior.

This agreement is valid from this date _____ to _____.

_____   _____
Signature Intern/Student Therapist   Signature Off-Site Supervisor

_____
Signature Agency Administrative Supervisor

Developed by P. Dwyer.

83

Resources For Supervising in Private Contracts

Hargrave, T. (1991). Utilizing inexpensive communication systems: Building one-way mirrors for private practice consultation and supervision. *Journal of Marital and Family Therapy, 17*, 89-91.

Kaslow, F. (1986). Seeking and providing supervision in private practice. In F. Kaslow (Ed.), *Supervision and training: Models, dilemmas, and challenges* (pp. 143-157). New York: Haworth Press.

> *There has been a significant decrease in the number of private practitioners engaged in privately contracted supervision according to a study of American Association for Marriage and Family Therapy Approved Supervisors.*

Nichols, W., Nichols, D., & Hardy, K. (1990). Supevision in family therapy: A decade restudy. *Journal of Marital and Family Therapy, 16*, 275-285.

Storm, C. (1990). Striking the supervision bargain. *Supervision Bulletin, 4*, 3-4.

II. PHILOSOPY:
PREFERRED IDEAS, VALUES, & BELIEFS

Supervisory Challenge 6: Comparing Supervision Models

Sophisticated supervisors are not only clear about their own philosophy of supervision, but are knowledgeable about the variety of supervision models. One way to test your knowledge of the many supervision approaches is to apply a variety of supervision models to a supervision scenario. After reading the one described here, ask yourself: If I were a supervisor with a _____ supervision philosophy, how would I view supervision? What personal and/or professional information, if any, would I need? How would I address the supervisees' concerns? What recommendations , if any, would I make regarding the cases?

Karen and Bill share the supervision hour. Karen is a 38 year old, Caucasian, divorced mother of a teen-ager. Bill is 25 years old, an African American, married, and has three young children. Both completed a MFT program and are employed in a local community mental health center. Although this is Bill's first professional job, Karen has worked in social services for over ten years. Karen prefers a solution-focused therapy approach while Bill's choice is his own unique mixture of the intergenerational approaches. However, their overall goals are similar. Both want to refine their approach particularly integrating their personal styles. Karen has brought a videotaped session of a divorcing couple who are in conflict over their children, who are suddenly having trouble in school and at home. Karen says she's overwhelmed with all of the issues and having difficulty knowing where to focus therapy. Bill's case is of a depressed single adult woman. Although she has not been suicidal, Bill finds himself worrying that her depression will worsen and he will not have done all he could. He has even found himself staying awake at night thinking about this case.

So, how did you do? How easy was it for you to move among the various models? If you were like the typical supervisor, some models were easier than others for you to apply. If there were supervision approaches that were still a bit fuzzy to you, perhaps its time to reread the chapters in the text. In either event, this exercise can be a helpful precursor to identifying your own theoretical leanings for your supervision philosophy.

85

Grid Comparing Supervision Models

Cheryl L. Storm

As you read about the many models of supervision, this form can be used to summarize each model. This exercise helps you compare the similarities and differences in the ideas and methods of the various models, and prepares you to apply them in supervision. On the form *Goal* refers to the major assumption(s) about the primary purpose of supervision (e.g., some models assume supervision is skill building while others view it as aimed at personal growth of supervisees). The second column, *Relationship*, refers to the type of supervisory relationship the model suggests (e.g. hierarchical, collaborative, and so on). *Methods*, the third column, refers to how supervision would typically be done and in what type of structure (i.e., individually, in groups, and so on). The final column, *Interventions*, refers to typical ways supervisors working from the model intervene.

COMPARISON OF SUPERVISION MODELS GRID

Criteria				
Model	*Goal*	*Relationship*	*Methods*	*Interventions*
Bowenian Family Therapy	Differentiation of therapist	Coach	Therapist works on own family-of-origin issues Presentation of own & clients genograms	Modeling of differentiation & agreed on activities to increase therapist's differentiation in his/her family

Tailored Supervision

Debby L. Schwarz Hirschhorn

My grandfather, I understand, was a tailor. I know, from the stories I have heard, that he felt the same suit might fit his customers' needs better at one stage of their lives than at another. Maybe that is why it makes sense to me that some modes of supervision fit supervisees better at some times than at others.

The first mode of supervision that I had was based on applying recognized systemic therapy models (e.g., brief therapy, solution-focused, and so on). In this mode a supervisor, highly competent in a particular theory of therapy, attempts to inculcate an appreciation of that model in the supervisee. It is the supervisor's job to reflect what has been gleaned from the supervision by applying (correctly) the supervisor's model to the supervisee's clients.

Another mode of supervision entails the supervisor attempting to assist supervisees in developing their own therapy style. In this mode of supervision supervisors allow supervisees to experiment with integrating the various models of therapy that they have been exposed to previously. In addition, if group supervision is used, the refusal of the supervisor to guide supervisees down a particular path creates an atmosphere in which group members feel comfortable turning to one another for ideas. Thus, supervision not only becomes an opportunity to integrate previous experiences, but also, through contact with colleagues, an opportunity to integrate unfamiliar models.

In experiencing these two supervision modes, what is useful to me is that each came at the right time to best help me in my professional development. Initially, I required something tangible to copy. I came from a nonsystemic background and was interested in shelving all previous learning for awhile to make room for new ideas. A supervisor who did not adhere to a particular model of therapy would have left me confused and frustrated. A supervisor giving concrete directions for adhering to a particular therapy model gave me a clear path on which to move forward.

87

This kind of supervision requires a balance on the supervisor's part between demanding adherence to a model and recognizing that, for the supervisee, it is not easy to suspend one's former "self" (Gergen, 1991) in order to function in a different way than before. For example, my first supervisor, who combined an Ericksonian and a Mental Research Institute model of doing therapy, developed engaging metaphors and expected that they be threaded through future family sessions. He would question closely to see if a family's interaction cycles were tracked, and he would model the types of interventions he thought suitable. Furthermore, if he liked a particular intervention, he believed in "pushing" it, something I had not been comfortable with. While I had to suspend my former "self," I learned how to do therapy without hedging.

My second supervisor was committed to solution-focused therapy. There was much comment, regarding my work, about avoiding "problem talk," not wasting precious minutes getting to the miracle question, and how to join with clients without focusing on problem description, but rather by inquiring about their interests.

In spite of the beneficial aspect of total immersion in a new model, one of the side effects of that mode of supervision is that supervisees may have very little to contribute to discussions. Interaction can center on how to best apply the particular model favored by the supervisor. Since the supervisee is in a one-down position relative to the supervisor as an expert in the use of the model, such discussions can merely become demonstrations that the supervisee is "catching on" to the use and philosophy of a new model. That is not at all bad -- quite the opposite. But after the catching on has been established, an opportunity to see if the model "fits" for the individual appears to me to be very helpful. When the supervisor prefers that a supervisee construct a personal model of therapy, the supervise does not need to impress the supervisor with his or her understanding of the model. The understanding necessary in such a situation in effect pits the supervisee against him or herself: How can I use my understanding of theory and practice to support the actions I am taking in the therapy room? Such an environment encourages open discussion and use of previous experience.

By the time I had a third supervisor, I felt like I needed space to try out some of the ideas I had formed in previous supervision. I was very impressed with solution-focused therapy, but wondered about how some aspects of it fit for me. I needed a clarification of the model and the flexibility to apply it somewhat differently. The timing for a supervision style in which a supervisee constructs his or her own model of therapy was perfect for me.

At the outset, my supervisor asked me what my goals were for professional development. I told him that I liked solution-focused therapy but was unsure if I could join and get to the miracle question as quickly as my last supervisor preferred. My new supervisor helped me to remain solution-focused by taking my time to join with families. He also blended in some of the learning I had acquired from my first supervisor by help ing to develop metaphors suited to each client. I felt encouraged for the first time to do therapy on the basis of my "own voice" (Rambo, Heath, & Chenail, 1993, p. 132) rather than on the basis of what fit the model I was working with. Practicing therapy on the basis of what feels right is a way of being that seems to me more suited to therapists with some experience behind them than to novice practitioners.

From the foregoing, it would seem that a beginning therapist might be more comfortable and absorb more under the supervision of someone preferring a particular model of therapy, while a more experienced therapist would perhaps flourish best within a spacious style that allows for personal exploration and modification of existing therapeutic models. Supervisors aware of the level of experience of their supervisees can then tailor supervision to fit the stage of their supervisees' professional development.

Note

The author is indebted to Dr. Jim Rudes for his "tailored supervision" and his encouragement.

Gergen, K. (1991). *The saturated self: Dilemmas of identity in contemporary life.* New York: Basic Books.

Rambo, A., Heath, A., & Chenail, R. (1993). *Practicing therapy: Exercises for growing therapists.* New York: W. W. Norton.

How To Assess Supervisees and Tailor Interventions

Sandra A. Rigazio-DiGilio

The assessment and intervention techniques provided to you here can be used in supervision regardless of your preferred supervision approaches or the preferred therapeutic approaches of your supervisees. Because systemic cognitive-developmental supervision (SCDS) facilitates the integration of many therapeutic and supervision techniques, it provides you with a general method to tailor your work to the individual needs and desires of your supervisees -- whether they wish to work within school-specific or integrative models of therapy. (You can find a full discussion of SCDS supervision in chapter 14 of the text.)

The Four Orientations

Cognitive-developmental orientations are used to identify various ways supervisees experience, view, and operate in the world and during therapy and supervision. SCDC focuses on the potentials and limits of supervisees' primary cognitive-developmental orientation. That is, how the orientations supervisees rely on organize the way they conceptualize and approach clinical and supervisory information. Supervisees are viewed as having different degrees of access to skills within each of the four orientations. Each orientation offers different conceptual, perceptual, executive, and relational resources that supervisees can draw upon during therapy and supervision.

In the chart on the next page, the four orientations are described with their accompanying competencies and constraints. *Competencies* are the skills available to supervisees. *Constraints* are the ways supervisees who over-rely on a particular orientation, might be limited by doing so. Constraints also reflect the ways supervisees may haphazardly use skills across orientations if they have not developed a sufficient foundation in any one of the orientations. The goal is to help supervisees to work within and master the primary cognitive, affective, and behavioral resources identified by each of the orientations so that they can enhance their therapeutic competence and their personal awareness.

THE FOUR COGNITIVE DEVELOPMENTAL ORIENTATIONS

Description	Competencies	Constraints
Sensorimotor/Elemental Use direct sensory experiences. Request help organizing information into hypotheses, clarifying intense emotional exchanges, & developing structured plans for sessions.	**Sensorimotor/Elemental** Draw upon here-and-now skills. Directly experience & track emotional exchanges without being reactive or overwhelmed. Identify own feelings permitting the working through of transference & countertransference.	**Sensorimotor/Elemental** Overly affected by intense emotional exchanges & prone to own hyperstimulation. Drawn to affective involvements which interfere with conceptual & executive skills. Interventions based on what feels right at the time resulting in random, haphazard treatment.
Concrete/Situational Describe events & articulate cause & effect transactions which permit predictability. Request help regarding accomplishing interventions & treatment plans. Often ask for validation.	**Concrete/Situational** Apply if/then reasoning. Develop linear hypotheses to better anticipate client reactions. Describe basic dynamics that occur in therapy & supervision that are usually keenly accurate.	**Concrete/Situational** Overly depend on one set of hypotheses or techniques. Difficulty seeing alternative perspectives, viewing situations from affective or reflective vantage points, applying circular reasoning, & recognizing how specific interventions fit into a wider treatment plan.
Formal/Reflective Analyze situations from multiple perspectives & use reflective & circular reasoning. Request help deciphering typical patterns within or across cases or in relation to self, & for assistance in examining theoretical/ therapeutic themes.	**Formal/Reflective** Synthesize ideas & strategies across various models & modify treatment plans based on clinical or supervisory feedback. Can examine how their own patterns impact on therapy & supervision. Directly link actions with an overall treatment plan.	**Formal/Reflective** Difficulty transferring assessments & plans to effective executive skills & recognizing or challenging assumptions. Minimize affective & behavioral data, preferring to analyze themes across situations.
Dialectic/Systemic Challenge assumptions undergirding their conceptualizations. Request help organizing their thoughts & questions into appropriate treatment plans. Seek assurance of their treatment plans because they recognize limitations inherent in any one choice.	**Dialectic/Systemic** Aware of wider contextual & historical influences. Seek solutions aimed at clients & broader environment. Assists clients through deconstruction & reconstruction of rules, assumptions, & themes.	**Dialectic/Systemic** Overwhelmed by multiple & contextual perspectives, so unable to commit to plan of action. Easily render any sense of reality as meaningless versus treating ideas as alternative & perhaps viable constructions. Clients often unable to deal with complexity of ideas.

Supervising Using the Orientations

Supervisees are seen as requiring different supervisory approaches throughout supervision, depending on their developmental, historical, contextual, and sociocultural circumstances. Supervisors strive to co-construct environments uniquely tailored to each supervisee's orientation in order to facilitate skill mastery and skill extension. In the next chart, supervisory objectives and modalities/techniques are summarized which help you accomplish this goal. This chart enables you to coherently select -- from among diverse supervisory options -- those that best fit the needs of those you supervise at any given point in supervision. It also allows you to incorporate your own practices, whether you work from a school-specific or integrative framework.

The final chart conveys examples of the types of questions that can be asked by the supervisor regarding four domains of experience: the client, the self-as-therapist, the therapeutic process, and the supervisory process. These questions are initially used to identify and work within supervisees' primary orientations and are later used to identify and explore ancillary orientations. The ultimate objective is to ensure that supervisees learn to work within developmentally appropriate orientations over time and in different circumstances. As a supervisor, you can first use the questions within the orientation of your supervisees across the four domains to establish a firm foundation within that orientation. Then you can help your supervisees tap resources within the other orientations by asking questions in one domain of experience across the orientations.

When supervisors are able to co-construct a supervisory environment, target appropriate objectives, and use supervision modalities and techniques that fit with supervisees' orientations, supervision is tailored to supervisees' needs. Because supervision fits them, supervisees are encouraged to examine the constraints of their world view and to explore alternative resources.

This exercise is reproduced here by permission of S. Rigazio-DiGilio, copyright 1995.

92

MATCHING ENVIRONMENTS, OBJECTIVES, AND MODALITIES/TECHNIQUES

Supervision Environment

Sensorimotor/Elemental
- Structured environment
- Created by directive supervisory style

Concrete/Situational
- Coaching environment
- Created by semi-directive style

Formal/Reflective
- Consulting environment
- Created by supervisor assuming consultant role

Dialectic/Systemic
- Collaborative environment
- Created by supervisor & supervisees engaging in collegial venture

Supervision Objectives

Sensorimotor/Elemental
- Develop skills in case conceptualization
- Clarify & directly experience client & therapist feelings
- Reduce anxiety
- Identify transference & countertransference issues

Concrete/Situational
- Learn/practice strategies & techniques
- Become proficient at if/then reasoning
- Enhance tracking skills
- Increase predictability
- Understand decision-making process

Formal/Reflective
- Reflect/analyze self & clinical data
- Generalize assessment & intervention skills
- Identify themes & patterns in self, client, therapy, & supervision
- Co-construct parallel analogs to help clients expand perspectives & actions

Dialectic/Systemic
- Recognize/challenge assumptions & rules
- Recognize/challenge developmental & contextual influences on worldview
- Evaluate parameters of one's beliefs & constructions

Sample Modalities/Techniques

Sensorimotor/Elemental
- Live supervision
- Supervisor/supervisee therapy teams
- Electronic & team supervision focused on case conceptualizations
- Instruction

Concrete/Situational
- Live supervision with pre/mid/post coaching
- Electronic supervision focused on conceptual & executive mastery
- Practice exercises focused on conceptual & executive skills

Formal/Reflective
- Edited electronic segments focused on identifying themes & patterns across cases and encounters
- Assistance in constructing & using integrative metaframeworks
- Independent self-analysis exercises

Dialectic/Systemic
- Focus on epistemological & ontological issues
- Cotherapy
- Peer consultation
- Co-constructing hypotheses & plans

SAMPLE QUESTIONS FOR SUPERVISORY ASSESSMENT AND INTERVENTION

Client	Self As Therapist	Therapeutic Process	Supervisory Process
Sensorimotor/Elemental	**Sensorimotor/Elemental**	**Sensorimotor/Elemental**	**Sensorimotor/Elemental**
How does this couple express emotions?	How do you feel as you descibe this couple?	How is the couple feeling toward you?	How does my reaction effect you?
Concrete/Situational	**Concrete/Situational**	**Concrete/Situational**	**Concrete/Situational**
What do they do & say to each other?	Can you tell me exactly what you did with this couple?	What did they do to prompt that reaction?	Could you describe what just occurred here?
Formal/Reflective	**Formal/Reflective**	**Formal/Reflective**	**Formal/Reflective**
What themes are evident that help you understand this couple?	Does your reaction to this couple seem familiar to you?	What approach seems to match this couple best?	How is our relationship similar to others in your life?
Dialectic/Systemic	**Dialectic/Systemic**	**Dialectic/Systemic**	**Dialectic/Systemic**
What rules does this couple operate from?	What rules are you operating from when working with this couple?	What rules guide the therapy relationship you have with this couple?	What rules guide the work we do here?

Resources For Comparing Supervision Models

Aponte, H. (1992). Training the person of the therapist in structural family therapy. *Journal of Marital and Family Therapy, 18,* 269-281.

Bagarozzi, D. (1980). Wholistic family therapy and clinical supervision: Systematic behavioral and psychoanalytic perspectives. *Family Therapy, 7,* 153-165.

Beck, R. (1984). The supervision of family of origin family systems treatment. In C. Munson (Ed.), *Family of origin applications in clinical supervision* (pp. 49-60). New York: Haworth Press.

Bernard, J., & Goodyear, R. (1992). *Fundamentals of clinical supervision.* Boston, MA: Allyn & Bacon.

> *Although no one model of supervision is preferred by supervisors, the theory most cited as influencing supervisor's philosophies is structural, followed closely by intergenerational.*

Wetchler, J. (1988). Primary and secondary influential theories of family therapy supervisors: A research note. *Family Therapy, 15,* 69-74.

Bobele, M., Gardner, G., & Biever, J. (1995). Supervision as social construction. *Journal of Systemic Therapies, 14,* 14-25.

Cantwell, P., & Holmes, S. (1995). Cumulative process: A collaborative approach to systemic supervision. *Journal of Systemic Therapies, 14,* 35-46.

Colapinto, J. (1988). Teaching the structural way. In H. Liddle, D. Breunlin, & R. Schwartz, (Eds.), *Handbook of family therapy training and supervision* (pp. 17-37). New York: Guilford Press.

Connell, G. (1984). An approach to supervision of symbolic-experiential psychotherapy. *Journal of Marital and Family Therapy, 10,* 273-280.

Duhl, B. (1986). Toward cognitive-behavioral integration in training systems therapists: An interactive approach to training in generic systems thinking. In F. Piercy (Ed.), *Family therapy education and supervision* (pp. 91-108). New York: Haworth Press.

Fine, M. (1992). Family therapy training: II. Hypothesizing and story telling. *Journal of Family Psychotherapy, 3,* 61-79.

Fisch, R. (1988). Training in the brief therapy model of the M.R.I. In H. Liddle, D. Breunlin, & R. Schwartz (Eds.), *Handbook of family therapy training and supervision* (pp. 78-92). New York: Guilford Press.

Frank, T. (1994). Solution-oriented supervision: The coaxing of expertise. *The Family Journal, 2*, 11-18.

Haley, J. (1996). *Teaching and learning family therapy.* New York: Guilford Press.

Haley, J. (1993). How to be a therapy supervisor without knowing how to change anyone. *Journal of Systemic Therapies, 4*, 41-52.

Haley J. (1988). Reflections on supervision. In H. Liddle, D. Breunlin, & R. Schwartz (Eds.), *Handbook of family therapy training and supervision* (pp. 358-367). New York: Guilford Press.

Hill, E. (1992). Marital and family therapy supervision: A relational-attachment model. *Contemporary Family Therapy, 14*, 115-125.

Holloway, E. (1992). Supervision: A way of teaching and learning. In S. Brown, & R. Lent (Eds.), *Handbook of counseling psychology* (2nd ed., pp. 177-214). New York: John Wiley & Sons.

Kaslow, F. (1991). Marital therapy supervision and consultation. *American Journal of Family Therapy, 19*, 129-146.

Kassis, J., & Adelfer, C. (1987). "Mixed doubles": An exercise of double description comparing structural and strategic-systemic supervision. *Journal of Strategic and Systemic Therapies, 6*, 51-56.

Keller, J., & Protinsky, H. (1985). Family therapy supervision: An integrative model. *Journal of Psychotherapy and the Family, 1*, 83-90.

Landau, J., & Stanton, M. (1983). Aspects of supervision with the "Pick-a-Dali Circus" model. *Journal of Strategic and Systemic Therapies, 2*, 31-39.

Liddle, H., Breunlin, D., & Schwartz R. (Eds.), (1988). *Handbook of family therapy training and supervision.* New York: Guilford Press.

Marek, L., Sandefer, D., Beach, A., Coward, R., & Protinsky, H. (1994). Supervision without the problem: A model of solution-focused supervision. *Journal of Family Psychotherapy, 5*, 57-64.

Mazza, J. (1988). Training strategic therapists: The use of indirect techniques. In H. Liddle, D. Breunlin, & R. Schwartz (Eds.), *Handbook of family therapy training and supervision* (pp. 93-109). New York: Guilford Press.

McDaniel, S., Weber, T., & McKeever, J. (1983). Multiple theoretical approaches to supervision: Choices in family therapy training. *Family Process, 22*, 491-500.

Mead, E., & Crane, D. (1978). An empirical approach to supervision and training of relationship therapists. *Journal of Marriage and Family Counseling, 4*, 67-76.

Merl, H. (1995). Reflecting supervision. *Journal of Systemic Therapies, 14* , 47-56.

Munson, C. (Ed.). (1984). *Family-of-origin applications in clinical supervision.* New York: Haworth Press.

Neal, J. (1996). Narrative training and supervision. *Journal of Systemic Therapies, 15,* 63-79.

Papero, D. (1988). Training in Bowen Theory. In H. Liddle, D. Breunlin, & R. Schwartz (Eds.), *Handbook of family therapy training and supervision* (pp. 62-77). New York: Guilford Press.

Pirotta, S., & Cecchin, G. (1988). The Milan training program. In H. Liddle, D. Breunlin, & R. Schwartz (Eds.), *Handbook of family therapy training and supervision* (pp. 38-61). New York: Guilford Press.

Protinsky, H., & Keller, J. (1984). Supervision of marriage and family therapy: A family-of-origin approach. In C. Munson (Ed.), *Family-of-origin applications in clinical supervision* (pp. 75-80). New York: Haworth Press.

Protinsky, J., & Preli, R. (1987). Intervention in strategic supervision. *Journal of Strategic and Systemic Therapies, 6,* 18-23.

Selekman, M., & Todd, T. (1995). Co-creating a context for change in the supervisory system: The solution-focused supervision model. *Journal of Systemic Therapies, 14,* 21-33.

Stoltenberg, C., & Delworth, U. (1987). *Supervising counselors and therapists: A developmental approach* . San Francisco: Jossey-Bass.

Storm, C., & Heath, A. (1982). Strategic supervision: The danger lies in discovery. *Journal of Strategic and Systemic Therapy, 1,* 71.

Storm, C., Heath, A. (1991). Problem-focused supervision: Rationale, exemplification, and limitations. *Journal of Family Psychotherapy, 2,* 55-70.

Taibbi, R. (1990). Integrated family therapy: A model for supervision. *Families in Society, 71,* 542-549.

Thomas, F. (1994). Solution-oriented supervision: The coaxing of expertise. *The Family Journal, 2,* 11-18.

Tucker, B., Hart, G., & Liddle, H. (1976). Supervision in family therapy: A developmental perspective. *Journal of Marriage and Family Counseling, 2,* 269-276.

Wetchler, J. (1990). Solution-focused supervision. *Family Therapy, 17,* 129-138.

Wetchler, J. (1988). Primary and secondary influential theories of family therapy supervisors: A research note. *Family Therapy, 15,* 69-74.

White, M. (1989/1990). Family therapy training and supervision in a world of experience and narrative. *Dulwich Centre Newsletter, Summer,* 27-38.

Wright, L., Luckhurst, P., & Amundson, J. (1990). Family therapy supervision as counter-induction. *Journal of Family Psychotherapy, 1,* 65-74.

Anderson, H. *Supervision with Harlene Anderson.* (Video #535). Washington, DC: The American Association for Marriage and Family Therapy (AAMFT).

Berg, I., Freidman, E., Liddle, H., & Todd, T. *Fielding supervision impasses.* (Video #531). Washington, DC: AAMFT.

Rigazio-DiGilio, S., & Anderson, S. *Cognitive developmental model.* (Video #530). Washington, DC: AAMFT.

Thomas, F. *Solution-focused supervision.* (Video #566). Washington, DC: AAMFT.

Chess, S., Gendlin, E., Haley, J., Geary, B. *Supervision panel.* Pheonix, AZ: The Milton Erickson Foundation Inc.

Fialkov, C., & Haddad, D. *Improvisation in postmodern supervision.* (Audio #706-315). Norcross, VA: Resource Link.

Glasser, W., Madanes, C., Yalom, Y., & Loriedo, C. *Supervision panel.* Pheonix, AZ: The Milton Erickson Foundation Inc.

Goulding, M., Marmor, J., Silverstein, O., Trenkle, B. *Supervision panel.* Pheonix, AZ: The Milton Erickson Foundation Inc.

MacKune-Karrer, B., Cohen, R., & Eldon, M. *Experiencing metaframeworks: Learning to be systemic.* (Audio #706-503). The Norcross, VA: The Resource Link.

Rigazio-DiGilio, S. *Systemic cognitive-developmental model.* (Audio #706-303). The Norcross, VA: The Resource Link.

Thomas, F., & Corley, D. *Competency & collaboration in supervision.* (Audio #706-203) The Norcross, VA: The Resource Link.

Supervisory Challenge 7:
Creating Your Own Philosophy

We both continue to be amazed as we watch even experienced MFT colleagues whom we respect freeze completely when asked to commit their philosophy of supervision to writing. Added pressure seems to come from being asked to write a comprehensive statement in a limited number of pages.

We are always convinced (although you may not be) that you already "have it in you" to begin to articulate your philosophy. Over the years, we have developed a variety of gimmicks to help supervisors-in-training "break the ice" and begin this process. Often we have included assignments such as answering the questions in the next article as part of our supervision courses. For beginning supervisors, Cheryl has recommended beginning with your model of therapy and then asking yourself which of your therapy assumptions about change also fit the supervision context.

There is no need to rely on elaborate assignments to get over the obstacles of writing. Any initial stimulus will do, including a chapter from the philosophy section of the text, comparing notes with another supervisor, or watching the supervision videos listed on the resource page. Whatever the stimulus, get started by jotting down your thoughts on the following: What assumptions made by the supervisor (i.e., chapter author, others you know, supervisors on the video, and so on) am I particularly comfortable with? Where would I make different assumptions? What supervisory interventions made by this supervisor would I also tend to make or avoid completely? What methods and structures (e.g., live supervision versus case report, individual supervision versus team, and so on) fit best for me? Go back over your answers and elaborate on why you have made particular choices, and you will find yourself well on your way.

Family Therapy Supervision Theory-Building Questions

Fred P. Piercy & Doug H. Sprenkle

Almost a decade ago we proposed a series of family therapy theory building questions to help family therapy students think through and develop their own evolving theory of therapy (Piercy & Sprenkle, 1988). Similarly, we believe that family therapy supervisors can use these theory building questions to develop their own integrative theory of family therapy supervision. Here we present illustrative family therapy supervision theory building questions for this purpose.

You can answer these questions for yourself individually or with another supervisor, or if you are training supervisors raise one or more of these questions with supervisors-in-training individually or in a group setting. We like to break large groups into triads where one person is the "focus person" and the other two ask that person selected supervision theory building questions. What results is not a group discussion, because only one person has the "floor" at any one time. After a half hour or so, someone else becomes the focus person.

You may wish to use these questions in other ways as well. For example, you could write brief answers on one or more of the theory building questions, or plan discussions with other supervisors around certain questions. Or you could videotape your answers to selected questions, and examine the videotapes at a later date to examine change in theory over time. You can also compare your answers to the thinking reflected in the literature on family therapy supervision.

We believe that the most important outcome in using these questions is the reflective process supervisors go through in developing their own supervision theory. That is, we hope that through raising these questions -- in whatever format -- you will be challenged to think, integrate, and grow as competent supervisors and scholars. We present the supervision theory building questions in this spirit.

Piercy, F. & Sprenkle, D. (1988). Family therapy theory-building questions. *Journal of Marital and Family Therapy, 14*, 307-309.

FAMILY THERAPY SUPERVISION
THEORY-BUILDING QUESTIONS

Influence

- What models of therapy have most influenced your supervision approach? What models of supervision have most influenced your approach?

- What books have had the most impact on your approach to family therapy supervision? What theorists? Why?

- How has the thinking of constructionist therapists such as Anderson and Goolishian, Andersen, White, deShazer, and others influenced your theory of supervision? What aspects of their work do you plan to employ in supervision? Why?

- In what other ways does your supervision theory relate to current marriage and family therapy (MFT) and supervision literatures?

Isomorphism

- In what ways is your model of therapy similar to your model of supervision? In what ways is it different?

- How do you integrate the concept of isomorphism (i.e.,patterns and sequences replicated at various systems levels) into your theory of supervision?

Change and Components of Supervision

- What do you attempt to do in the supervision you provide? What does this tell you about your theory of supervision?

- How do supervisees change in supervision and how does that relate to what you do as a supervisor?

- What are several theoretical tenets (assumptions) that guide your supervision?

- What are your main supervision goals? Defend these goals.

- How is what you do in supervision consistent with your supervision theory and supervision goals?

- How important are the following in your evolving supervision theory:
  Supervisor-supervisee relationship
  Empowerment
  Transference and countertransference
  Skill building
  DSM IV
  Family-of-origin issues

- To what extent do you see supervision as education? In what ways is it similar and in what ways is it different?

- Discuss how one or more of these constructs or principles fit or do not fit into your evolving theory of supervision: power, hierarchy, social constructionism, choice, individuation/differentiation, transference, behavioral rehearsal, collaboration, paradox, triangles, self-disclosure, therapeutic stories, humor, and internal resources.

- What relative importance do you give affect, cognition and behavior change in your approach to MFT supervision?

- How do you foster the development and creativity of therapists rather than simply fostering imitation of yourself?

Developmental Stages of Supervision

- What developmental stages do you conceptualize in the supervision process?

- To what degree are developmental stages of the supervision process important in your approach to supervision? Why?

- How is what you do different in each of these developmental stages? Why is it different?

Self of Supervisor

- How have your personal values, beliefs, life experiences, and theoretical assumptions had an effect on your philosophy and practice of supervision?

- What personal qualities do you believe are important for the therapist to demonstrate in supervision?

- What personal or family-of-origin issues should you be aware of when you provide supervision? What about areas of discomfort or inexperience? In what ethical ways do you plan to deal with these issues?

- Are there certain supervision issues for which you should seek consultation or refer? What are they?

- How do you plan to renew yourself as a supervisor? How do you plan to keep "up" with the supervision literature?

Gender Issues

- How has the feminist critique of MFT informed your approach to supervision?

- What gender issues should you be aware of as a supervisor? In what ways might your gender and the gender of your supervisee affect the way you do supervision?

- How do you as a supervisor deal with power differential in the supervisory relationship and in the families that your supervisees treat?

Diversity Issues

- How does your evolving supervision theory incorporate issues of culture, ethnicity, class, sexual orientation, disability, and other aspects of diversity?

- In what ways have you learned to work productively with supervisees from different cultures and backgrounds?

- When should cultural differences be accepted in therapy and supervision and when should they be challenged? What is your rationale?

- In what ways do you change your approach to supervision to "fit" the culture or unique background of your supervisees?

Accountability/Assessment

- What are the components of your supervision contract with your supervisees? How do you develop this contract? In what way do you involve your supervisee in the development of this contract?

- How do you evaluate your progress in supervision? How do you reliably evaluate the skill level of your supervisees? What written feedback do you provide your supervisees? What opportunities do they have to respond to this feedback?

- How do you incorporate supervisee feedback into the supervision process?

Ethical Issues

- How do you negotiate dual relationship issues in supervision?

- What are important ethical and legal responsibilities of the supervisor?

- How do you deal with issues such as client confidentiality, informed consent, videotaping and live observation, and professional boundaries?

An Example of an Integrative Supervision Philosophy

Mona DeKoven Fishbane

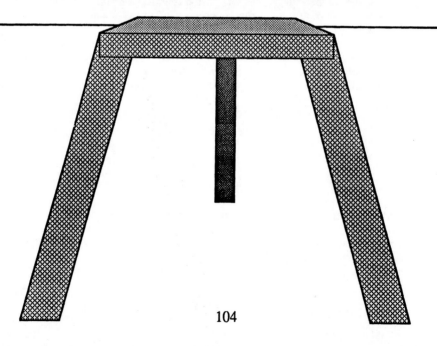

SUPERVISOR PROFILE: Mona DeKoven Fishbane

At the Time of Supervisory Training:

Education: Doctoral degree in psychology from the University of Massachusettes in 1979.
Contextual Influences: 49 year old, Caucasian, Jewish female.
Therapy Experience: 5 years in agency & 15 years in private setting.
Theoretical Influences: Worked intensively with prominent therapists from a number of "schools," including Umbarger (structural), Weakland and Fisch (Mental Research Institute Model), Silverstein (systemic), and White (narrative). Also considers the contextual model of Boszormenyi-Nagi and the family systems model of Bowen to have been important influences.
Supervision Experience: Supervisor for over 14 years.
Supervision Orientation: Integrative

Since Becoming a Supervisor:

Designation as an Approved Supervisor: 1994
Professional Setting: Faculty member, Chicago Center for Family Health.
Supervision Experience: Conducts a consultation group for therapists exploring their own family-of-origin issues in a marriage and family therapy institute.

Theoretical Influences on Therapy

My therapeutic orientation reflects my integration of several models --
primarily systemic, family-of-origin, object relations, and narrative. I have also
been influenced by the strategic schools, although I do not consider myself a
strategic therapist per se. New theories on gender differences and the feminist
critique of marriage family therapy (MFT) inform my work as well.

Respect for clients, and a resource-based rather than a pathology-based
approach is the foundation of my work in therapy; a similar respect informs my
approach to supervision. A brief description of my approach to therapy will serve
as a backdrop to my theory of supervision, as there are many parallels between the
two. My starting point is an appreciation of context. Clients' context includes their
life-cycle stage, cultural and ethnic legacies, gender, and health and financial
factors, among others. I want to know the context of their decision to see me, as
well as their prior therapy experiences. Early on I work out a contract with clients.
Their definition of the problem, and their goals -- in conjunction with my early
formulation -- form the basis of the contract. I help them take ownership of the
change process, with me as "assistant" (Nichols, 1988). The therapeutic contract
includes goals for change as well as time and financial considerations. At this early
stage, I am also joining with them and beginning the complex process of building
trust.

As a systemic therapist, I teach clients about circularity (Silverstein, 1983); I
encourage them to track their own sequences, to look for interactive patterns. I
explore with them their beliefs, premises, assumptions -- their narrative. I consider
with them how they construct their world. The idea of self as a creator helps them
challenge the idea of self as a victim. (However, I am not a radical constructivist; I
believe that injustices, abuse, and imbalances of power do exist and do affect
people. When these are present currently or historically in a family system, I
address them in therapy.) I am interested in each person's "survival strategies"--
the core positions they adopted as children to survive in their family-of-origin -- and

how these survival strategies interface and conflict in their current relationships. For me the sharing of these insights with their partners, and the witnessing of each other's work -- which enhances empathy -- are critical parts of the therapy. I help them look at their "dances," and at the processes of projective identification in the relationship. I find object relations helpful in understanding these processes. I look at my own feelings during the therapy, at the "resonances" (Elkaim, 1992), which I feel with these patients. This gives me information about them and about me as their therapist.

I help couples and families become more empowered about change with techniques such as externalizing the problem (White, 1989). When they become stuck, I explore dilemmas around stability and change (Keeney & Silverstein, 1986; Nichols, 1988). I may link the family's need for stability to intergenerational legacies and loyalties (Boszormenyi-Nagy & Spark, 1973). I do not believe in "resistance," but see it as either clients' loyalty to family-of-origin, or as a sign of a tension between therapist and family -- usually, with the therapist pushing for change, and the family pushing for stability. My job is not to change clients, but to help them make choices (Papero, 1988).

Throughout this work the holding therapeutic relationship is central. I am active, curious, empathic; I use humor where appropriate. At times I teach -- about gender differences, boundaries, childrearing dilemmas, and so on. I also learn about clients' world views, about courage, and about the many different ways people interact in families. I encourage feedback; I take criticism seriously. I prefer to be transparent about the work (White, 1993) rather than secretive, and to share power with clients (Wheeler et al., 1989). I maintain clear boundaries, and I am alert to ethical and legal issues.

Theoretical Influences on Supervision

There are many similarities in my approach to supervision. As in therapy, I want to know the context of both this supervision and of the therapist in his/her life. Is this a beginner, or a colleague well on her way? As with therapy, timing is critical, and I gear my approach to the needs and ability of the therapist. As we work out a contract and specific goals, the process is shaped by the therapist's needs and orientation as well as mine, and by external constraints such as licensing, the criteria set by the American Association for Marriage and Family Therapy's (AAMFT), and so on. We look at the institutional context of the therapist's clinical work and of our supervision (Liddle, 1988). In setting goals, I consider with the therapist his/her learning style so we can develop a good fit (Liddle, 1988; Wheeler et al., 1989). I am sensitive to contextual differences between us -- of gender, ethnicity, culture, age, and so on -- and how they might impact on the work. As with clients, I encourage the therapist to bring the lived data to our work. In supervision, this is done with a combination of detailed description, audio- and videotape, and live one-way mirror consultations I help the therapist clarify his/her beliefs and assumptions, as well as the clients , and to look at the interplay of these beliefs of the therapist and family system. Help the therapist actively consider the context of clients -- issues of power and gender, culture, family-of-origin, economic stability, and so on. I want to know how the therapist formulates hypotheses, and how these inform the therapeutic interventions (Tomm & Wright, 1979). I teach the therapist to identify interactional sequences and patterns, and to think and intervene systemically in sessions.

Impasses -- whether within the family, between therapist and family, or between therapist and supervisor--offer opportunities to deconstruct relationship dilemmas, and to explore individual assumptions, behaviors, and survival strategies which contribute to the impasse. Exploration of the layers of resonances (Elkaim, 1992; Prosky, 1992), in which isomorphic dilemmas are experienced by the family, therapist, and in the therapist/supervisor relationship, is often fruitful (Schwartz et al., 1988; Storm & Heath, 1985). My approach to helping a therapist with an impasse depends on the developmental stage of the therapist. With a less experienced marital and family therapist, I focus on skills and techniques. I help the therapist achieve a systemic understanding of the case, and consider ways of intervening to resolve the impasse. When a more experienced therapist who has mastered technique and systems thinking becomes stuck, I may additionally explore with him/her personal resonances using family-of-origin and genogram data. However, I access this level as a supervisor very carefully and respectfully to be sure to honor privacy and boundaries, and to differentiate supervision from therapy.

As with therapy, in supervision the relationship is a central factor, the basis of good work. I combine teaching of theory, techniques, and so on -- with dialogue with the therapist, working in a co-evolutionary and transparent manner (Todd, 1992; White, 1993). In that regard, if a team is used behind the one-way mirror, I am most comfortable using a reflecting team, which promotes collaboration, rather than hierarchy, for the couple or family, the therapist, and the team. Underlying this is an assumption of resources and wisdom in both clients and therapist, and a belief in a dialogical, respectful process (Liddle, 1988; Schwartz, 1988). I am aware that I am the supervisor, and not the therapist on the case (Liddle, 1988), so I work with the therapist as the focus in his/her work with the family or couple. Furthermore, I am sensitive to the dangers of "robotization" (Schwartz et al., 1988), and help the therapist develop his/her own style and approach rather than mimic mine. The degree of hierarchy in the supervisory relationship depends on the context, level of the therapist, and goals of supervision. My supervision with a more advanced therapist tends to be more collaborative (Liddle et al., 1988).

Evaluation and Feedback in Supervision

Evaluation and feedback are an essential part of supervision. As with clients, with therapists I frame mistakes as an opportunity to learn, and base my feedback on an appreciation of the therapist's strengths as well as weaknesses (Schwartz, 1988). I am aware that for the therapist to hear feedback, the arousal level should be moderate (Breunlin et al., 1988); excessive anxiety interferes with learning. I track with the therapist his/her development over the course of the supervision; I encourage self-evaluation by the therapist (Todd, 1992; Wheeler et al., 1989) as well. If I find evidence of deficits or gaps in the therapist's knowledge or skill mastery, I make suggestions to remedy the situation, such as further training. The nature of the evaluation varies with the stage of the therapist's development and the goals of the supervision. I provide written evaluations as required by institutions, licensing boards, AAMFT, and so on; in these I assess the therapist's strengths and weaknesses. In ensuring the safety of the supervision, I guard against dual relationships (Storm, 1993) and maintain confidentiality and an awareness of ethical and legal implications of the work.

Differences Between Supervision and Therapy

In my mind there are some significant differences between therapy and supervision. One relates to the balance of active teaching in supervision versus a more gradual evolutionary process of change in therapy. While I may confront and challenge in both modalities, I am likely to push harder in supervision. In therapy I am comfortable with the paradoxes of change, and address the change/stability dilemmas carefully, patiently, and systemically. Unless someone is in danger, I do not assume a controlling position in therapy, but rather work with the system. In supervision, the educational mandate is stronger. Furthermore, if a therapist is acting in a manner that concerns me, I am aware of my obligation to the clients, to the therapist, to the profession, and to society to evaluate and critique the therapist. As a supervisor I bear a level of responsibility to the clinical case as well as to the therapist and the field. Even if there is no serious problem or concern the evaluative role of the supervisor is built into supervision. The double agenda of supervision -- to nourish the growth of the therapist, and to evaluate -- differentiates supervision from therapy.

Supervision Case Study

T, a social worker, came to me for supervision in couple and family therapy. Her original training was psychodynamic, and she had completed post-graduate training in MFT as well. When she came to me she was already operating at a sophisticated level as a marital and family therapist. She was bright and well-read in the field. Two factors could have contributed to our developing a dual relationship or to competition: 1.) we knew each other as colleagues in the community, and 2.) her advanced level of development. We were, in fact, careful to preserve the boundaries of our supervisory relationship and did not confuse our task. T saw her clients in her private practice. We met once a week over the course of a year for supervision. Our contract was clearly negotiated as to time, place, fees, and goals. She provided me with a periodic written and oral summary of her overall practice; our focus was on several couples and family cases over time. Our primary medium was case consultation, with some audio- and videotaped, and live supervision. This was consistent with her advanced skill level and with my supervision philosophy, which emphasizes therapist narratives and internal process as well as systemic, interactive abilities.

We clarified goals and objectives at the beginning of our supervision. T had, in her prior training, learned an integrative approach to family therapy, and wanted to continue in that direction, integrating especially the systemic, individual, and integenerational levels in her work. She wanted to explore her own patterns of reacting to couples and families which might impede or facilitate therapy. She wanted to be challenged in supervision, especially to learn to take criticism. She shared her fear of making mistakes. She also wanted to be able to give me feedback in supervision. She was interested in learning new techniques in our work, and especially in honing her use of self as a therapist. I judged her goals to be appropriate given her skill level.

To assess T's interpersonal and learning styles, I asked her how she learns best and how I could best help her as a supervisor. She described herself as self-directive. She noted her tendency to take charge, even of her own supervision, and her ambivalence about getting help. I asked how she could let me help her. She said that a mutual respect in our learning would facilitate the process for her. These initial conversations about goals and learning styles were highly relevant to our subsequent work, and I believe we were true to the tasks we set out to accomplish.

T had two couples in her caseload who were at an impasse and considering divorce. In both cases the couple's original quid pro quo changed as the wife became more assertive and gained power in her life. T was sensitive to the gender and power issues in these cases. However, she was dismayed and frustrated because each couples was unable to renegotiate a new contract incorporating the wife's newfound power, and contemplated divorce instead. In our work, T related her desire to save these marriages to her own triangled position in her family-of-origin. This connection helped her shift her position with the couples, and she was able to help them grieve and let go of their old contract, and to consider their choices in a less constrained way. It was apparent that T's impasse with these couples was not based on technical ignorance; therefore I considered exploring her own family-of-origin resonances appropriate and productive.

T at times became over-responsible as a therapist, especially with clients in crisis. This led to her occasionally feeling frustrated and discouraged. I helped her identify and examine these moments of therapeutic disappointment or impatience. She readily saw that her position was keeping her stuck. She related her over responsibility to her role in her family-of-origin, and worked hard in our supervision to challenge this tendency in herself. I helped her share responsibility for therapy with her clients, to help them make choices in their lives. As she did this, she found she was better able to empathically connect with their dilemmas and their pain, and was less focused on changing them.

T treated a family whose members were overwhelmed and angry at their ill, demanding, elderly father. T became over-responsible and overwhelmed herself in the work. I suggested a strategic reframe -- that the sick father was feisty -- and had T coach the father to be more effective in his feistiness, so his caregivers would be more attentive. T and I also addressed the loss issues in the family. T made the link to the loss of her own father when she was a child; she saw that rescuing and over-responsibility were her answers to loss. This connection freed her up with the case and she became energetic and curious again with the family.

At one point when I gave T feedback about her pattern of taking on too much responsibility and feeling overwhelmed with this family, she heard me as criticizing her for complaining. This interaction in our supervision was isomorphic with the case: The ill father was a complainer, and the family criticized him for it. I clarified that I had felt connected with her in my observation, not critical. She found this interchange helpful. Although painful, this was an important moment of feedback between us.

In the course of our supervision we were attentive to T's strengths as a therapist as well as difficulties. She joins well, and stays with difficult clients and works on the therapeutic relationship with them. She handles crises and emergencies in a responsible, professional manner. Her mastery of systems is impressive. She sees sequences and patterns. She helps clients reframe their dilemmas in ways that empower them to make new choices. In working with families she is adept at detriangling a child and helping the parents work out their own issues. She is attentive to contextual issues such as culture, gender, and life cycle stages.

We were both committed to making our supervisory relationship collaborative, respectful, and honest. In the beginning of our work I wondered if I could be helpful to T; she leads so much with her competence. But she did indeed let me in and shared her doubts and vulnerabilities as well as her strengths. It was clear to both of us that this was supervision and not just collegiality or friendship. Furthermore, we were both clear that our relationship was supervision and not therapy; although we would explore the personal resonances for T of the impasses in her work, our focus was always on T as therapist. These boundaries around our work were essential for good supervision. We were aware of our shared gender, race, and socioeconomic status, but had different ethnic backgrounds. Although T was able to learn from me, I did not feel that she was "robotized" or imitating me. It was important to both of us that in our work T could explore her own issues and grow creatively as a therapist.

T's progress as a therapist was evident during our year of supervision. She became more adept at helping clients face their own dilemmas and choices, with T assuming appropriate, but not excessive responsibility. Her ability to work through relationship impasses with clients and her formulation of systemic hypotheses developed significantly. She achieved her goals in our supervision on receiving a and giving feedback and criticism. Although these moments are potentially painful, she faced them honestly and openly.

My Learning as a Supervisor-in-training

In evaluating my work as a supervisor this year with my own supervisor, in reading the supervision literature and formulating my supervision philosophy, Ilearned a great deal. I became more conscious of the levels in the supervisory process. I was aware of my role as outsider to the therapy, and while I made suggestions for therapeutic interventions, I was careful not to assume the role of therapist in the case. I kept in mind the relationship between T and myself in the supervision, and she and I periodically processed and reflected on it. I learned to appreciate the complex interplay between the different levels in this supervisory structure -- clients, therapist, and the levels of supervisory relationships. Being aware that I was accountable in this work on so many levels -- to myself, to T, to her clients, to my supervisor, to AAMFT and the field -- helped me evaluate my work and become more thoughtful about it. My supervision with T was consonant with her advanced stage of development. When I supervise less experienced therapists, I assume a more directive teaching role, and teaching of technique, live and videotaped supervision become more prominent. My personal challenge is to balance that more hierarchical teaching structure with the respectful, resource-based stance which is at the heart of my supervision and therapy. I look forward to this ongoing challenge in my future work as a supervisor.

Anderson, C., & Walsh, F. (Eds.), *Women in families: A framework for family therapy.* New York: W.W. Norton.

Boszormeyi-Nagy, I., & Spark, G. (1973). *Invisible loyalties: Reciprocity in integenerational family therapy.* New York: Harper & Row.

Breunlin, D., Karrer, B., McGuire, D., & Cimmarusti, R. (1988). Cybernetics of videotape supervision. In H. Liddle, D. Breunlin, & R. Schwartz, (Eds.), *Handbook of family therapy training and supervision* (pp. 194-206). New York: Guilford Press.

Elkaim, M. (1992, June). Comments at interest group on International Family Therapy Training Programs, AFTA, Amelia Island, Florida.

Keeney, B., & Silverstein, O. (1986). *The therapeutic voice of Olga Silverstein.* New York: Guilford Press.

Liddle, H. (1988). Systemic supervision: Conceptual overlays and pragmatic guidelines. In H. Liddle, D. Breunlin, & R. Schwartz, (Eds.), *Handbook of family therapy training and supervision* (pp. 153-171). New York: Guilford Press.

Liddle, H., Davidson, G., and Barrett, M. (1988). Outcomes of live supervision: Trainee perspectives. In H. Liddle, D. Breunlin, & R. Schwartz, (Eds.), *Handbook of family therapy training and supervision* (pp. 386-398). New York: Guilford Press.

Nichols, W. (1988). An integrative psychodynamic and systems approach. In H. Liddle, D. Breunlin, & R. Schwartz, (Eds.), *Handbook of family therapy training and supervision* (pp. 110-127). New York: Guilford Press.

Papero, D. (1988). Training in Bowen theory. In H. Liddle, D. Breunlin, & R. Schwartz, (Eds.), *Handbook of family therapy training and supervision* (pp. 62-77). New York: Guilford Press.

Prosky, P. (1992). Letter to the editor. *The Supervision Bulletin, 5,* 3 & 4.

Schwartz, R. (1988). The trainer-trainee relationship in family therapy training. In H. Liddle, D. Breunlin, & R. Schwartz, *Handbook of family therapy training and supervision* (pp. 172-182). New York: The Guilford Press.

Schwartz, R., Liddle, H., & Breunlin, D. (1988). Muddles in live supervision. In H. Liddle, D. Breunlin, & R. Schwartz, (Eds.), *Handbook of family therapy training and supervision* (pp. 183-193). N ew York: Guilford Press.

Silverstein, O. (1983). Private training group in systemic therapy. Cambridge, MA.

Storm, C., & Heath, A. (1985). Models of supervision: Using therapy theory as a guide. *Clinical Supervisor, 3,* 87-96.

Storm, C. (1993). Dual relationships: Broadening our understanding. *Supervision Bulletin, 6,* 1.

Todd, T. (1992). Self-supervision: A goal for all supervisors? *Supervision Bulletin, 5,* 3.

Tomm, K., & Wright, L. (1979). Training in family therapy: Perceptual, conceptual and executive skills. *Family Process, 18,* 237-250.

Wheeler, D., Avis, J., Miller, L., & Chaney, S. (1989). Rethinking family therapy training and supervision: A feminist model. In M. McGoldrick, C. Anderson, & F. Walsh (Eds.), *Women in families: A framework for family therapy.* (pp. 135-151). New York: W.W. Norton.

White, M. (1988/89). The externalizing of the problem and the reauthoring of lives and relationships. *Dulwich Center Newsletter, Summer,* 5-28.

White, M. (1993). Intensive workshop in narrative therapy. Evanston, IL: Evanston Family Therapy Center.

An Example of a Consistent Supervision Philosophy

Teresa McDowell

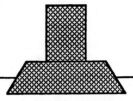

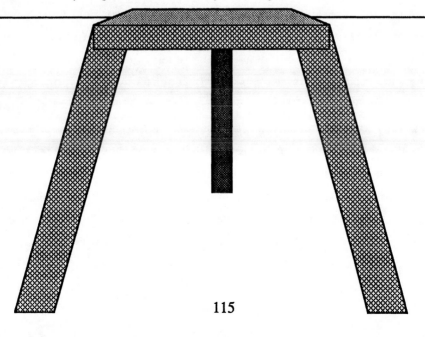

SUPERVISOR PROFILE: Teresa McDowell

At the Time of Supervisory Training:

Education: Masters degree in Marriage & Family Therapy (MFT) from Pacific Lutheran University in 1985.
Contextual Influences: 39 year old, Caucasian female, living in a rural setting.
Therapy Experience: 3 years in an agency & 5 years in private practice.
Theoretical Influences: Trained in structural, strategic and Mental Research Institute Brief Therapy models. Solution-focused and narrative approaches have also been highly influential.
Supervision Experience: Supervised masters level therapists & paraprofessionals in social service agencies such as Family Reconciliation Services, Head Start, and The Family Service Center.
Supervision Orientation: At the time primarily structural.

Since Becoming a Supervisor:

Designation of Approved Supervisor: 1992
Professional Setting: Private practice and part-time faculty member at MFT masters program, Pacific Lutheran University.
Supervision Experience: Supervisor for a MFT masters program and some supervision of MFT post-graduates in a variety of settings.

Supervision Assumptions

My philosophy of supervision is based on how I do therapy and my beliefs about change. As a clinician, I maintain an awareness of the structure of the systems I am working with and work towards clarification of boundaries and hierarchical congruity. My beliefs about change go beyond structural theory, blending in ideas from brief and solution-oriented approaches. Supervision differs from therapy in many ways, including the supervisor's responsibility for the development of the therapist, the addition of more levels of interaction; the colleagial relationship between supervisee and supervisor, and the inherent hierarchy involved in professional gatekeeping. There are enough similarities between supervision and therapy, however, to justify the use of well developed therapy approaches in defining a supervisory approach (Heath & Storm, 1983; Mazza, 1988; McDaniel et al., 1983; Papero, 1988; Storm & Heath, 1985).

I recognize that there is a hierarchical difference between the supervisor and supervisee that can be used as leverage for change, and that a clear boundary between the supervisee and the supervisor needs to be maintained. Throughout the supervisory relationship I attempt to maintain an awareness of the systems involved through the use of a "supervision map." This map initially includes the supervisee, members of the supervisee's work systems, the supervisor, and members of the supervisor's work systems. The use of this map is based on structural therapy which assumes that the hierarchy within the supervisory system needs to be clear for the supervisor/supervisee system to function well. Upon entering a supervisee's work system, I feel it is important to join with the appropriate level of the hierarchy to gain understanding and support of the supervision process. The need to attend to this structure varies greatly from a private practice setting where there is virtually no hierarchical structure to a highly organized social service organization with a clear philosophy, set of procedures, and chain of command. The supervision map expands with each case to include the family and those systems which are currently involved with the family. The supervisor attends to the various levels of this overall system and is aware of isomorphism (Liddle & Saba,

1983) and dysfunctional patterns which may occur and need interrupting (Storm, York, & Sheehy, 1990; Tucker & Liddle, 1978). This map also allows the supervisor to take into account the context in which the supervisee is working and any expectations or limits that may be imposed on the supervisee within that context.

It is my belief that while certain qualities necessary to becoming a therapist may be innate or learned through life experience, the bulk of therapeutic skill is learned through understanding and adhering to a theoretical approach. This is enhanced by systematic training and an incorporation of the use of self within the theoretical framework. I do not believe it is necessary for the supervisor's approach in supervision to duplicate the theory being learned by the supervisee. Instead, I view the theory being learned as part of the content of the supervision process.

The supervisor and supervisee expect that through their relationship the supervisee will improve her ability to help families change. Throughout my relationship with supervisees I expect to negotiate specific goals to meet this end. I believe it is important for the supervisee to evaluate her own areas of difficulty and to identify areas of potential growth. I also believe, however, that it is part of the supervisor's role to identify problem areas and areas of needed growth for the supervisee. While some of these goals may begin in the form of a supervisor's "hidden agenda," interventions are made to encourage these areas to become mutually agreed upon and acknowledged goals. I further believe it is up to the supervisor to evaluate the skill level and individual strengths of the supervisee, taking into account multiple factors including the supervisee's level of education and training, ability to view families systemically, recognition of the difference between process and content, knowledge of a theoretical framework and ability to apply theory. The supervisor also takes into account the individual aspects of the supervisee such as age, gender (Warburton et al., 1989; Wheeler et al., 1989), socioeconomic background, ethnicity, and family-of-origin relationships. With this information, the supervisor is better able to assist the supervisee in meeting goals and to encourage a greater use of self within a theoretical framework. The supervisor also attends to these areas as potential blocks to necessary change. These blocks are overcome by direct intervention, such as enactments, or by identification which leaves the supervisee responsible for change, such as referral to therapy to resolve ongoing family-of-origin issues. The supervisor must also help the supervisee be sensitive to contextual issues such as class, gender, ethnicity, and religious background, and how these factors may impact her work with clients.

Methods of Supervision

I view the supervisor as responsible for finding methods of supervision which meet the unique needs and learning styles of the supervisee, allowing for a wide variety of interventions. My methods of supervision typically rely on interventions which promote mutuality of goals and make use of the supervisee's strengths and successes to encourage change. My view of how change is best inspired in the therapy room as well as within the supervision context is that the positive expectation of change and the emphasis on even small successes encourages a generalizable shift in behavior. The supervisee is encouraged to use her own resources and to generalize from what has worked in the past and what she knows about theory that can guide her. When alternative solutions are lacking, I frequently "brain storm" with supervisees offering numerous alternatives for the supervisee to choose from to maintain and increase the supervisee's sense of responsibility and competence. I also frequently point out behaviors or interactions which show change and success in the goal areas. The degree of direction offered a supervisee depends on her overall experience, level of confidence, and knowledge of the specific areas in question. While legal and ethical issues are mutually discussed, I am clearly directive when needed (Engelberg & Heath, 1990; Solvenko, 1980).

There is considerable amount of literature describing the use of case report, videotape, and live supervision (Beroza, 1983; Birchler, 1978; Breunlin et al, 1988; Heath, 1983; Liddle & Schwartz, 1983; Montalvo, 1973; Whiffen, 1982). I find it most useful to employ live supervision when working on areas such as skill development, overcoming anxiety in the therapy room, and interrupting repetitive, nonproductive interactions between the therapist and client. I find videotaped supervision most useful for being able to identify the supervisee's underlying beliefs and experiences in the therapy room, pointing out successful change in therapist behavior, offering alternative interventions, and helping supervisees recognize isomorphic patterns and their own positions in systems. Case reports are valuable when there are many cases to review, when specific information about a type of case is needed, or when legal or ethical issues arise which must be immediately discussed.

Supervision Case Study

I supervised Alice over a four month period during her second practica in a marriage and family therapy masters program. She was married, in her twenties, with a quiet, pleasing demeanor. In talking with Alice it was apparent that she was very bright, as evidenced by her quick grasp of theoretical concepts and creative intervention ideas. Her first practicum supervisor noted her high level of competence when discussing her with me and on her evaluation, which he had reviewed with Alice.

Our contract for supervision was predetermined to a large extent by the university setting. During our first meeting, we reviewed our contract noting that we would meet for one and a half hours weekly for the duration of one practicum, and that there would be an evaluation which included a pass/fail grade. We agreed that she would follow certain procedures in preparing for supervision and that we would rely heavily on raw data. Alice agreed to notify me immediately if she had any cases which involved emergency situations. During this initial contracting session, we clarified which theoretical approaches she would be using and how these interfaced with the rest of her graduate training program. She identified several areas for growth and we established an initial set of goals. These goals included applying structural family therapy and increasing her sense of direction during the middle phases of therapy. We acknowledged that other goals would develop as we began to explore her work in more depth.

As Alice and I began to work together initially by viewing a series of video-tapes, it became clear that she often attempted to please clients, frequently allowing them to disrupt her plans and goals for the therapy session. By watching her own interactions with clients, she could see how her concern over clients feeling supported by her sometimes left her stuck in sessions without the necessary leverage to produce change. Alice added to her original goals the goal of sticking with her agenda for sessions without being rigid, directing the flow of conversation including developing a variety of ways to produce enactments, and being less concerned with clients liking her.

Numerous interventions were made to help Alice begin to meet her goals. As we reviewed cases together, I would first ask Alice to identify what her goals were for the case and for the individual session at hand. I emphasized reliance on structural theory and mapping to determine these goals and the choice of interventions. As Alice relied more on theory to guide the direction she was taking in therapy, she was able to do longer range planning, allowing for greater direction during mid-therapy sessions. By viewing videotapes, we were able to stop at decision points and discuss alternative interventions using a structural approach. In order to continually expand her repertoire, we frequently brainstormed alternative interventions. I felt it was important that Alice be given suggestions and alternatives, but that final choices be left to her to increase her sense of confidence in being in charge of therapy.

Once Alice increased her confidence in planning what she wanted to accomplish in any given therapy session, we worked on ways for her to make sure she was able to follow through. I continually focused on Alice's successes, frequently stopping a videotape or pointing out after a live session times when she was able to stick with her agenda. We developed numerous ways for her to stay on track including writing down a plan before entering a session, leaving a session briefly when she felt confused, redirecting interaction, and repeating unanswered questions.

Helping Alice meet her goal of being able to direct the flow of conversation and produce enactments was accomplished in part by the viewing of videotapes and brainstorming interventions at various decision points. I also asked Alice to role play directing behaviors. I pointed out to Alice each time she was successful in redirecting conversation or getting a couple to talk directly. We discussed and I frequently challenged Alice's underlying belief that she always needed to be polite. By recognizing this as not helpful for clients, she gave herself permission to explore "not-so-polite" behaviors such as interrupting, insisting that people talk directly, and not making eye contact.

Engaging in these new behaviors not only allowed Alice to meet her goals of staying on track and being more directive, but also allowed her to confront some of her fears about clients not liking her. We were also fortunate in having a client get very angry with her during the course of therapy. This allowed me an opportunity to help Alice interpret the client's anger theoretically rather than personally.

As expected during the early stages of development as a therapist, Alice felt she needed more information in numerous areas to be effective therapeutically. She frequently sought my direction in finding reading materials and some of our supervision included giving direct information. I encouraged Alice to use this information in a way which fit her theoretical model and own way of working. We discussed the need to confer with other professionals involved in cases and acknowledged when it was preferable to bring in a cotherapist or to refer a case.

Alice struck me as more competent than she recognized. I wondered if this might be gender related, especially after working with her on her need to please clients. Near the middle of the practicum, Alice brought a male cotherapist in on a case. She had worked on this case in supervision and had made great progress in her ability to structure sessions and direct enactments. She had moved herself out of a triangulated position with this client couple. Alice reported that after the first session with her cotherapist, who actually had less experience than she had, he had expressed great insight into how she was "stuck" with the couple. She accepted his

121

insight as useful, admiring his abilities. Later, I received input from the co-therapist's supervisor that Alice had presented this case as a class project. The videotape of her work revealed she made a very successful intervention which she dismissed, giving credit for change to the introduction of her co-therapist. During the supervision, she described how a session plan had been aborted because her co-therapist had come up with better ideas which she followed in session. At one point, the clients even asked if the cotherapist was her supervisor. I did not see the same pattern of deferral in Alice's work with female cotherapists.

It was helpful to me to have in mind a "supervision map" to make decisions about intervening in this pattern. The map included those involved in the context of supervision as follows:

SUPERVISION MAP

Female Supervisor-of-supervision	Cotherapist's Male Supervisor (Head of MFT Program)	Other Male Supervisors

Female Supervisor-in-training (Working for MFT Program)

Male Supervisee Female Supervisee

Male Client Female Client

There was isomorphism between the client level of the system and the cotherapist level which, given the nature of the roles within the supervision system, could have easily been repeated there. The issue at hand was addressed within the supervision team. There was agreement about the need to intervene in a way which would encourage the growth of both supervisees involved. The male cotherapist's supervisor and I collaborated in making interventions with both supervisees that were congruent with our goals.

I made numerous interventions aimed at empowering Alice and confronting her apparent gender issue. I asked Alice what her plan had been for a session that had been derailed by her cotherapist, validating and congratulating her on her original ideas. I confronted her with why she had chosen to abandon her ideas so rapidly. I asked her to call time out in therapy the next time she felt the agenda changing so she and her cotherapist could agree on the course of action. I also invited her to bring her cotherapist into our next supervision session.

During our next session, with the cotherapist present, we viewed another tape. I asked them to identify their original plan and whether or not they had stuck with it. We were fortunate to view a session in which the pattern of triangulation occurred between the client couple with the male cotherapist rather than with Alice. I was able to emphasize the therapist/client system in recognizing this triangulation versus seeing the pattern as specific to one therapist. This helped equalize the cotherapists. We discussed how they might present themselves as a team since this was what they were working on with the couple. While watching the videotape we were able to see the male cotherapist repeatedly take the lead. I challenged the team to consider the message they were giving the couple regarding gender. By considering how they were coming across to the couple, it appeared both therapists were able to look more clearly at their own values and behavior.

In the following sessions, the cotherapists were able to agree more in planning sessions. They positioned themselves in the room as a team, gave each other more equal air time, looked to each other, took breaks during the session to insure they were working together, and used more "we" statements with the couple. Alice reported sticking with her ideas and defending her position more actively with her cotherapist. The team became increasingly successful in working with the couple.

The evaluation at the end of the practicum offered another opportunity to empower Alice. During the evaluation we were able to once again build on her strengths by pointing out her increased ability to direct the flow of sessions, affirm that with her new planning skills mid-therapy direction had become less problematic, review her now quite large repertoire of interventions which allowed her to successfully engage clients in enactments, and validate her understanding and use of the structural therapy she had been learning. We were also able to identify areas in need of continuing growth including confrontation skills and tolerating disapproval from clients. I made a strong statement to Alice that I felt she had the potential to be a highly competent therapist and that I felt she underestimated her own abilities. I also told her that I felt this may be connected to how she viewed her role as a female. By this point in supervision, Alice had become aware that she did sometimes defer to men and had done so in her cotherapy relationship. She stated she had been surprised to discover this about herself, yet she knew that she underestimated her abilities. She believed this was due to having been raised in a very traditional family. Her awareness of this issue, her decision to identify this area as an ongoing goal for her next practicum, and her ability to shift her behavior, led me to feel confident that she would be able to progress in this area.

My Growth As A Supervisor

This supervision experience with Alice, as well as my experience with the other supervisees with whom I worked, was very helpful in my development as a supervisor. I learned a tremendous amount from my supervisor as she helped me ferret out areas of needed development in each of my supervisees and encouraged me to trust my own judgement. My supervisor brought a great deal of structure into my supervision process by continually incorporating our agreed upon goals into specific cases. This allowed me to consistently progress and to recognize my own change. I attempted to assimilate this style in working with my supervisees which allowed me to remain responsible for change in the goal areas, focus on the supervision process rather than just case content, and to evaluate supervisee progress in an ongoing way. I found that this approach fit my goal directed style which builds on small changes. The academic setting's reliance on clear contracting and evaluating helped me recognize the need for formal contracting and periodic evaluations in the non academic setting. Through my supervision I was able to explore the use of evaluations as an intervention tool. My repertoire of interventions increased significantly and by the end of the process I felt more confident and empowered.

To develop as a supervisor I plan on attending workshops and to continue to read the supervision literature. I am going to continue to provide supervision, confer with colleagues, and to be part of supervision groups whenever possible.

Postscript

Becoming an Approved Supervisor was an exciting and challenging step in my career as a marriage and family therapist. I admired my supervisors and wondered how I would be able to offer others what I had valued so much in my own training. The supervision course opened my eyes to a whole new set of ideas and revealed a level of interaction I had not seen as a supervisee. As I read and listened to the supervisors who had gone before me, I began to form a framework that I could use to guide my thoughts about supervision. I recognized that what I knew about therapy, as well as my skills and style as an experienced therapist, were important and transferable tools. Writing my Supervision Philosophy and Case Study to gain the Approved Supervisor designation from the American Association for Marriage and Family Therapy helped me identify and commit to a beginning stance in my work with supervisees.

Even though I had some experience supervising, I was still at the point where it was difficult to clearly identify my ideas about supervision. Writing the Supervision Philosophy Statement encouraged me to determine and articulate my beliefs and own unique style. However, it also felt somewhat academic as I reached for ideas and made decisions based more on the knowledge of others than on my own limited experience. There were many decisions to make about theory, intervention style, use of raw data, contracting, evaluating, and so on. Developing

125

a concise framework from which to base supervisory decisions required the integration of my own ideas with what I had learned in my training as a supervisor and from the literature on supervision. Writing the Supervision Case Study helped me recognize that much of my philosophy had been informed by my own work and that in turn, I was already able to apply the template I had fashioned from my own unique approach, my experience as a therapist, the guidance I received from supervision-of-supervision, and the many ideas offered by other supervisors.

Nearly five years and dozens of supervisees later, I find myself wondering about how developing a beginning philosophy has affected my work long term. I also wonder about what has changed in my original ideas. As I look back, I realize that thinking through my beliefs about supervision early in my experience as a supervisor was an important developmental step. Realizing the need, and developing the ability, to form a model of supervision has allowed me to use a theoretical framework to guide my decisions and interventions. This has helped me avoid supervising mindlessly or relying on a poorly connected set of techniques. Adhering to a beginning philosophy also provided me with a base from which to grow.

Many of the ideas that I understood on an academic level, such as isomorphism and the multiple levels of systems, have become second nature. I believe this has occurred because of the introduction of these ideas during supervision training and my decision to include them in my philosophy. Some of the concepts I placed in the forefront at the beginning such as the "supervision map," are now in the background, leaving room for new ideas. As the field changes and therapy and supervision evolve, I find myself revisiting my thoughts about the supervisory relationship and my interventions with supervisees and the families they see. For example, postmodern thought has lead me to be more collaborative and transparent than I used to be, and allowed me to explore new techniques like being an active participant of a reflective team that I am also supervising. I have become more flexible in blending of a variety of MFT theory in supervision and often shift the way I work to incorporate interventions from the model a supervisee is learning. I have become increasingly aware of the importance of a positive supervision context and have a much clearer understanding of the developmental needs of supervisees.

I ended my Philosophy of Supervision Statement with what I thought was a perfunctory remark about my ideas being in an ongoing state of development as I incorporated new concepts and experiences into my beliefs about change. As it turns out, this viewpoint has had an important affect on my ability to use a model of supervision while remaining open to change, and, in fact could still be the "last line" of my supervision philosophy!

Beroza, R. (1983). The shoemaker's children. *Family Therapy Networker*, 31-33.

Bircher, G. (1975). Live supervision and instant feedback in marriage and family therapy. *Journal of Marriage and Family Counseling, 11*, 331-342.

Bruenlin, D., Karrer, B., McGuire, D., & Cimmarusti, R. (1988). Cybernetics of videotape supervision. In H. Liddle, D. Breunlin, & R. Schwartz, (Eds.), *Handbook of family therapy training and supervision* (pp. 194-206). New York: Guilford Press.

Engleberg, S., & Heath, A. (1990). Legal liability in supervision. *Supervision Bulletin, 3*, 2-4.

Heath, A., & Storm, C. (1983). Answering the call: A manual for beginning supervisors. *Family Therapy Networker, March/April*, 36-37, 66.

Liddle, A., & Saba, G. (1983). On context replication: The isomorphic relationship of training and therapy. *Journal of Strategic and Systemic Therapies, 2*, 3-11.

Mazza, J. (1988). Training strategic therapists: The use of indirect techniques. In H. Liddle, D. Breunlin, & R. Schwartz, (Eds.), *Handbook of family therapy training and supervision* (pp. 93-109). New York: Guilford Press.

McDaniel, S., Weber, T., & McKeever, J. (1993). Multiple theoretical approaches to supervision: Choices in family therapy training. *Family Process, 22*, 491-500.

Montalvo, B. (1973). Aspects of live supervision. *Family Process, 12*, 343-359.

Papero, D. (1988). Training in Bowen theory. In H. Liddle, D. Breunlin, & R. Schwartz, (Eds.), *Handbook of family therapy training and supervision* (pp. 62-77). New York: The Guilford Press.

Slovenko, R. (1980). Legal issues in psychotherapy supervision. In A. Hess(Ed.), *Psychotherapy supervision* (pp.87-96). New York: John Wiley & Sons.

Storm, C., & Heath, A. (1985). Models of supervision: Using therapy theory as a guide. *Clinical Supervisor, 3*, 87-96

Storm, C., York, C., & Sheehy, P. (1990). Supervision of cotherapists: Cotherapy liasons and the shaping of supervision. *Journal of Psychotherapy and the Family, 1*, 65-74.

Tucker, B., & Liddle, H. (1978). Intra- and interpersonal process in the group supervision of family therapists. *Family Therapy, 5*, 13-28.

Warburton, J., Newberry, A., & Alexander, J. (1989). Women as therapists, trainees, and supervisors. In M. McGoldrick, C. Anderson, & F. Walsh (Eds.), *Women in families: A framework for family therapy* (pp. 135-151). New York: W. W. Norton.

Whiffen, R. (1982). The use of videotape in supervision. In R. Whiffen, & J. Byng-Hall (Eds.), *Family therapy supervision: Recent developments and practice* (pp. 39-46). New York: Grune & Stratton.

Resources For Developing A Philosophy of Supervision

Bagarozzi, D., & Anderson, S. (1989). Training and supervision in marital and family therapy. In D. Bagarozzi & S. Anderson (Eds.), *Personal, marital, and family myths: Theoretical formulations and clinical strategies.* (pp. 274-298). New York: W. W. Norton.

Everett, C. (1980). An analysis of AAMFT supervisors: Their identities, roles, and resources. *Journal of Marital and Family Therapy, 6,* 215-226.

Everett, C. (1980). Supervision of marriage and family therapy. In A. Hess (Ed.), *Psychotherapy supervision: Theory, research, and practice* (pp. 367-379). New York: John Wiley.

Everett, C., & Koerpel, B. (1986). Family therapy supervision: A review and critique of the literature. *Contemporary Family Therapy, 8,* 62-74.

The overwhelming majority of supervisors define themselves as integrationists.

Wetchler, J. (1988). Primary and secondary influential theories of family therapy supervisors: A research note. *Family Therapy, 15,* 69-74.

Hardy, K., & Keller, J. (1991). Marriage and family therapy education: Emerging trends and issues. *Contemporary Family Therapy: An International Journal, 13,* 303-314.

Heath, A., & Storm, C. (1983). Answering the call: A manual for beginning supervisors. *Family Therapy Networker, March/April,* 36-37, 66.

Holloway, E. (1995). *Clinical supervision: A systems approach.* Thousand Oaks, CA: Sage publications, Inc.

Liddle, H. (1991). Training and supervision in family therapy: A comprehensive and critical analysis. In A. Gurman, & D. Kniskern (Eds.). *Handbook of family therapy* (vol. 2 , pp. 638-697). New York: Brunner/Mazel.

Liddle, H. (1988). Conceptual overlays and pragmatic guidelines for systemic supervision. In H. Liddle, D. Breunlin, & R. Schwartz (Eds.), *Handbook of family therapy training and supervision* (pp. 153-171). New York: Guilford Press.

Liddle, H. (1982). Family therapy training and supervision: Current issues, future trends. *International Journal of Family Therapy, 4,* 81-97.

Liddle, H. (1982). On the problems of eclecticism: A call for epistemological clarification and human scale theories. *Family Process, 21,* 243-250.

Liddle, H., & Halpin, R. (1978). Family therapy training and supervision literature: A comparative review. *Journal of Marriage and Family Counseling, 4,* 77-98.

Olsen, D., & Stern, S. (1990). Issues in the development of a family therapy supervision model. *Clinical Supervisor, 8,* 49-65.

Piercy, F., & Sprenkle, D. (1986). Supervision and training. In F. Piercy, D. Sprenkle, & Associates (Eds.), *Family therapy sourcebook* (pp. 288-321). New York: Guilford Press.

Storm, C., & Heath, A. (1985). Models of supervision: Using therapy theory as a guide. *Clinical Supervisor, 3,* 87-96.

Berg, I., Freidman, E., Liddle, H., & Todd, T. *Fielding supervision impasses.* (Video #531). Norcross, VA: The Resource Link.

Liddle, H. *Clinical supervision.* (Audio #706-404). Norcross, VA: The Resource Link.

III. RELATIONSHIPS:
POWER, PROBLEMS, & COMPLEXITY

Supervisory Challenge 8:
Creating Effective Supervisory Relationships

All supervisors have at some time in their careers been supervisees. Not too long ago Cheryl asked a group of supervisors-in-training to discuss their best supervision experiences. How did their supervisors create positive supervisory experiences? The group, having difficulty focusing on positive experiences, chose instead to share their "horror stories". These horror stories ranged from an isolated, temporarily uncomfortable moment in supervision to supervisory relationships of the "grin and bear it" type.

Although we agreed that it is easy to fall into remembering the bad times and forgetting the good, the perplexing (and upsetting) finding for us was the silence that surrounded these experiences. Overwhelmingly, the participants reported that their supervisors did not have an inkling of their dissatisfaction. The supervisees pretended all was well. Some remembered their supervisors as disinterested in their point of view. Others felt the supervisory relationship itself, because of the inherently hierarchical and evaluative role of the supervisor, prevented them from conveying their true feelings even though they were fairly confident their supervisors might have been responsive to their concerns. And still others felt the risks involved were too great. What if their supervisors were permanently offended by their feedback? How would this color their supervisors' beliefs about their competency?

If your supervisees recounted their honest feelings about their supervision with you, what would they say? What steps do you take to reduce supervisee silence?

Questions of Power

Marshall Fine & Jean Turner

The intention of this activity is to increase awareness of gender and position as two intersecting sources of power in supervision relationships. The questions are designed to bring forth dominant and subordinated or unspoken ideas regarding how power connected with gender and position influences behavior and emotions in supervision.

When supervisors openly acknowledge the power associated with their position and gender they are less likely to inadvertently constrain others and themselves. When therapists are invited by their supervisors to address the power relationships between themselves, their supervisors and their clients, they have the opportunity to clarify the power dynamics and to question their own contribution to the relationships with their supervisors and their clients.

The reflective questions can be addressed in open conversation between supervisor and therapist with each person sharing their response to the same set of questions. Alternatively, the questions can be pondered independently by each supervision participant. In either case the strengths and pitfalls of gender/position intersects are rendered transparent in a process that generates greater choice of action.

The following questions can be answered from the perspective of supervisor in relation to therapist, therapist in relation to supervisor, and therapist in relation to client. We refer to all persons in the supervision system as "supervision participants." We suggest that you explore how your answers would be different if the participant to whom you are referring were male or female, supervisor or therapist.

QUESTIONS ABOUT OTHER'S ATTRIBUTIONS TO YOU

- In what ways might supervision participants with whom you have interacted have attributed power to you on the basis of your sex? On the basis of your position?

- In what ways might power not have been attributed to you by supervision participants because of your sex? Because of your position?

- What might be the amount of power attributed to you by supervision participants by virtue of your sex and position? How comfortable do you feel about this amount of attributed power?

- Think of a time in the past when you thought a supervision participant attributed a gender/position stereotype to you that felt comfortable or fit with your self -- image in that context. What were the circumstances?

- Think of a time when you thought a supervision participant attributed a gender/position stereotype to you that was not comfortable or fitting with your self-image in that context. What were the circumstances? What did you think and do? In retrospect, would you have preferred to do anything different?

- If you were to ask supervision participants who have worked with you in the past, which times they felt the most/least powerful in relationship to you, what do you think they might say? What aspects of their view might be related to gender and position?

QUESTIONS ABOUT YOUR OWN ATTRIBUTIONS

- Think of a time when you used gender–related and/or position–related power with someone in the supervision system in a manner that felt comfortable for you. What were the circumstances?

- Think of a time when you used gender–related and/or position–related power with someone in the supervision system in a manner that felt uncomfortable for you. What were the circumstances?

- What aspects of your way of working do you believe are different from the typical gender or position stereotypes?

- How do you think these atypical power attributions work to constrain or facilitate the supervision interaction?

AWARENESS OF PERSONAL POWER

- Which gender/position issues do you think you are most aware of? Which would you feel most comfortable talking with a supervisor/therapist about?

- Which gender/position issues do you think you are most blind to? Which would you feel least comfortable talking with a supervisor/therapist about?

- Where do you feel you have made the most positive shifts in dealing with gender/position issues?

What is Your Style? The SSI

Janie Long & John J. Lawless

The Supervisory Styles Index (SSI) is a 22 item self-report inventory that you can use to explore your supervisory style. Style has been described as the way in which the personality and convictions of the supervisor are demonstrated in the supervisory relationship. Some scholars believe it is not possible to address client issues without first addressing the supervisory relationship, as this is where the problem areas are mirrored.

Three sets of complimentary supervisory styles are examined in the SSI: affiliative and authoritative; nondirective and directive; and self-disclosing and non-self-disclosing. An affiliative style of supervision encourages collaboration and fosters egalitarian relationships. An affiliative style of supervision is employed when supervisors value the opinions and experience of supervisees as holding equal value to their own. Mutuality in the relationship is encouraged. An authoritative style encourages hierarchy and boundaries between the supervisor and supervisee. An authoritative style of supervision is employed when supervisors believe that supervisees will learn more from the supervisor's experience and expertise. A directive style of supervision establishes the supervisor as the expert who directs the supervisee in how to do therapy. A nondirective style of supervision removes the supervisor as the expert and recognizes the supervisee's competencies and individuality in working with clients. A nondirective style encourages original contributions and critical thinking related to case conceptualization. A self-disclosing style of supervision supports connection within the supervisory process and reinforces commonalities of experience. A non-self-disclosing style of supervision encourages distance in the supervisory relationship and allows the supervisor to remain hidden.

EXAMPLES OF SUPERVISOR RESPONSES
OF EACH OF THE STYLES

Affiliative Supervisor:

What would you like to get out of your supervision experience, and how can I be helpful?

Authoritative Supervisor:

What we will be focusing on in supervision is how your own sexist bias influences your therapy.

Directive Supervisor:

When you see this couple next, you should...I know you see it differently, but I want you to try it my way.

Nondirective Supervisor:

Tell me what you think is going on with this couple. So, how are you going to handle this when they come in?

Self-disclosing Supervisor:

When I first started seeing clients I was very   nervous. In my family, I was always the family clown so when things got tense in the session I tended to joke around.

Nonself-disclosing Supervisor:

What I do in that situation is really not the issue. I'm more interested in why you react the way that you do?

In order to get a broader perspective of your style, it is helpful for you to fill out the SSI for several of your supervisees, and to ask several supervisees to fill out the therapists' form of the SSI(SSI-T). The wording between the two forms has been slightly changed for clarity allowing the supervisor and supervisee to rate the same item without changing the meaning of that item.

Scoring the SSI and SSI-T

Several items on the SSI and SSI-T need to be reverse scored. In other words, subtract the score on these items from 6 before totaling your score for each subscale. For example, if you scored a 2 on these items your true score would be

135

4. This number would be added with the other item scores in that subscale to attain your total subscale score. Two of the subscales have items to be reverse scored.

Statements 1-9 in the SSI and SSI-T represent the affiliative/ authoritative subscale (AFF/AUTH). Items 2,5,6,7,and 8 should be reverse scored. Scores will range from 9-45 given that you answer all questions. Scores from 36-45 are indicative of a more affiliative style. Scores from 9-18 are indicative of a more authoritative style. Scores falling between 19-35 indicate that you vascillate between the two styles. Looking at your style with several supervisees will probably provide a clearer pattern of your general style. Looking at multiple supervisees is important for all the scales.

Items 10-15 measure the nondirective/directive subscale (ND/D). All the items in this subscale need to be reverse scored. Scores will range from 6-30. Scores from 24-30 indicate that you have a nondirective style. Scores from 6-12 show that you are a more directive supervisor. Scores falling between 13-23 indicate that you alternate between the two styles.

Items 16-22 represent the self-disclosing/non-self-disclosing subscale (SD/NSD). None of the items on this subscale are reverse scored. Scores will range from 7-35. Scores from 28-35 exhibit that you have a self-disclosing style. Scores from 7-14 show that your style is nonself-disclosing. Scores falling between 15-27 indicate that you fluctuate between the two styles.

It is important to note that each subscale is distinct and the scores should not be totaled. The categories of style described above and assessed with this instrument are not exhaustive but rather a starting place from which to begin your examination of your supervisory style.

Interpreting the SSI and the SSI-T

You are encouraged not to think of style as dichotomous but rather as continuous. While you may tend to be more affiliative in overall style, you may find that you become more authoritative with certain presenting problems or with particular supervisees. It is not the intent of the instrument to identify any style as being superior to any other. Depending on the context of supervision, it is expected that certain styles of supervision will be more effective in some situations than in others.

SUPERVISION STYLES INDEX: SUPERVISOR FORM

The following survey explores the supervisory relationship. This questionnaire will ask you several questions about yourself, how you do supervision, and about some of your thoughts concerning the process of supervision. For these questions you are asked to rate your perceptions of yourself in the supervision setting with a minimum of one of your supervisees. If you rate more than one supervisee, it is suggested that you rate each supervisee independently of the other.

A=All of the time   **M=Most of the time**   **S=Some of the time**

R=Rarely   **N=Never**

		A	M	S	R	N
1.	I solicit the opinions of my supervisee.	A	M	S	R	N
2.	My understanding about what is going on with the client(s) is more accurate than the supervisee's.	A	M	S	R	N
3.	If the supervisee's ideas about the case differ from my own, I support the supervisee's ideas.	A	M	S	R	N
4.	I recognize the supervisee as a person with expertise.	A	M	S	R	N
5.	I expect my supervisee to consult with me concerning all aspects of case management (i.e., case notes, follow-up phone calls).	A	M	S	R	N
6.	During supervision I direct the conversation.	A	M	S	R	N
7.	During live supervision I am in charge of the session.	A	M	S	R	N
8.	I choose the videotape segments to be processed.	A	M	S	R	N
9.	I spend time joining with the supervisee.	A	M	S	R	N
10.	The supervisor phones in directives at least 3 times per hour.	A	M	S	R	N
11.	I develop the final intervention to be used in a session.	A	M	S	R	N
12.	I have primary responsibility to develop the homework tasks given to the client(s).	A	M	S	R	N
13.	I enter the session when I feel the supervisee is not being effective.	A	M	S	R	N
14.	I am in charge of the video equipment.	A	M	S	R	N
15.	I insist on strict adherence to my directives.	A	M	S	R	N
16.	I openly share examples from my own experience as a therapist.	A	M	S	R	N
17.	I am willing to discuss how my family of origin issues affect my performance in as therapist.	A	M	S	R	N
18.	I acknowledge my own limitations as a therapist.	A	M	S	R	N
19.	I disclose how current issues in my life affects the supervision process.	A	M	S	R	N
20.	I will admit when I make a mistake in supervision.	A	M	S	R	N
21.	I talk about my own life experiences.	A	M	S	R	N
22.	I discuss my clinical work.	A	M	S	R	N

Instrument developed by J. Long and J. Lawless.

SUPERVISORY STYLES INDEX: SUPERVISEE FORM

The following survey explores the supervisory relationship. This questionnaire will ask you several questions about yourself, your perception of supervision, and about some of your thoughts concerning the process of supervision. For these questions you are asked to rate your perceptions of yourself in supervision settings.

A=All of the time　　**M=Most of the time**　　**S=Some of the time**
R=Rarely　　**N=Never**

	A	M	S	R	N
1. The supervisor is respectful of my opinions about the therapy process.	A	M	S	R	N
2. The supervisor considers her/his understanding about what is going on with the client(s) to be more accurate than my own.	A	M	S	R	N
3. If the supervisor's ideas about the case differ from my own, the supervisor supports my ideas.	A	M	S	R	N
4. The supervisor recognizes me as a person with expertise.	A	M	S	R	N
5. The supervisor expects me to consult with her/him concerning all aspects of case management (i.e., case notes, follow-up phone calls).	A	M	S	R	N
6. The supervisor directs the conversation.	A	M	S	R	N
7. During cotherapy the supervisor is in charge of the session.	A	M	S	R	N
8. The supervisor chooses the videotape segments to be processed during supervision	A	M	S	R	N
9. The supervisor spends time joining with me.	A	M	S	R	N
10. The supervisor phones in directives at least 3 times per hour.	A	M	S	R	N
11. The supervisor develops the final intervention to be used in a session.	A	M	S	R	N
12. The supervisor has primary responsibility for developing homework tasks given to the client(s).	A	M	S	R	N
13. The supervisor enters the session when he/she feels that I am not being effective.	A	M	S	R	N
14. The supervisor is in charge of the video equipment.	A	M	S	R	N
15. The supervisor insists on strict adherence to his/her directives.	A	M	S	R	N
16. The supervisor openly shares examples from his/her experience as a therapist.	A	M	S	R	N
17. The supervisor is willing to discuss how his/her family-of-origin issues affected his/her performance in therapy.	A	M	S	R	N
18. The supervisor acknowledges his/her own limitations as a supervisor.	A	M	S	R	N
19. The supervisor discloses how current issues in his/her life affects the supervision process.	A	M	S	R	N
20. The supervisor admits mistakes.	A	M	S	R	N
21. The supervisor is open about his/her own life.	A	M	S	R	N
22. The supervisor discusses his/her clinical work.	A	M	S	R	N

Instrument developed by J. Long and J. Lawless.

The Story of the Therapist

Bruce Kahl

There are times when therapists are invited to feel overwhelmed, incompetent, and self-doubting. This is often a multifaceted process involving several elements of therapists' lives. Frequently, this can include a separation from a story or time in which they believed in themselves. This is the story of one such therapist.

The therapist was a supervisee named J., a white male in his early thirties, who recently completed his master's degree in school psychology, and was working in his third year as a school psychologist. J. was part of a group of five other school psychologists -- three women and three men, all white, and all of whom were being seen for both individual and group supervision by myself, a supervisor-in-training at the time for the American Association for Marriage and Family Therapy.

The case under discussion was that of Jacquan, an African American youngster who had been placed in foster care, along with four other siblings, 16 months ago. Jacquan and an older sister, age 11, had come home from school one day to find that their mother had made arrangements to place the children in foster care without any further explanations. The mother was a crack addict, and could no longer care for the children. After placement, she made no effort to contact the children. Jacquan was 10 years old, in the fourth grade, having been "held over" once, and receiving extra school services along with mandated counseling once a week. The school was located in an inner-city district in Brooklyn, New York, and composed of predominantly African American students and teachers. The principal was also African American. Jacquan's foster mother of 14 months signed a release to have a reflecting team present during therapy, but refused any video-aping or audiotaping, or the use of a one-way mirror.

In the fourth counseling session, J. explained to the foster mother that Jacquan was developing an alternative story of himself, and how this had been

139

reflected in improved self-control and completion of assignments in school. The foster mother acknowledged that he did seem to be improving in his schoolwork, and that she hadn't been called up to school lately because of his behavior problems. However, unbeknown to J., she had already decided to ask that Jacquan and his siblings be transferred to another foster home, and had signed the necessary release papers. She was unwilling to reconsider this decision because Jacquan and his older sister were causing severe problems in the household. Her mind had been made up, and "there was nothing further to discuss." As the session ended, Jacquan began to cry, and the foster mother replied that she had repeatedly warned him and his sister, and was not about to rescind her decision now.

J. and the team began to process this rapid turn of events, both in individual and group supervision, with J. feeling very discouraged, incompetent, and self-doubting. He felt that he should have been able to see this coming and to have forestalled it. With his permission, I decided to have a narrative conversation with J. regarding this case in front of the group.

I chose to use a series of questions designed to highlight how therapists can also be invited into self-blame and self-accusation. In essence I asked J., "If you ask clients to become better at identifying ways in which they can escape from a problem-saturated story, can you experiment along with them in being able to do that yourself?" This narrative dialogue with J. seemed to trigger off a process in the group in which each person had, at one time or another, misplaced accounts of themselves in which they were competent.

"...each person had, at one time or another misplaced accounts of themselves in which they were incompetent."

I decided that this was an appropriate time to use an exercise borrowed from White (1989/90) as a way of combating negative influences and stories about our professional roles. The supervisees were asked to share stories about their experiences as therapists. These included how they came to be involved in this type of work, how the meaning of being a therapist has changed over time, and how they have made significant progress in their professional growth. Each supervisee was asked about the nature of personal crises they had experienced in their careers; what triggered those crises; how they surmounted them; the new realizations and conclusions that occurred as they surmounted each crisis; and the effects that these realizations had on the shape of their subsequent careers as therapists. They were also asked to identify and retrieve some of their very early statements of conscious purpose relating to being therapists, however unsophisticated these might have been, and reflect on what this suggested about their commitment to this work. They were asked to share some of their experiences of life that have contributed to a further clarification of their purposes in taking up this work, and how these purposes related to their own notion of commitment; experiences of life that have generated realizations about the particular contributions that each had a determination to make during the course of his/her life. They were further asked to discuss those experiences they were having in the course of this exercise, associated with engaging in the process of bearing witness to, elevating, and honoring their conscious purpose and commitment. And, finally, the supervisees were asked to talk about how this elevation and honoring of these conscious purposes and commitment could affect: a) the shape of their work, b) their experiences of themselves in relation to their work, and c) their relationship with themselves.

As the impact of this exercise wound its way through the group, several effects could be observed. First, as people began to overcome their initial shyness and reticence, despite having worked together as a team for several months, they started to recount experiences from much earlier periods in their lives, some going back to childhood and adolescence, in which they wanted to help members of their family, or to be of service to the community. Otheres recounted idealized ideas about helping people in trouble. Second, although they were aware of how unsophisticated their motives were, they never discarded their initial desire to "help and be of service to others," but only became increasingly focused on how they intended to bring this about. Some had early dreams temporarily derailed by

141

personal crisis, gender biases, lack of support, and so on, but each in some way found the means to return to their original purpose. This exercise helped them elevate and honor their conscious purpose and commitment to their work. As a result, the group seemed to congeal around a set of shared values and goals, and a sense of renewed pride in their professional roles and identities. The exercise seemed to "center" the group and allow them to reclaim their temporarily misplaced competence.

The exercise seemed to allow supervisees to reclaim their temporarily misplaced competence.

J., with the group's help, decided to continue seeing Jacquan until he was placed in a new school, with a new foster mother. J. was torn about how to handle these final sessions, since this new placement seemed to confirm Jacquan's notion of being abandoned because he was a "bad kid." After suggesting in individual supervision that J. raise the issue of self-blame, Jaquan began to talk about his sense of having been deserted by his mother "because he was a bad kid and was always causing her problems." J. patiently explained to Jacquan that his mother was a sick woman and could no longer care for her children, but Jacquan didn't seem to "buy" this revision, especially given his current experience with his foster mother. The reflecting team decided to offer Jacquan an odd-even day ritual. On odd days, Jacquan was free to believe that his mother deserted the children because they were causing her too many problems, but on even days he was to make a concerted effort to believe that his mother was a sick person who was not up to the job of caring for her children, and had no choice but to put them in foster care. Jacquan was intrigued by the ritual, and the freedom to make a choice, and he promised to write down in a little book given to him by the team, how these beliefs would affect his behavior on a daily basis. J. decided to continue helping Jaguan develop an alternative story about himself and to continue therapy with Jaquan.

White, M. (1989/90). Family therapy training and supervision in a world of experience and narrative. *Dulwich Centre Newsletter, Summer,* 27-38.

Reverse Live Supervision:
Leveling the Supervisory Playing Field

D. Blake Woodside

For many, live supervision has become a critical portion of the training stream. The usual benefits of this type of supervision appear obvious -- direct observation of the supervisee's performance, and the opportunity to provide instantaneous corrective feedback. One of the problems, however, is that such sessions can become performances, stilted and artificial -- especially in settings where time is short and the opportunities for live observation are few. Because many supervisees have never had the experience of live supervision, anxiety about it may heighten the unnatural quality of the experience. Add the effect of a "team" of supervisees plus supervisor usually in a darkened room behind a mirror, a team who may hastily deliver interventions to the anxious supervisee.

In our setting, we have had the luxury of regular access to live sessions as part of a family therapy clinic in a comprehensive inpatient, day hospital and outpatient program for the treatment of eating disorders. The family therapists attached to these units hold a joint clinic weekly, where families from any one of the units are seen. The therapists and their supervisees function as a "team." This arrangement is useful from a programatic point of view, as patients are often transferred across the treatment programs. From the point of view of training, it increases the mass of therapists and provides students a superior educational experience. While training in this setting myself, I went through a stage where I was having some difficulty in formulating treatment plans for my cases. My supervisor, perhaps in desperation, hit upon the idea of asking me to function as the voice from the team when she was seeing families. Thus, she forced me to think actively about this particular aspect of the work. While it was first awkward to be giving my supervisor "direction," this reverse live supervision led to a demystification of the whole process. Previously, commentary from the team had come as a rather mysterious, intimidating event. It also forced me to think actively about what my supervisor had been doing while I was working with families in front of the mirror. Thus, I began to think in a much more focused way about how to monitor the process of change in a family.

There is a significant difference in observing one's supervisor as compared to being behind the mirror observing another supervisee. In the latter circumstance, one's supervisor is almost certainly present. Despite all efforts to the contrary, the supervisor ends up leading any discussion or commentary. Difficulties observed in the conduct of the session will be interpreted differently -- usually as evidence of the supervisee's lack of experience. This can enhance supervisees' fear of exposing potential problem areas. Viewing tapes of the supervisor's work usually suffers similarly since tapes are almost always chosen to highlight the supervisor's competence or brilliance. When was the last time any of you saved a tape of a really bad session to show your supervisees?

I use reverse live supervision as a standard part of my repertoire and believe that it has a number of benefits. By allowing supervisees to experience the process from a different perspective, this technique breaks down some of the artificial barriers in supervisory relationships, particularly those relating to the inherent power differential between those in front and those behind the mirror. Demanding that supervisees periodically provide such commentary also allows more rapid development of the ability to observe oneself. A supervisor need not lose his/her authoritative stance -- there is still lots of opportunity to demonstrate your knowledge while discussing your mistakes. Supervision tends to become more collegial after such an experience. Supervisees are much more likely to express opinions which may not match those of their supervisors. The effect of observing their supervisor struggle with a difficult case, appear at a loss, or just come from behind the mirror and say, "Boy, I wish I hadn't gotten out of bed today" cannot be overstated. Inevitably supervisees feel more at ease with their mistakes, and improve the quality of material brought to supervision. Finally, such experiences may simply humanize the experience of supervision a bit more. It is really hard to remain too formal when your supervisees have just observed you making one of those classical errors that you have been warning them about for months.

Resources For Effective Supervision Relationships

Anderson, H., & Swim, S. (1995). Supervision as collaborative conversation: Connecting the voices of supervisor and supervisee. *Journal of Strategic and Systemic Therapy, 14*, 1-13.

Braver, M., Graffin, N., & Holahan, W. (1990). Supervising the advanced trainee: A multiple therapy training model. *Psychotherapy, 27*, 561-567.

Everett, C. (1980). An analysis of AAMFT supervisors: Their identities, roles, and resources. *Journal of Marital and Family Therapy, 6*, 215-226.

Handley, P. (1982). Relationship between supervisors' and trainees' cognitive styles and the supervision process. *Journal of Counseling Psychology, 29*, 508-515.

In a review of studies of supervisees' perceptions, of supervision, Liddle concludes supervisees uniformly report stress, especially when live or videotaped supervision is part of the supervision experience.

Liddle, H. (1991). Training and supervision in family therapy: A comprehensive and critical analysis. In A. Gurman, & D. Kniskern (Eds.),*Handbook of family therapy* (vol. 2, pp. 638-698). New York: Brunner/Mazel.

Holloway, E., & Wolleat, P. (1981). Style differences of beginning supervisors: An interactional analysis. *Journal of Counseling Psychology, 28*, 373-376.

Heppner, P., & Handley, P. (1981). A study of interpersonal influence in supervision. *Journal of Counseling Psychology, 28*, 437-444.

Kadushin, A. (1974). Supervisor-supervisee: A survey. *Social Work, May*, 288-297.

Shanfield, S., Matthews, K., & Hetherly, V. (1993). What do excellant psychotherapy supervisors do? *American Journal of Psychiatry, 105*, 1081-1084.

Snyder, M. (1996). Supervision, co-vision, meta-vision, and alter-vision. *Supervision Bulletin, 9*, 3.

Wetchler, J. (1989). Supervisors' and supervisees' perceptions of the effectiveness of family therapy supervisor interpersonal skills. *American Journal of Family Therapy, 17*, 244-256.

Wilcoxon, S. (1992). Criteria for the selection and retention of supervisees: A survey of approved supervisors. *Family Therapy, 19*, 17-24.

Haddad, D., & Falicov, C. *Creating a context for talking about supervision.* (Video #526). Washington, DC: The American Association for Marriage and Family Therapy (AAMFT).

Heath, A., & Thwarp, L. *What really happens in supervision?* (Video #532). Washington, DC: AAMFT.

Multi-levels of supervision. (Audio #706-103). Norross, VA: The Resource Link.

Nazario, A., Early, G., Steir, H. *Power differentials in supervision.* (Audio #706-403). Norcross, VA: The Resource Link.

Haber, R., & Ridgeley, E. *Supervising the position and person of the therapist.* (Audio #706-603). Norcross, VA: The Resource Link.

Wark, L. *Family therapy supervision: Hierarchical or collaborative?* (Audio #705-518). Norcross, VA: The Resource Link.

A Supervisory Challenge 9:
Managing Multiple Relationships

In the world of therapy, the admonition regarding multiple relationships is simple: "Don't do it!" Even after the conclusion of therapy, most therapists probably prefer not to encounter former patients socially or in a non therapeutic context, partly to allow possibly resuming therapy in the future. In the world of supervision, as was discussed in chapter 18 of the text, the situation is much less clear-cut, and the ideal situation harder to specify.

At the completion of successful supervision, supervisor and supervisee are professional peers, with much less hierarchical distance than therapists and former clients. Even during supervision, they are peers to some extent, depending on the level of training of the supervisee and on the context (e.g., agency versus degree-granting program). A variety of professional relationships are permissible and even desirable from the standpoint of successful mentoring. These can include co-authoring a publication, attending a conference together, doing co-therapy, and so on.

Ethical standards clearly discourage multiple relationships that have the potential for exploiting the supervisee or contaminating the objectivity of the supervision process. In theory this is fine, but what safeguards are necessary in practice? You may believe your motives to be pure and your objectivity unaffected, but how do you check the veracity of these assumptions? Does the supervisee share your faith? How do you ensure that a proposed multiple relationship is as advantageous for the supervisee as it is for you? That the supervisee truly experiences a free choice of accepting or refusing? Regarding contamination, how can you cross-check your objectivity with a peer or mentor of your own?

Multiple Relationships in Supervisory Practice

Ingeborg E. Haug

Let us assume that Roger Tuller and his wife had seen you for marital therapy over a period of ten months. At the time, Roger was in his second semester as a graduate student in marriage and family therapy, and he and his wife were adjusting to being new parents. Now, three years later, Roger is placed as an intern at the agency where you are the primary supervisor. You are uneasy about the impending "dual relationship" and consult a colleague, without revealing Roger's identity, on how to handle this situation professionally and ethically.

Multiple relationships between clients and therapists have long been recognized as difficult and potentially harmful to all parties involved. Multiple relationships between supervisors and supervisees are more complex, since the purpose of supervision is to help supervisees attain the status of a fully credentialed professional colleague.

In preparation, you review the guidelines concerning supervisory multiple relationships of the following mental health professions, listed in alphabethical order according to their acronyms: The American Association for Marriage and Family Therapy (AAMFT) (1993, 1996) the American Association for Pastoral Counselors (AAPC) (1994), the American Counseling Association (ACA) (1995) and its founding division, the Association for Counselor Education and Supervision (ACES) (1993), the American Psychological Association (APA) (1992), and the National Association of Social Workers (NASW) (1989, 1994, 1996). (See the grid on the next page for a comparison across the organizations.)

All five mental health professions, without exception and in similar language, strongly advise supervisors to protect supervisees from being harmed or exploited in the supervisory relationship. They also all explicitly and categorically prohibit sexual relationships between supervisor and supervisee. The language used to convey this prohibition, however, could be seen as open to interpretation: No written document addresses sexual intercourse per se, but instead prohibits "sexual intimacies" (AAMFT), "sexual behavior" (AAPC), "sexual contact" (ACES), "sexual relationships" (APA), and "sexual activities or contact" (NASW)

MULTIPLE RELATIONSHIPS GRID

Organization	Sexual Relationship with Supervisee	Sexual Harassment	Non Sexual Multiple Relationship	Therapy with Supervisees	Supervision of Family Member or Close Relationship
AAMFT	Prohibited	Prohibited	Make effort to avoid; if unavoidable use caution	Prohibited	Prohibited
AAPC	Prohibited & defined	Prohibited & defined	Make every effort to avoid with current & former supervisees	Prohibited	Prohibited
ACA (ACES)	Prohibited	Prohibited	Clearly identify boundaries	Prohibited	Prohibited
APA	Prohibited	Prohibited & defined	May be unavoidable, aware of potential for harm	Not specifically addressed	Prohibited
NASW	Prohibited	Prohibited	No dual relationships when risk of exploitation exist	Not specifically addressed	Prohibited

between supervisor and supervisee. This could be construed to either include or exclude what might be termed "sexualized" contact such as holding, stroking, or hugging. AAPC's ethics code provides the most specific and inclusive definition: "Sexual behavior is defined as, but not limited to, all forms of overt and covert seductive speech, gestures, and behavior as well as physical contact of a sexual nature"... "All forms of sexual behavior with ... supervisees...is unethical" (APC, 1993, p. 4).

All professional codes and standards prohibit sexual or other harassment of supervisees. APA provides an explicit definition of what constitutes sexual harassment.

You are at this time particularly interested in the guidelines the various professional groups provide in regards to nonsexual multiple relationships of a social, business, or professional nature. AAPC takes the most stringent position by applying its guidelines to current and former supervisees. Members are advised to "make every effort to avoid dual relationships that could impair judgement or increase the risk of personal and/or financial exploitation" (AAPC, 1993, p. 4). While AAMFT also admonishes its members to diligently avoid dual relationships, this directive does not extend to former supervisees. APA addresses the issue by acknowledging that it can be difficult to avoid social or other nonprofessional contact with supervisees. However, it is the psychologist's responsibility to anticipate the consequences of such relationships and to refrain from entering into them if it seems likely that they might result in harm (APA, 1992). ACA, in a similar vein, states that many supervisors fulfill multiple roles and need to be mindful of the differential in power that exists between supervisor and supervisee (ACES, 1993).

In addition to the general guidelines regarding multiple non–sexual relationships, AAMFT, AAPC, and ACA specifically prohibit supervisors from accepting supervisees as therapy clients. AAMFT, ACA, and NASW also do not accept supervision provided to family members or close relatives.

Having informed yourself, you consider the potential conflicts inherent in the proposed professional set up. If the two of you were to establish a supervisory relationship, you could never again serve as therapist to Roger and/or his wife. What responsibility do you have to Roger's wife to clarify the impact on her if you were to serve as Roger's supervisor? As a supervisor you will have an evaluative role — what might be the unintended consequences down the road of your possessing personal information about Roger? What, if any, might be the potential consequences of your prior relationship with Roger with regard to the other interns at the agency? Does the agency director need to be informed about this dilemma and be part of the search for solutions? What is the potential for harm or even exploitation of all involved?

Given all the complications, you decide to initiate a frank and thorough discussion of these issues with Roger and investigate with him other options for supervision. If no other possibilities are feasible, you will propose to Roger that you jointly determine from the outset how potential conflicts down the road will be addressed and formalize your agreements in a written supervisory contract.

American Association for Marriage and Family Therapy (AAMFT) (1996). *AAMFT code of ethics.* Washington, DC: Author.

AAMFT (1993). *AAMFT Approved Supervisor designation: Standards and responsibilities.* Washington, DC: Author.

American Association of Pastoral Counselors (1994). *Code of ethics.* Fairfax, VA: Author.

American Counseling Association (1995). *Code of ethics and standards of practice.* Alexandria, VA: Author.

Association for Counselor Education and Supervision (1993). *Ethical guidelines for counseling supervisors.* Alexandria, VA: Author.

American Psychological Association (1992). *Ethical principles of psychologists and code of conduct.* Washington, DC: Author.

National Association of Social Workers (NASW) (1996). *Code of ethics of the NASW.* Washington, DC: Author.

NASW (1989). *NASW standards for the practice of clinical social work.* Washington, DC: Author.

NASW (1994). *Guidelines for clinical social work supervision.* Washington, DC: Author.

See p. 10 on how to contact these organizations.

What is the Difference Between Personal Therapy & Person-of-the-Therapist Supervision?

Brent J. Atkinson

In my supervisory relationships, the distinction between therapy and supervision is discussed at length and clarified before supervision begins. However, because my professional colleagues do not have the benefits of these discussions, there is potential that they may become confused about the distinction, particularily if they hear my supervisees talk about exploring their emotions or discussing aspects of their personal lives during supervision with me. Am I doing therapy or supervision with these interns? I wrote this paper mainly for the benefit of those who come into indirect contact with my work as a supervisor, and are not supervisors themselves. Since writing this paper, however, I have found it useful to share with interns to supplement our conversations before beginning supervision.

Article 4.1 in the American association for Marriage and Family Therapy Code of Ethics cautions supervisors to make every effort to avoid dual relationships that could impair their professional judgement or increase the risk of exploitation, and lists the dual roles of supervisor and therapist as one such possible relationship.

However, over the years, a number of prominent family therapists have suggested that good supervision always involves some qualities that are therapy-like (Aponte, 1994; Kantor & Mitchell, 1992; Storm, 1991; Tomm, 1993). This is particularly true when supervision focuses on exploring the therapist's experience with clients (including automatic internal and behavioral reactions), rather than just focusing on how to apply theory and technique to the practice of assessment, interviewing, case planning, and so on. Like good therapy, good supervision promotes introspection, attention to one's emotional reactions, and exploring ways to alter reactions when they interfere with one's goals.

So what makes supervision different than personal therapy? For me, there are two aspects of supervision that distinguish it from personal therapy. First, there are some activities in supervision that are totally distinct from activities that occur in therapy. These activities include learning what to do next as a therapist, where and how to direct therapy, what to give attention to, and what to ignore. In my work as a supervisor, about half of the time in supervision is spent on these activities. The other half of the time in supervision is focused on exploring various reactions and internal experiences therapists have when they are with clients. It is here that supervision can sometimes become confused with therapy, unless understandings and expectations between supervisor and therapist are clear.

When I function either as a therapist or supervisor, I am careful to create explicit understandings regarding goals and responsibilities. The contract in therapy is very different than the contract in supervision. When clients begin therapy with me, they are generally asking me to help them resolve distress they are experiencing in their personal lives, or to assist them in finding greater fulfillment in their lives. In contrast, when therapists come to me for supervision, they are asking me to help them improve their professional functioning. In therapy, I assume a certain level of responsibility for helping clients find a way to function better in their personal lives. In supervision, neither therapists nor I are interested in such an agreement. Any improvement in the therapist's personal life during supervision is incidental to the process of becoming a better therapist. Supervision sometimes may be therapeutic, but it is not therapy unless supervisor and therapist agree that the supervisor will help the therapist resolve sources of distress in the therapist's personal life. I do not make such agreements, and generally, therapists are not interested in them either.

Therapists' are, however, sometimes interested in discussing aspects of their personal histories or present circumstances in supervision, particularly if it occurs to therapists that some of the reactions they are having with clients parallel the ones they are having (or have had) in their own lives. Therapists are also often interested in improving specific skills related to their ability to be sensitive to the nuances of their emotional states and cognitions, and want to use supervision as a context for practicing. These are activities I will do in supervision. In fact, I encourage therapists to use a certain portion of supervision for such activities if they believe that doing so will improve their skills as therapists (as I generally do). This is not personal therapy, but it does involve exploring reactions and circumstances that are sometimes highly personal. It might become personal therapy if the reactions and circumstances explored were contributed to or triggered by personal distress in a therapist's life, and if the supervisor agreed to work with the therapist on the goal of resolving the personal distress. This is an agreement I will not make. When therapists' level of personal distress is interfering with their professional functioning, or if therapists show interest in receiving help in resolving personal distress, I refer them for personal therapy.

Most of the time a referral is not necessary. Therapists are simply interested in developing their fullest potential to know themselves well and to use this increased self-awareness as a resource in their work with clients. This doesn't mean that supervision doesn't contribute to a greater sense of fulfillment in therapists' personal lives. It often does. Any time individuals become more sensitive to their internal reactions or more interpersonally skillful in any context, there may be side benefits in their most intimate relationships. It's just important to be clear that an increase in therapists' personal fulfillment is not the goal of supervision, and even if therapists experience profound personal growth as a result of supervision, the ultimate goal is not complete until this growth is used as a resource for their work with clients.

In seeking to be careful about potential exploitation in supervision, it is not enough to caution against the dual relationships of therapist/client and supervisor/supervisee. There is potential for exploitation any time there is an imbalance of risk in relationships (Atkinson, 1993). The supervisory relationship is no exception, especially when supervision includes an exploration of the therapist's internal experience during therapy sessions. For a discussion of the risks in person-of-the-therapist supervision, and safeguards for preventing exploitation, see my earlier article in the first section of this guide.

Aponte, H. (1994). How personal can training get? *Journal of Marital and Family Therapy, 20,* 3-15.

Atkinson, B. (1993). Hierarchy: The imbalance of risk. *Family Process,* 32, 167-170.

Kantor, D., & Mitchell, E. (1992). Letter to the editor. *Supervision Bulletin,* 5, 4.

Storm, C., & Freidman, E. (1991). Changing the line: An interview with Edwin Friedman. *Supervision Bulletin,* 6, 1 & 2.

Tomm, K. (1993). Defining supervision and therapy: A fuzzy boundary? *Supervision Bulletin,* 6, 2.

Resources For Managing Multiple Relationships

Amerian Association for Marriage and Family Therapy (AAMFT). (1996). *AAMFT Code of ethics.* Washington DC: Author.

AAMFT. (1991). *AAMFT Approved Supervisor designation: Standards and responsibilities.* Washington DC: Author.

Aponte, H. (1994). How personal can training get? *Journal of Marital and Family Therapy, 20,* 3-15.

Bograd, M. (1992). The duel over dual relationships. *Family Therapy Networker,* 33-37.

> ***Supervisees involved in multiple relationships report harmful effects occur when there is a dual agenda that is duplicitous and kept covert.***
>
> Peterson, M. (1992). *At personal risk: Boundary violations in professional-client relationships.* New York: W.W. Norton.

Bernard, J., & Goodyear, R. (1992). *Fundamentals of clinical supervision.* Needham Heights: Allyn & Bacon.

Cormier, L., & Bernard, J. (1982). Ethical and legal responsibilities of clinical supervisors. *Personnel and Guidance Journal, 60,* 486-490.

Goodyear, R., & Sinnett, E. (1984). Current and emerging ethical issues for counseling psychologists. *The Counseling Psychologist, 12,* 87-98.

Humphrey, F. (1994). Dual relationships. In G. Brock (Ed.), *Ethics casebook* (pp. 173-190). Washington, DC: AAMFT.

Kitchener, K. (1988). Dual role relationships: What makes them so problematic? *Journal of Counseling and Development, 67,* 217-221.

Leslie, R. (1989). Dual relationships: The legal view. *The California Therapist, September/October,* 9-13.

Newman, A. (1981). Ethical issues in the supervision of psychotherapy. *Professional Psychology, 12,* 690-695.

Peterson, M. (1992). *At personal risk: Boundary violations in professional-client relationships.* New York: W.W. Norton.

Peterson, M. (1993). Covert agendas in supervision: Identifying the real culprit. *Supervision Bulletin, 6,* 1 & 7.

Pope, K. (1991). Dual relationships in psychotherapy. *Ethics & Behavior, 1,* 21-34.

Preister, S. (1991). AAMFT code of ethics changes. *Family Therapy News, 23,* 20.

Ryder, R., & Hepworth, J. (1990). AAMFT ethical code: "Dual relationships." *Journal of Marital and Family Therapy, 16,* 127-132.

Storm, C. (1994). Defensive supervision: Balancing ethical responsibility with vulnerability. In G. Brock (Ed.), *Ethics casebook* (pp. 173-190). Washington, DC: AAMFT.

Storm, C. (1992). Nonsexual dual relationships examined. *Family Therapy News, 24,* 12 & 29.

Storm, C. (1991). Supervisors as guardians of the profession. *Supervision Bulletin, 4,* 4.

Storm, C., & Freidman, E. (1991). Changing the line: An interview with Edwin Friedman. *Supervision Bulletin, 6,* 1, 2.

Tomm, K. (1993). Defining supervision and therapy: A fuzzy boundary? *Supervision Bulletin, 6,* 2.

Tomm, K. (1991). The ethics of dual relationships. *The Calgary Participator: A Family Therapy Newsletter, 1,* 11-15.

Panel. *Where to draw the line?* (Video #534). Washington, DC: AAMFT.

Panel. *Dual relationships in supervision.* (Video #565). Washington, DC: AAMFT.

Peterson, C. *MFT supervision: Evaluating and managing dual relationships.* (Audio #706-615. Norcross, VA: The Resource Link.

Peterson, M. *Boundary dilemnas in supervision.* (Audio #703-234). Norcross, VA: The Resource Link.

IV. PRAGMATICS: METHODS & INTERVENTIONS

Supervisory Challenge 10: Developing Your Blueprint

Initial supervision contracts function as the blueprint you and your supervisees follow as you build your supervision relationship. Although supervision contracts are as varied as the personalities of those who develop them, they usually cover the basics: outline logistics, clarify the supervisory relationship, identify goals, describe methods, review clinical issues, comply with requirements of credentialing bodies, employers, and educational institutions; and specify evaluation procedures. (See chapter 19 for a discussion of each of these components.)

Although we agree contracting is critical for an effective supervision relationship and our ultimate contracts are similar in many ways, Cheryl's tendency to plan everything and Tom's tendency to let things flow create very different contracting environments with our supervisees. Some supervisors prefer an overall outline for the negotiation process, and their contracting consists of discussing a series of topics or questions. Below we offer two examples of this type of contract. Other supervisors use a prewritten contract which can be altered to fit each supervision situation. Below we offer excerpts from these types of contracts which illustrate the variety of styles of supervisors.

What is your preferred style? Do you like to have as much as possible discussed and negotiated with your supervisees before you begin supervision? Or, do you prefer to develop your agreements as you go? Is it important for you to have an attorney endorse your contract or are you comfortable with a "gentlemen's or gentlewomen's agreement?" If you supervise in a different setting than your usual one, to what degree can your contracting methods remain unchanged?

A Guide: The Initial Supervision Session Checklist

Layne Prest & Toni Schindler Zimmerman

All of us who have been in supervision -- as supervisor, supervisor-in-training, or supervisee -- know that it is a complicated process. By and large, most of the important issues are probably addressed most of the time. But wouldn't it be nice if there was a guide to remind or give permission to all of the participants to discuss important issues? Issues besides those having to do with getting client systems unstuck? The Initial Supervision Session Checklist (ISSC) was developed for just this purpose. Based on in-depth interviews and focus groups with experienced supervisors and supervisees, the checklist represents the many facets of the supervisory relationship. It was developed as a guide to the important first stages of supervision during which you are negotiating the "contract" for supervision between supervisees and yourself. These contracts are developed on different levels, spoken and unspoken. The outcome of these negotiations is often shaped by unacknowledged power dynamics. The checklist may prompt you and your supervisees to make a greater portion of the negotiation process overt. If this type of instrument is used in the early stages of the process, you and your supervisees may feel more permission to discuss key issues. The ISSC should be introduced and discussed in the first meeting, and if you and your supervisee agree, used throughout the supervision process in order to keep track of important issues, including attainment of goals. The ISSC can be used in a variety of contexts by both you and your supervisees, no matter how experienced either of you are, to facilitate development of an effective contract for supervision.

INITIAL SUPERVISION SESSION CHECKLIST (ISSC)

This checklist is designed for use by both supervisor and supervisee during the initial session(s) of the supervisory process. The ISSC facilitates a clear contract for supervision, maximizes the fit between supervisor and supervisee, and encourages goal attainment.

Education, Training and Clinical Experiences
Inquire about the following characteristics of the supervisee/supervisor:
___ educational background
___ training experiences
___ setting(s), number of years
___ theoretical orientation(s)
___ clinical competence with various issues (e.g., ethnicity, gender, substance abuse, alternative lifestyles, abortion), models, populations, problems, & family forms
___ sense of mission/purpose in the field
___ educational plans & professional goals of the supervisee

Philosophy of Supervision
Explore supervisee's/supervisor's philosophy of the supervision process, including:
___ philosophy of therapy & change
___ purpose of supervision

Previous Supervision Experiences
In order to assess the range of the supervisee's competence, discuss the following points:
___ previous supervision experiences (e.g., format, setting)
___ strengths & weaknesses as therapist/supervisee (as indicators of developmental level)
___ supervisee's competence with stages of therapy process: initial call, intake, joining, middle phase, termination, & referral
___ level of development in terms of case planning, notes, collateral support, & networking
___ supervisory competence with various issues (e.g., ethnicity, gender, age, alternative lifestyles, abortion), models, techniques, populations, & family form
___ methods for managing supervisor-supervisee differences

Supervision Goals
In order to establish and evaluate goals of supervision, address the following:
___ goals (personal and professional)
___ process of goal evaluation & time frame (e.g., weekly)
___ requirements for which supervisee is seeking supervision (e.g., licensure or certification)
___ requirements met by supervisor's supervision

Supervision Style and Techniques
An optimum fit in terms of supervisory style may be facilitated by addressing:
___ specific expectations regarding roles, hierarchy, etc
___ types of supervision which would facilitate clinical growth of the supervisee
___ preferred style (e.g., didactic, therapeutic, experiential, collegial)
___ parallels between therapy & supervision models
___ focus (e.g., therapist's development, cases, or both)
___ if case focused, in what manner (e.g., few cases explored in-depth, crisis management)
___ modality (e.g., audio, video, verbal, cotherapy with supervisor, live observation)

Instrument developed by Prest, Schindler Zimmerman, & Sporakowski.

Reprinted by permission of Haworth Press from the article Prest, L., Schindler Zimmerman, T., & Sporakowski, M. (1992). The initial supervision checklist (ISSC): A guide for the MFT supervision process. *The Clinical Supervisor, 10*, 117-133.

Theoretical Orientation

Recognizing that a good theoretical fit is important to the supervisory process, address:

__ models or specific schools trained in for therapy &/or supervision

__ extent to which these models have been used clinically

__ populations, problems, &/or family forms with which models have been most effective

__ interest in learning new approaches

__ integration of theoretical models

Legal/Ethical Considerations

The legal & ethical parameters for the supervision process must be defined. These include:

__ responsibility for clients discussed in supervision in different contexts (e.g., licensed vs. unlicensed therapist, private practice vs. academic setting)

__ number of cases for which the supervisor will be responsible

__ emergency & backup procedures available (e.g., supervisor accessibility)

__ awareness of professional ethical codes (e.g., AAMFT, APA)

__ confidentiality regarding supervision discussions (e.g., supervisee's family of origin)

__ confidentiality issues when more than one supervisee is involved

__ specific issues related to dual roles (e.g., professor-student or colleague-colleague supervisory relationships)

__ process for dealing with issues such as burnout & transference/countertransference

Use of Self/Personal Issues

Supervision may include a focus on "use of self" or other personal issues, including:

__ utility of "use of self" in supervision

__ supervisee's current family & other relationships

__ issues related to supervisor's & supervisee's race, ethnicity, & gender

__ discussion of techniques (e.g., genograms, coaching supervisee's differentiation process)

__ conflicts between personal values & beliefs, & goals for supervision

__ significant life events or contexts shaping supervisee's clinical work

Practical Issues

The supervision process is a contractual one in which the supervisor provides a service to the supervisee/consumer. The following practical considerations must be addressed:

__ fee & arrangements for payment

__ location, schedule, & duration of meetings

__ duration of supervision (e.g., semester, number of hours)

__ how will time & fees be split among supervisees

__ format (video, audio, or case presentation; individual or group supervision)

__ modality (e.g., experiential techniques, live observation)

__ the role of other supervisees (e.g., spectator, co-supervisor, co-supervisee)

__ supervision session guidelines (e.g., smoking, punctuality, cueing of tapes ahead of time)

__ process for handling conflictual issues between members of the supervision group

__ process & responsibility for documenting supervision (e.g., forms, verification)

__ exchange of regular & emergency phone numbers

Supervisee's Workplace

These ecosystemic considerations are important for the small private practice or large inpatient unit, especially when members are joined to create a new supervision system:

__ supervisee's place of employment/practice

__ "agency" dynamics (e.g., administrative control, theoretical conflicts)

__ "agency" structure (e.g., other supervisors involved in cases, responsibility & liability)

__ referral system (e.g., court ordered, self-referred)

__ supervisee's support system

The Many Styles of Contracts: Formal to Casual

There are many ways to approach the contracting process for you to choose from -- from using a more formal prepared, standard contract to using an initial supervision discussion to cover the basics. Supervisors recognize that the supervision agreement changes over time. As a result, some supervisors set specific times to renegotiate the initial contract, while other supervisors check with their supervisees about changes that need to be made in the contract on an ongoing informal basis during supervision. In either case, contracting is not a one shot effort, but a continual process during supervision. The approach you use will be greatly influenced by your interpersonal style of supervising as well as the setting in which you supervise and in which your supervisees work.

Some supervisors begin the contracting process by ensuring they and their supervisees are informed consumers by exchanging basic information about themselves and the supervision process. Many supervisors swap resumes so that they and their supervisees have comprehensive information about each others' background. Others use a standardized form, such as *The Professional History Form* (Mead, 1990). If you are an Approved Supervisor of the American Association for Marriage and Family Therapy (AAMFT), you may want to follow Case's (1990) lead and provide your supervisees with a copy of the ethical code guiding your work and the *AAMFT Approved Supervisor Designation: Standards and Responsibilities* so that your supervisees know what they can expect of you.

No matter what your preferred style is, we encourage you to document the process in some way. Documentation of your initial agreement and any changes made along the help you and your supervisees be on the "same page," preventing miscommunication and misunderstanding. Your documentation can take be a written standardized agreement or a narrative outlining the terms you have negotiated. In either case, signatures indicating supervisors and supervisees have discussed the terms of their working agreement are a must!

Some supervisors use a "business style" in their documentation, frequently being very specific regarding the terms of the agreement, while others write theirs in an informal "conversational style" with the terms of the agreement being more general. Compare the following two examples:

A "Business Style" Contract	*A "Conversational Style" Contract*
I agree to provide ongoing feedback to the supervisee regarding the progress. If I have reason to anticipate the supervisee will not be ready as viewed unsupervised practice of MFT within the orginally projected period and minimum hours, I will warn the supervisee of this assessment as soon as possible, with a minimum of three months remaining for the supervisee toremedy these shortcomings.	We have discussed the evaluation process, and agreed that if there is any concern on the part of the supervisor regarding the supervisee's progress we will talk about it as soon as the supervisor is aware of being concern. We will work out an appropriate plan to address the concern.

There are several areas that supervisors frequently include in their contracts which are meant to prevent your supervisees from feeling blindsided when you take action in a certain manner. Consider including the following:

- If unethical behavior occurs, I will be required to notify the appropriate professional bodies. We will address the situation as needed in supervision.

- If the supervisee cancels supervision in less than x number of hours, full fee is to be paid. If the supervisor cancels in less than x number of hours, the supervisor will provide an hour of supervision at no charge (Finlay, V., 1991).

- As a part of supervision, you may be asked to do additional readings, attend certain classes, or participate in additional supervision hours if additional education is needed for you to adequately practice as a therapist.

- If personal issues seem to be effecting your therapy negatively, you may be required to seek personal therapy.

As you choose your style of contracting, remember contracts are most effective when they are continually renegotiated and not left to gather dust!

Case, N. (1990). Personal communication.

Finlay, V. (1991). Personal communication.

Mead, D. (1990). *Effective supervision: A task-oriented model for the mental health professions.* New York: Brunner/Mazel.

Resources For Contracting

Beavers, W. (1985). Family therapy supervision: An introduction and consumer's guide. *Journal of Psychotherapy & the Family, 1,* 15-24.

Bridge, P., & Bascue, L. (1990). Documentation of psychotherapy supervision. *Psychotherapy in Private Practice, 8,* 79-86.

Fox, R. (1990). Contracting in supervision: A goal oriented process. *The Clinical Supervisor, 1,* 37-49.

McDowell, T. (1991). Contracting from the top down. *Supervision Bulletin, 4,* 3-4.

Prest, L., Schindler-Zimmerman, T., & Sporakowski, M. (1992). The initial session supervision checklist (ISSC): A guide for the MFT supervision process. *The Clinical Supervisor, 10,* 117-133.

Dwyer, P., & Bridge, P. *Document Supervision: Contracts, progress, & evaluations.* (Video # 703-334). Norcross, VA: The Resource Link.

Supervisory Challenge 11:
Selecting Structures & Formats

In a perfect world, supervisors would have the opportunity to conduct supervision with individuals or groups, given the needs of a particular supervisee while also having access to the full range of formats to support the supervisee's learning goals. If a supervisee was isolated from other family therapists, the supervisor would have a group that the supervisee could join. If a supervisee felt frozen when a particular family dynamic occurred, a one way mirror would be immediately available so the supervisor could offer timely assistance or model a response. As chapters 20 through 25 in the text convey, no one structure nor format "fits all."

In the real world however, supervisors (and supervisees) are frequently limited -- whether by numbers of supervisees available, schedules, facilities, and so on -- in the structures and formats that they can employ in supervision. It is also common for supervisors to fall into "ruts" of doing supervision in a certain way because it is easy or because they just like doing it that way. When we have fallen into such ruts, it has sometimes taken a supervision session that hasn't gone well to remind us that what is convenient, or what we prefer, may not be what a supervisee can most benefit from. At these times we have found that we can usually get out of our rut and find a better way for supervision to occur given this situation and this particular supervisee.

How will you ensure that the structures and formats you use in supervision provide the best learning experience for your supervisees? Since structures and formats all have their pluses and minuses, how will you decrease the negatives if you are supervising in a less than desired structure or format for your supervisee's needs? How will you change your methods as supervisee needs change over time?

Highlighting Success In Groups:
Empowering & Energizing Supervisees

Carla Pond

The practice of therapy requires an ongoing source of energy and support without which therapists often find themselves tired, drained, frustrated, and bored. Those especially prone to this burnout may be therapists who work in larger systems (agencies, hospitals, and so on) where they have little or no control. However, private practice can also engender these feelings when it is isolating or stressful. The group supervision exercise below can help energize supervisees.

The exercise, which developed out of the solution-focused model of therapy, highlights the competence of each supervisee. Supervisees, I found, often arrived at supervision with a distinct lack of energy and sometimes even tried to convince me that their cases were hopeless. As a reaction to this I decided, in an isomorphic way, to apply to supervisees the same solution-focused approach I was trying to teach them to apply to clients. At the beginning of a supervision group I asked each supervisee in turn to describe a successful intervention that they had used since our last meeting. It was acceptable to highlight any successful interchange in therapy, however slight or seemingly insignificant. The rest of the group was asked, each in turn, to respond to the person who had just presented their intervention. Responses varied from simple praise or affirmation, the report of similar interventions, or the invention of new ideas. Interest and excitement began to build regarding cases.

Before the end of each turn, each supervisee was also asked to talk about what it was like to present their idea, to receive reactions and to respond. Often, lively discussions followed. This processing turned out to be a crucial part of the exercise. Comments like "I forgot I could do this" surfaced. Follow-up questions were asked when appropriate: How could you stay in touch with your successes on an ongoing basis? What could happen that could get you to forget you are competent? What could get in the way of building your successes? How could you sustain the feeling about your work you have right now?

Noticeable results emerged immediately from this process. Generally speaking, supervisees had not been used to having time to focus on their successes, usually only stopping to process cases when they are stuck. When given the chance, supervisees' natural resources surfaced, often putting them in touch with their original reasons for becoming a therapist, and reminding them how exciting it can be to positively affect clients' lives. As supervisees experienced themselves as more competent, anxiety subsided.

Another benefit of directly hearing about others' successes was the broadening of viewpoints. Supervisees developed self-confidence as they received public acknowledgment. The exercise helped normalize difficulties supervisees might have been having and helped them transfer their focus from how they were feeling to skill-building and problem-solving.

One supervisee made the following comments about participating in the exercise. She felt that it helped her to be empowered as a therapist "and to recognize the things that can get ignored...its easier to have an awareness of clients but not of ourselves. It's helpful to hear other people energizing us and developing us...the process put value on what I do...I felt encouraged, challenged, and anxious to keep going...put me back in focus."

This exercise can be repeated often, even weekly, with a group. As the group gets used to presenting ideas and is able to sustain energy, the format can be shortened to simply highlight and share techniques. When used sporadically it is best to use the entire exercise and allow ample time so supervisees can experience the shift in their self-perception and get their creativity flowing. It can also be used in individual supervision where the amount of attention from the supervisor hopefully offsets the loss of the group interaction.

The process presented here, as is true of all solution-focused work, is more than just "focusing on the positive" because it is designed to energize supervisees without denying or ignoring the negative. It is clear to supervisees that this exercise is not a substitute to presenting difficult cases or situations that they are grappling with, but rather a way to prepare them to tackle challenges.

As we see supervisees become increasingly competent therapists, we, as supervisors isomorphically experience ourselves as capable. This approach requires us to believe that each supervisee has the ability and potential to be an effective therapist, according to that person's own style. We can define our own competence as the ability to facilitate this process.

Energy, on the surface, is a concept that may seem nonsystemic or intrapsychic. But perhaps it might be useful to look at it as a reaction rather than a condition. If we are energized as a response to a stimulus, then energy can be seen as an interactional process. As supervisors we can commit ourselves to behaviors that elicit energy from supervisees, helping to produce therapists who may be described as self-confident, able to generate appropriate custom-made interventions, and who know when to ask for help and how to get help. This exercise is one way we can train supervisees to be self-energizing, competent therapists.

The Fly on the Wall:

Layne Prest

Reflecting Team Supervision

Supervisors who work with groups of supervisees and are looking for new and challenging ways to work with the supervision process might want to try Reflecting Team Supervision (RTS). Roberts, in chapter 24 of the text, extensively discusses the underlying philosophy of RTS and offers ideas for using it in a variety of settings. Here I briefly review the ideas then discuss my experiences in RTS and what I believe are the advantages to the process.

The Basic Ideas

The idea is fairly straightforward. In theory, RTS borrows ideas from constructivism. In supervision from a constructivist perspective no one person (i.e., supervisor) is presumed to have knowledge which makes him or her the unqualified expert. Both the supervisor and the supervisee(s) (as well as the client system) are presumed to have professional and other life experiences which can be tapped in the therapy and supervision process. The truth about a situation is thought to be influenced by each person's perspective. As a result there are many "realities" about any given situation. And the reality which becomes predominant is thought to evolve as a result of the interaction among those involved.

In practice, the RTS structure and process is based on Anderson's (1989) reflecting team model. In reflecting team therapy, a group of therapists as the reflecting team observes part of a therapy session (usually from behind a one-way mirror, but the mirror isn't necessary). After they observe approximately half of the session, there is a break. During the break, members of the therapist-client system and the reflecting team switch places. The members of the reflecting team then discuss their perceptions and ideas about the session while the therapist and client(s) watch. Following this, the therapy session is resumed as the therapist and client(s) discuss what they have heard members of the reflecting team say.

The reflecting team supervision process is similar. A supervision group (consisting of a supervisor, supervisee, and up to five others) meet to discuss a case. The supervisee presents the case using notes and/or a videotape. (RTS could actually take place in conjunction with a live case as well. In this event, the therapist/supervisee would take a break from the therapy session to meet with the supervision group.) Behind the mirror or in another part of the room the reflecting team observes the supervision process. The reflecting team members attempt to focus their attention on the process of supervision and the connections among the client family, family/therapist, and supervision group processes. They try not to focus on the content of client(s)' or therapist's report.

After 30-45 minutes of supervision, the process shifts. Two groups switch rooms or chairs in the same room. Or instead of actually moving, the focus could just change so that the reflecting team is the one being observed. However the process is structured, the reflecting team members then discuss their observations of the various levels of process while the supervision group members watch and listen.

When the reflecting team discussion concludes, the supervision process can resume. Once the direct supervision of the case is concluded, the members of the two groups (supervision and reflecting) can meet together to discuss observations and experiences of the supervision and reflecting team process. The level of disclosure is obviously influenced by the degree to which participants are able to share honestly, openly, and non-critically.

It isn't necessary to have a large group to make this happen. I have been involved in RTS in which the supervision group and reflecting team included a total of as few as five or as many as 15 people. For example, a supervisor, and two supervisees (one of whom is presenting a case) could form the supervision group, while two or three others could form the reflecting team. The number of people isn't as important as a willingness to listen to and value a variety of perspectives.

In addition, the group process allows, and even depends on, fluid membership in each group. In other words, it is helpful if the same people aren't in the supervision group or in the reflecting team all of the time.

In terms of facilities, you can use either one large room or two smaller, adjoining rooms separated by a one-way mirror. Consequently, the reflecting team model can be adapted to a variety of settings: private practice groups, community mental health agencies, private agencies, hospitals, and training programs. The group can have a designated leader (a formal supervisor) or a rotating system where members of the group act as the supervisor for that session (as in peer supervision or consultation groups).

Supervisory Gains From Using RTS

Whatever the setting, you and your supervisees stand to gain several things from utilizing this structure and process. In RTS are generated not only the variety of opinions, impressions, hypotheses, and interventions which often come out of the group supervision process, but also another layer of perspectives which are offered by the reflecting group. As described earlier, this layer consists of comments on the process of the therapy and supervision groups, and the reciprocal interaction between the two. According to RTS participants with whom I have spoken, the "difference which makes a difference" in therapy and supervision is more likely to emerge given this richness of perspectives. Supervisors and supervisees both gain an added perspective. The meta-position of the reflecting team is a unique vantage point from which to observe and offer feedback to the supervision group. And the corresponding "fly on the wall position" (Prest, Darden, & Keller, 1990) that the therapist/supervisee and supervisor can take allows each of them to feel safe, while also getting honest feedback. Another benefit is that participants are given the opportunity to scrutinize and discuss the way in which the different system levels fit together. Triangles and other relationship dynamics can be observed to take place at more than one level of the treatment/supervision system. It is even more interesting if you are supervising a

170

live session (as opposed to utilizing a videotape of a therapy session) because three levels are operating and can be observed at the same time. The isomorphism can be astounding. Members of each group (therapist/supervisee, supervisor, and other participants, including clients if it is a live session) spend time under the glass. And this is another reward of RTS: it challenges you as a supervisor. You have to adopt a position of not being the expert, the "one who knows." As a result, many people with whom I have worked have experienced RTS as embodying a more egalitarian and less hierarchical process.

Additional anecdotal evidence in the form of feedback from supervisees (and clients if they are involved) suggests that the process is useful in helping people become empowered and systems to become unstuck. And for supervisors who feel their style of supervision works okay but who are feeling the need for a rejuvenating experience, reflecting team supervision can provide a challenging but liberating perspective on the supervision process.

Anderson, T. (1987). The reflecting team: Dialogue and meta-dialogue in clinical work. *Family Process, 26*, 415-428.

Prest, L., Darden, E., & Keller, J. (1990). "The fly on the wall" reflecting team supervision. *Journal of Marital and Family Therapy, 16*, 265-273.

Live Supervision Form

The Live Supervision Form developed by Heath (1983) was one of the first published forms created with the explicit acknowledgment that the use of such a form can significantly impact the structuring of the supervision process. While the form is immediately useful for live supervision, we include it here because it has many components that can stimulate you to think about making observations during live supervision that fit your model of supervision and selecting a live supervision format that is consistent with the learning goals and objectives of your supervisees. We highlight some of the components below. Your task is to reflect on how you would modify the form to fit your live supervision better.

The form addresses contracting issues. It provides a log of supervision hours and is printed on carbonless paper so that supervisees can keep a copy. (Other forms in this guide log supervision and clinical hours separately.) Recording recommendations and giving supervisees a copy (another copy can be placed in client charts) also structures accountability for supervisory follow-through. The format includes space for noting "prearranged" features of the live supervision agreement. This can remind you of the need to negotiate these specifics in advance. You can select other features to match a different supervision format other than supervision of one supervisee, such as live supervision of teams. While not elaborated on extensively in this form it includes spaces for noting goals for therapists' skill development and supervisors' observations. Although you can use the form across models, it collects data that is not equally relevant for all models of therapy and supervision. These include "session objectives," "session themes," and "homework assigned."

Using this form as a starting point, what would you keep, modify, or discard if you wanted a custom-tailored form for documenting supervision?

Heath, A. (1983). The live supervision form: Structure and theory for assessment in live supervision. In B. Keeney (Ed.), *Diagnosis and assessment in family therapy* (pp. 143-154). Rockville, MD: Aspen Press.

The Live Supervision Form

Date	Time	Room	Session/Contract

Therapist: _____ Clients: _____

Session Objectives:
1. Follow-up on assignment

2.

3.

4.

Prearranged Live Intervention Format:
☐ Phone-in ☐ Knock ☐ Walk-in
Midsession Conference at: +30____ +40____ Other _____
Specific Intervention Style: _____
Other Request of Observers:

Therapist's Theoretical Orientation:

Skill Development Goals:

Session Themes and Hypotheses:

Observations and Comments: _____
_____
_____
_____
_____
_____
_____

Messages and/or Assignment: _____
_____
_____
_____

Summary of Observations and Comments:
1.

2.

3.

Recommendations for Future Sessions:
1.

2.

3.

Next Appointment:

Day	Date	Time

AAMFT Approved Supervision Credit

	.	

Hours & Minutes

Supervisor's Initials

Reprinted from the Forms Book, Copyright 1991, American Association for Marriage and Family Therapy. Reprinted with permission.

Adapting Supervision Forms For A Custom Fit

Thomas C. Todd

For several years I have been assigning supervisors-in -raining the task of taking an existing supervision form, such as the Heath Live Supervision Form, and adapting it to fit their supervision context and model of supervision. In 1991 I was unexpectedly given a taste of my own medicine as part of a presentation on Solution-focused Supervision at Pacific Lutheran University. In anticipation of a live consultation I had sent a copy of the Case Summary Form on the next page to the clinician who was presenting a case for consultation. (For further details on this consultation session, see Selekman & Todd, 1995.)

Participants in the seminar noted that the form was more problem-focused than solution-focused. We used this as an opportunity to incorporate the language and ideas of solution-focused therapy. The careful reader will note many places where the form was modified to incorporate the presupposition that change and progress were already taking place and would continue, beginning with renaming the form as a Case Progress form and ending with the assumption that the supervision session was going to be helpful. Depending on your model of supervision, what you want supervisees to provide in preparation for supervision, and what you want to emphasize, you can modify these forms or any other supervision forms to provide a better fit.

Selekman, M., & Todd, T. (1995). Co-creating a context for change in the supervisory system: The solution-focused model. *Journal of Systemic Therapies, 14,* 21-33.

CASE SUMMARY

Therapist:_____   Date:_

Family:_____

Family Composition (Names, ages, and so on):
_____
_____

# of Sessions to date_____with whom?
_____

Presenting problem and accomplishments so far:
_____

Case formulation/hypothesis:
_____

Recent interventions and response of the family:
_____

Goals for supervision:
_____

FROM

TO

SUMMARY OF CASE PROGRESS

Therapist:_____   Date:_

Family:_____

Family Composition (Names, ages, and so on):
_____
_____

# of Sessions to date_____with whom?
_____

Client goals and scaling of accomplishments so far:
_____

Solution sequence and exceptions:
_____
_____

What has worked best so far? _____

How is supervision going to be helpful?
_____

Resources For Selecting Supervision Structures & Formats

Amundson, J. (1995). Supevision as an exercise of mythic proportions: The healer, the magician, the warrior, the seer, and the sage. *Journal of Systemic Therapies, 14*, 26-34.

Berger, M., & Dammann, C. (1982). Live supervision as context, treatment, and training. *Family Process, 21*, 240-248.

Biggs, D. (1988). The case presentation approach in clinical supervision. *Counselor Education and Supervision, 27*, 240-248.

Birchler, G. (1975). Live supervision and instant feedback in marriage and family therapy. *Journal of Marriage and Family Counseling, 1*, 331-342.

A study of supervision practices found case consultation was the most frequently used method of supervision. Taped supervision was next. Live supervision was the least frequently used method.

Wetchler, J., Piercy, F., & Sprenkle, D. (1989). Supervisors' and supervisees' perceptions of the effectiveness of family therapy techniques. *American Journal of Family Therapy, 17*, 35-47.

Bistline, J., Mathews, C., & Frieden, F. (1985). The impact of live supervision on supervisees' verbal and nonverbal behavior: A preliminary investigation. *Journal of Marital and Family Therapy, 11*, 203-205.

Breunlin, D., & Cade, B. (1981). Intervening in family systems with observer messages. *Journal of Marital and Family Therapy, 7*, 453-460.

Breunlin, D., Karrer, B., McGuire, D., & Cimmarusti, R. (1988). Cybernetics of videotape supervision. In H. Liddle, D. Breunlin, & R. Schwartz (Eds.), *Handbook of family therapy training and supervision* (pp. 194-206). New York: Guilford Press.

Brodsky, J., & Meyers, H. (1986). In vivo rotation: An alternative model for psychotherapy supervision. In F. Kaslow (Ed.), *Supervision and training: Models, dilemmas, and challenges* (pp. 95-104). New York: Haworth Press.

Bullock, D., & Kobayashi, K. (1978). The use of live consultation in family therapy. *Family Process, 5*, 245-250.

Cohen, M., Gross, S., & Turner, M. (1976). A note on a developmental model for training family therapists through group supervision. *Journal of Marriage and Family Counseling, 2,* 48-56.

Connell, G., & Russell, L. (1986). In-therapy consultation: A supervision and therapy technique of symbolic-experiential family therapy. *American Journal of Family Therapy, 14,* 313-323.

Coppersmith, E. (1978). Expanding uses of the telephone in family therapy. *Family Process, 19,* 411-417.

Cornwell, M., & Pearson, R. (1981). Cotherapy teams and one-way screen in family therapy practice and training. *Family Process, 20,* 199-209.

Elizur, J. (1990). "Stuckness" in live supervision: Expanding the therapist's style. *Journal of Family Therapy, 12,* 267-280.

Fennell, D., Hovestadt, A., & Harvey, S. (1986). A comparison of delayed feedback and live supervision models of marriage and family therapist clinical training. *Journal of Marital and Family Therapy, 12,* 181-186.

Friedman, R. (1991). Ten commandments for the family therapist. *Clinical Supervisor, 9,* 181-186.

Gallant, J., Thyer, B., Bailey, J. (1991). Using bug-in-the-ear feedback in clinical supervision: Preliminary evaluation. *Research on Social Work Practice, 1,* 175-187.

Gershenson, J., & Cohen, M. (1978). Through the looking glass: The experiences of two family therapy trainees with live supervision. *Family Process, 17,* 225-230.

Hare-Mustin, R. (1976). Live supervision in psychotherapy. *Voices, 12,* 21-24.

Hargrave, T. (1991). Utilizing inexpensive communication systems: Building one-way mirrors for private practice consultation and supervision. *Journal of Marital and Family Therapy, 17,* 89-91.

Heath, A. (1982). Team family therapy family training: Conceptual and pragmatic considerations. *Family Process, 21,* 187-194.

Heath, A. (1983). The live supervision form: Structure and theory for assessment in live supervision. In B. Keeney (Ed.), *Diagnosis and assessment in family therapy* (pp. 143-154). Rockville, MD: Aspen Press.

Keeney, B. (1990). Supervising client conversation: A note on a contextual structure for evoking therapeutic creativity. *Journal of Family Psychotherapy, 1,* 51-56.

Kingston, P., & Smith, D. (1983). Preparation for live consultation and live supervision when working with one-way screen. *Journal of Family Therapy, 5,* 219-234.

Kramer, J. (1985b). Working with therapists in a group. In J. Kramer (Ed.), *Family interfaces: Transgenerational patterns* (pp. 231-326). New York: Brunner/Mazel.

Keith, D., Connell, G., & Whitaker, C. (1992). Group supervision in symbolic experiential family therapy. *Journal of Family Psychotherapy, 3*, 93-110.

Kramer, T., & Reitz, M. (1980). Using videotape playback to train family therapists. *Family Process, 19*, 145-150.

Lambert, P. (1989/90). Live supervision: The co-evaluation of a learning context. *Dulwich Centre Newsletter*, 15-19.

Latham, T. (1982). The use of co-working (cotherapy) as a training method. *Journal of Family Therapy, 4*, 257-269.

Lewis, W., & Rohrbaugh, M. (1989). Live supervision by family therapists: A Virginia survey. *Journal of Marital and Family Therapy, 15*, 323-326.

Liddle, H., Davidson, G., & Barrett, M. (1988). Outcomes of live supervision: Trainee perspectives. In H. Liddle, D. Breunlin, & R. Schwartz (Eds.), *Handbook of family therapy training and supervision* (pp. 386-398). New York: Guilford Press.

Liddle, H., & Schwartz, R. (1983). Live supervision/consultation: Conceptual and pragmatic guidelines for family therapy training. *Family Process, 22*, 477-490.

Montalvo, B. (1973). Aspects of live supervision. *Family Process, 12*, 343-359.

Myerstein, I., & Kompass, F. (1987). Teaching the mechanics of design, collaboration, and delivery of the final intervention in a team based live supervision group. *Journal of Strategic and Systemic Therapies, 6*, 39-51.

Olson, U., & Pegg, P. (1979). Direct open supervision: A team approach. *Family Process, 18*, 463-470.

Piercy, F., Sprenkle, D., & Constantine, J. (1986). Family members' perceptions of live observation/supervision: An exploratory study. *Contemporary Family Therapy: An International Journal, 8*, 171-187.

Prest, L., Darden, E., & Keller, J. (1990). "The fly on the wall" reflecting team supervision. *Journal of Marital and Family Therapy, 16*, 265-273.

Quinn, W., Atkinson, B., & Hood, E. (1985). The stuck case clinic as a group supervision model. *Journal of Marital and Family Therapy, 11*, 67-74.

Richman, J., Aitken, D., & Prather, D. (1990). In-therapy consultation: A supervisory and therapeutic experience from practice. *Clinical Supervisor, 8*, 81-89.

Rickert, V., & Turner, J. (1978). Through the looking glass: Supervision in family therapy. *Social Casework, 59*, 131-137.

Roberts, J. (1981). The development of a team approach in live supervision. *Journal of Strategic and Systemic Therapies, 1*, 24-35.

Roberts, J. (1983). Two models of live supervision: Collaborative team and supervisor guided. *Journal of Strategic and Systemic Therapies, 2*, 68-78.

Roberts, J. (1983). The third tier: The overlooked dimension in family therapy training. *Family Therapy Networker, 7*, 30, 60-61.

Roberts, J., Mathews, W., Bodin, N., Cohen, D., Lewandowski, L., Novo, J., Pumilia, J., & Willis, C. (1989). Training with O (observing) and T (treatment) teams in live supervision. *Journal of Marital and Family Therapy, 15*, 397-410.

Shilts, L., & Aronson, J. (1993). Circular hearing: Working through the muddles of supervision. *Journal of Family Psychotherapy, 4*, 57-68.

Smith, C., Smith, T., & Salts, C. (1991). The effects of supervisory interruptions on therapists and clients. *American Journal of Family Therapy, 19*, 250-256.

Smith, D., & Kingston, P. (1980). Live supervision without a one-way screen. *Journal of Family Therapy, 2*, 379-387.

Sonne, J., & Lincoln, G. (1964). Heterosexual cotherapy team experience during family therapy. *Family Process, 4*, 177-197.

Storm, C., York, C., & Sheehy, P. (1990). Supervision of cotherapists: Cotherapy liaisons and the shaping of supervision. *Journal of Family Psychotherapy, 1*, 65-74.

Tucker, B., & Liddle, H. (1978). Intra- and interpersonal process in the group supervision of beginning family therapists. *Family Therapy, 5*, 13-28.

West, J., Bubenzer, D., Pinsoneault, T., & Holeman, V. (1993). Three supervision modalities for training marital and family counselors. *Counselor Education and Supervision, 33*, 127-138.

West, J., Bubenzer, D., & Zarski, J. (1989). Live supervision in family therapy: An interview with Barbara Okun and Fred Piercy. *Counselor Education and Supervision, 29*, 25-34.

Wetchler, J., Trepper, T., McCollum, E., & Nelson, T. (1993). Videotape supervision via long-distance telephone. *American Journal of Family Therapy, 21*, 242-247.

Whitaker, C. (1976). Comment: Live supervision in psychotherapy. *Voices, 12*, 24-25.

Wright, L. (1986). An analysis of live supervision "phone-ins" in family therapy. *Journal of Marital and Family Therapy, 12*, 187-190.

Zarski, J., Sand-Pringle, C., Greenbank, M., & Cibik, P. (1991). The invisible mirror: In-home family therapy and supervision. *Journal of Marital and Family Therapy, 17*, 133-143.

Zarski, J., & Zygmond, M. (1989). Negotiating transitions: A supervision model for home-based family therapists. *Contemporary Family Therapy: An International Journal, 11*, 119-130.

Bruenlin, D. *Enhancing training and therapy with video supervision.* (Video #567). Washington, DC: The American Association for Marriage and Famiy Therapy.

Supervisory Challenge 12: Evaluating Supervision

If you are like many, if not most, supervisors, evaluating your supervisees is not a favorite part of your job as a supervisor--in fact, it may be your least favorite. Yet, most supervisees need an evaluation by you for advancement of their career, whether that means qualifying to sit for an examination, fulfilling credentialing requirements, or receiving a raise from their employer. In addition, most supervisees anxiously await your responses regarding how well they are doing in their work. Similarly, if you are like most supervisors, you too wait for clues regarding how well you are doing as a supervisor.

Consequently you must decide how you will evaluate your supervisees and how you will ensure they evaluate you. Although supervisors generally agree that there are certain gross abilities all therapists must have, there is wide variation within the field regarding the specific skills and qualities therapists must exhibit. For example, everyone would probably agree that if a therapist monopolizes the conversation and obtains little or no input from clients regarding their concerns, the therapist is far from achieving basic competence. However, there is a lot of disagreement among supervisors regarding issues such as the degree to which therapists should let therapy sessions unfold versus structuring them.

So, one of the first decisions you must make is how you define therapeutic competence beyond the broad outline of consensus that exists within the field. You must decide to what degree you use an apriori standard (whether of your own development, proposed by a model of therapy, and so on) or create a standard based on the unique situation of your supervisees. As you make this decision, you must simultaneously decide to what degree you involve your supervisees in the decisions regarding evaluation. Once decided, what procedures will you use? How will you provide ongoing evaluation information? At what points in time will you provide more formal feedback? How will you incorporate your supervisees' view of their progress? Then, you must reconsider these same decisions regarding your work as a supervisor. What does your evaluation decision tree look like?

Positive Self-monitoring:
Positive Images Lead to Positive Actions

Cheryl L. Storm

Positive self-monitoring or focusing on what one does well has been found to be highly effective in the learning of new tasks. Kirschenbaum (1984) compared two groups of new bowlers who both received lessons on the components of effective bowling. In one group, videotapes were reviewed with the bowlers for what they were doing well. In the other group, instructors highlighted ways the bowlers could perform differently. The group that focused on the positives improved more than 100 percent! Other research confirmed these results -- for learning social skills, math, and golf. But, what do these results have to do with supervision? If we consider supervision to be about learning, than these results are significant for our work. They suggest supervisees may learn more from being helped to identify their successful therapeutic moves rather than focusing on bringing "stuck cases" to supervision. Conducting a microanalysis of the helpful actions of supervisees during therapy sessions may be more successful than reviewing videotapes for alternative responses. Further, supervisors may be more effective if they assist their supervisees to monitor their work on an ongoing basis *for what they want to repeat rather than for what they want to avoid.* Since positive self-monitoring enhances learning, excellent supervision may be developing this capacity in supervisees.

For supervisors, there are benefits to focusing on competencies rather than "growth areas" in therapists. Supervisors' images of supervisees dramatically change. Supervisees with limited English language skills are also therapists highly skilled in connecting with clients nonverbally. Supervisees uncomfortable with conflict are seen as masters at finding compromises. These positive images of supervisees alter supervisory responses. Cooperrider (1990), reviewing research on the ways that positive images lead to positive action, notes that teachers who have positive images of their students have been found to be more emotionally supportive to these students, offer clearer, more immediate and increased positive feedback regarding students' performances; and provide better opportunities for students to perform and learn more challenging material. These positive actions which are beneficial to supervisees can also

Supervisors may be more effective if they assist their supervisees to monitor their work on an ongoing basis for what they want to repeat rather than for what they want to avoid.

lead to supervisors feeling more effective in their work. Supervisors, as teachers, may find positive self-monitoring an effective method for themselves as well as for their supervisees.

Cooperrider, D. (1990). Positive image, positive action: The affirmative basis of organizing. In S. Srivasta, D. Cooperrider, & Associates (Eds.), *Appreciative management and leadership: The power of positive thought and action in organizations* (pp. 91-125). San Francisco: Josey Bass.

A Supervisor Begins with Supervisee Self-evaluation

David Ivey

Supervisees' assessments of themselves can be used in combination with information about supervisees' backgrounds, credentials, and supervision goals to 1.) determine whether supervision should be arranged, 2.) identify its scope, and 3.) decide its structure. I have supervisees self-assess: success in reaching professional/career goals, supervision goals, positives and negatives of previous supervision, their abilities (five point scale below), and areas of significant limitations and strength. This information helps me determine whether further steps should be taken towards negotiating a contract and if I do, what should be included and emphasized in our agreement.

On a five point scale from excellent to very poor, score yourself on:

__ Case management
__ Case conceptualization/theoretical application
__ Ability to collaborate with other professionals
__ Ability to promote client growth/change
__ Treatment implementation/clinical technique
__ Empathic ability
__ Listening ability
__ Ability to provide feedback & suggestions
__ Ability to develop rapport
__ Ability to join with a family
__ Sensitivity to individual differences
__ Sensitivity to gender issues
__ Sensitivity to racial issues

__ Sensitivity to personal issues
__ Sensitivity to ethnic issues
__ Sensitivity to ethical issues
__ Treatment planning
__ Relationships with colleagues
__ Relationships with supervisors
__ Response to supervision
__ Record keeping
__ General professional conduct
__ Recognition of personal limitations
__ Self-confidence
__ Personal identification as an MFT

For complete self-assessment guidelines contact David Ivey, Texas Tech University, Box 41162, Lubbock, TX 79409-1162.

Tures (1993) similarly asks his supervisees to conduct a self-assessment. However, he is interested in finding out problems that may recur across cases, family-of-origin issues that effect supervisees' therapy and any personal work they may have done regarding those issues, and any difficulties supervisees anticipate may occur in supervision with him.

Tures, B. (1993). Personal communication.

Postmodern Evaluation Practices

Jean Turner & Marshall Fine

We developed the following practices to decrease the constraining aspects of the power imbalance in the supervision relationship while promoting accountability and greater collaboration.

Being "Transparent" About Power Differences

Being transparent as a supervisor involves being up-front about the power you have accepted as part of your supervisory position and about your responsibility to work according to particular professional standards. We combine the acknowledgment of the power dynamics with an invitation to critique and dialogue. The following text segment from a longer document written by Marshall is one example of this practice:

> The supervision relationship is a very special one for me, so I will try to be as collaborative and generative as possible. I am interested in getting to know who you are as a therapist. I think you will also get to know more about me. I am in an evaluative position and, as such, I have more power in the relationship. I realize that because of this and some other factors, the supervision relationship can never be totally collaborative. On a rare occasion, I might feel the need to go against one of your proposed therapeutic actions. If this were to happen, I would be open with you and you would have the opportunity to convince me otherwise.

Report-writing: Practices of Power and Proportion

We live in a society where people generally ascribe power to written language. Any written text that relates to a person's work is likely to be used to define, constitute, or establish their personhood. The constitutive power accorded to written documents means that they can be very useful in helping to shape the therapist's professional career and in assuring quality control for consumers of therapy services. Equally these documents can be destructive if misapplied or misunderstood. To reduce hazards and increase accountability, we have developed what we call "practices of proportion" which are intended to adjust or reckon the relationship of our supervisory voice to other sources of information about the therapist's work. Our actions of proportioning attend to both the strength and the jurisdiction of the evaluator's voice in the report. These practices mean we are less likely to create documents that might be misinterpreted as claims of "truth". At the same time we prevent ourselves from understating the claims that we need to make in order to act responsibly as supervisors, such as recording concerns about the ethics of a therapist's work.

Disclaimers

Jean has often used the following as a preface for her evaluation reports:

Over time people revise both the way they approach their work and the skills they bring to it. The text which follows concerns my observations with respect to this therapist's work over the period from January to April 19XX. My observations highlight certain aspects and only partially capture the richness and breadth of this therapist's work.

This disclaimer locates the evaluation report in historical/social context. It sets boundaries around the content of the document, acknowledges the evaluator' spartial, time-specific vision, and evokes the notion that the therapist's work has dynamic and fluid properties.

Co-authoring

Supervisors can offer therapists the choice of writing part of the text for their evaluation report. The following excerpt is the result of this interactive process:

Kevin: One of my strengths is my ability and willingness to be open and honest about the relationship between my therapist self and my non-therapist self. One thing which stands out for me is feeling as though I have moved another step away from wanting to get the therapy "right," to trusting my intuition, and drawing more confidently on my own experience. A strength of mine has been in identifying issues of concern for myself or the client in therapy and I have found myself growing dramatically in my trust to draw upon my own learning, beliefs, knowledge, and experience in making decisions and setting a therapeutic direction. *Marshall: I think that Kevin has made great strides in this area. He is a very thoughtful and self-reflective therapist who openly critiques himself. He works hard at finding places to "be himself" in the therapy room. I encourage Kevin to continue to work on this integration of self in therapy as I believe that as a person and therapist he has a great deal to offer clients. In particular I encourage him to continue to free himself up more when working with children. I saw this side of him and would hope that he can bring this forth more often in the future when he has the opportunity to work with more children.*

Preserving the two separate voices of evaluator and therapist enables the reader to hear the similarities and differences in their views. The sequencing of the authorship encourages the reader to attend to what the therapist has written since those comments provide the context for what the supervisor has to say. The supervisor responds to what the therapist has written but also has in mind others who might read the report.

Adding Voices

One way to address the partiality of evaluation reports is to include more commentators. Other professionals or colleagues who have worked with the therapist can fill in some of the spaces that are outside the vision of the supervisor. What follows is an excerpt from such a "third voice" document authored by Jean:

Context. At George's request he and I met with Kevin to hear Kevin's comments about working as a cotherapist with George. They had worked together with three clients over the semester and often took time for post-session discussions.

Comments. A number of times and in different ways Kevin expressed his pleasure about having the opportunity to work with George. I noted his emphasis on the following: How easy it was to talk together; George's ability to trust in the process, in clients and in himself; George's respectfulness; the generative questions he asked during therapy. Kevin also highlighted what he saw as George's ability to be empathic with clients' emotional pain. Kevin noted that this seemed especially significant for him when men are talking with men. The part that stood out for me (Jean) from this meeting was what Kevin said about the transfer of a client he has seen for more than a year and who will work with George when Kevin's time in the program ends. He expressed his confidence in George to "meet the client where he is and go on from there."

Inviting other voices can be particularly appropriate to facilitate bridging significant experiential gaps in the supervision relationship, as is the case when supervisor and therapist are different in terms of sex, social class, ethnicity, sexual orientation, and so on.

Note
We would like to express our appreciation of Kevin Stafford and George Bieley, former students in the University of Guelph program, for their consent to use passages from their evaluation reports.

Reprinted with permission from *Journal of Systemic Therapies, (1995), 14,* 62-67. Copyright 1995.

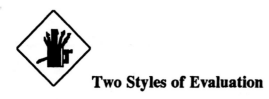 **Two Styles of Evaluation**

1. A Supervisor Uses a Narrative Style of Evaluation

Frederick Wegener

When evaluation occurs using my tool, my supervisee and I respond in narrative text to questions such as those below. We include concrete observations and examples whenever possible, and then share and discuss our writings.

- Do you meet the professional qualifications required by the certification you are seeking?

- Are your clients achieving outcomes congruent with your model?

- What is your ability to conduct yourself to promote your own professional growth and development?

- Did we address in supervision the learning goals set forth in our contract?

For a copy of the instrument, contact Fred Wegener, Northwest Pastoral Counseling, 3549 Bridgeport Way West, Tacoma, WA, 98466.

2. Another Supervisor Uses GAS Procedures

Goal Attainment Scaling (GAS) (Daley, 1987) is especially effective with 1.) supervisees who are more advanced and who have a fair amount of previous supervisor input enabling them to create appropriate and relevant goals, and 2.) supervisees who are self-directed learners who easily set personal development goals for themselves. One of the advantages is that it is supervisee centered.

PERSONAL GOAL	PLAN FOR ACCOMPLISHING	PLAN FOR EVALUATION
To identify patterns more clearly.	*To review videotapes of therapy for one hour weekly & identify information that I overlooked.*	*To bring to supervision three tapes with examples of complex patterns.*

Daley, B. (1987). Goal-attainment scaling: A method of evaluation. Part one. *Journal of Continuing Education in Nursing, 18,* 200-202.

Others Create Instruments: The PCD

Cheryl L. Storm, Charles D. York, & Associates

You and your supervisees can use the instrument presented here to judge supervisees' readiness for advancement to the next level in the clinical sequence of an educational program, for employment advancement in an agency, or to determine supervisees' supervision needs and progress.[1] Although the Post Graduate Competency Document (PCD) reflects the educational philosophy, learning objectives, and theoretical biases of the developers, it can easily be revised to fit your supervision ideas, goals, and setting. It has been adapted for use in doctoral programs, masters programs, agency settings, and by supervisors with private supervision contracts with therapists with varying degrees of experience.

Description of The Instrument

The PCD is based on the idea of supervision being aimed at supervisees' progressive learning of clinical competencies. The competencies are agreed on by consensus of a relevant group of professionals -- in our case a combination of

All it takes to create a similar instrument is for a relevant group -- of supervisors, or supervisees and supervisors -- to define the abilities within each competency area that indicate to them therapists are demonstrating competence.

educators in the field and the supervisors developing the tool. The overall competencies targeted were defined in the now classic paper by Tomm & Wright (1979) and are noted in the chart on the next page. Then, we agreed on specific abilities within each competency. They are abilities we believe competent therapists should demonstrate and we should work for in developing in our supervisees during supervision. These are stated as behavioral objectives. There is also an overall rating.

COMPETENCIES EVALUATED

General Case Management Competencies
Therapists' ability to fulfill agency responsibilities and coordinate their caseload.

Therapeutic Relationship Competencies
Therapists' skill at establishing and maintaining an ongoing relationship with clients.

Perceptual Competencies
Therapists' ability to observe interaction.

Conceptual Competencies
Therapists' skill at integrating these observations with theory.

Structuring Competencies
Therapists' ability to adequately direct therapy.

Intervention Competencies
Therapists' abilities of purposely behaving in a way to facilitate change.

Professional Development Competencies
Therapists' ability to use resources to promote their growth
& present themselves as marriage and family therapists.

The emphasis on the competencies tends to vary over, time based on the developmental stage of supervisees. We have found the following to reflect the normal highs and lows of emphasis according to supervisees' stages in their career. The version presented here is tailored for an intermediate supervisee who is receiving post graduate supervision shortly after completing a masters degree. You can receive a copy of the CD developed to be used with novice therapists by writing Cheryl L. Storm, Pacific Lutheran University, East Campus, Tacoma, Washington, 98447.

COMPETENCIES EMPHASIZED OVER TIME

Supervisee Development

Competencies	Novice Supervisee	Intermediate Supervisee	Advanced Supervisee
Case Management	H	M	L
Therapeutic Relationship	H	M	L
Perceptual	H	M	L
Conceptual	L	H	H
Structuring	H	M	L
Intervention	L	H	L
Professional Development	L	M	H

H = High Emphasis, M = Moderate Emphasis, L = Low Emphasis

Use of the Instrument

You and your supervisees rate the supervisees' ability on the items and are free to write comments explaining ratings, identifying strengths or growth areas not directly addressed or described well in the CD, or to write supplemental data. Although the instrument provides some standardization to the evaluation process, it also allows flexibility for you and your supervisees to add your specific point of view. For example, on one of the items within the Conceptual Competency section a supervisor wrote the following:

5. Therapist ASSESSES EXTRA-FAMILIAL STRESS (i.e., family-of-origin, school or work, other professionals, etc.) upon the system and INTERVENES ACCORDINGLY.

I----------I-----------I-----------I-----------I----------I----------I-----------I-----------I
Unacceptable   Below   Expected   Above   Advanced

Skilled in assessing impact
of extra-familial stress,
~~often intervenes by~~
~~including others~~
*Hesitant to act yet
has good ideas regarding
who to bring together*

Skilled at convening
meetings involving
clients & professionals
regarding treatment

191

In our experience, this instrument is most useful when considered as part of a wider, more encompassing process of evaluation which is highlighted in the box. In otherwords, the areas of competency are always part of the ongoing process of supervision.

OVERVIEW OF SUPERVISION EVALUATION PROCESS

- Supervisory ongoing discussions regarding supervisee progress during supervision.

- Ongoing and formal evaluation of supervision by supervisee.

- Regular discussion among supervisors of supervisees' progress.

- Formal evaluation with supervisee at specified points in time by supervisors.

- Reviews by supervisors and supervisees of client evaluations of therapy.

- Inclusion of supplemental data (e.g., agency personnel, area professionals, and so on).

When used in this way, the PCD becomes a "working document" that pulls together information about supervisees' progress toward the competencies from several sources and from several points in time.

Advantages of This Type of Instrument

If you are supervising within an educational program, training institute, or agency there are a number of advantages for supervisors developing a common evaluation instrument. Doing so encourages supervisors to determine their educational goals for supervision across the clinical experience, which can then be routinely conveyed to new supervisors and supervisees, thus providing continuity and structure to the evaluation process. Supervisees can conduct personal assessments of their progress; and supervisors' thinking, observations, and interventions are channeled in a similar direction. The use of a common instrument, such as this one, can lead to the identification of supervisees' strengths and growth areas which can easily be conveyed from one supervisor to the next, increasing the follow-through of supervision.

We have found this instrument particularly helpful because a pattern forms across items, since they are not mutually exclusive. For example, a supervisee may discover he has difficulty with competencies that involve direct clinical contact (i.e., therapeutic relationship, structuring, or intervention competencies), while he does well in those areas that do not involve client interaction (e.g., perceptual, conceptual, or case management competencies). In this case, the supervisor and supervisee may decide that a career as a therapist is not a good "fit" for the supervisee. If a supervisee is not ready for advancement or there is a serious question regarding a supervisee's appropriateness to become a marriage and family therapist, this tends to emerge clearly as supervisor's and your supervisee's ratings fall below expected on item after item on the instrument.

However, one of the drawbacks of this evaluation instrument is that it is based on a developmental view of competency with the acquisition of abilities assumed to be a steady upward line. Yet, certain abilities may be easier for supervisees at some points rather than at other points in time. Some competencies may even emerge as challenges for a supervisee, when it has appeared that he or she has been steadily developing this competency. For example, one of our supervisees appeared to regress on items addressing engagement, when, in fact, there was not ample opportunity for the issue to surface. She had done exceptionally well with engaging families in treatment as a novice therapist, scoring above expected on the items in the Therapeutic Relationship competency category. However, over time she began to have difficulty maintaining clients engagement after the initial engagement period, when a pattern developed of clients dropping out. Although supervisors stress that supervisees are being assessed as therapists in a particular stage of their development, we have also on occasion had difficulties with some supervisees interpreting their positive evaluations as indicating they have essentially mastered the competencies. They have then overstated their competency and noticeably changed their openness to supervision. Thus, the instrument can suggest supervisees are not increasing their competency when they actually are, or provide a false sense of ability by indicating more competency than exists.

Guidelines for Creating Your Own PCD

All it takes to create a similar instrument is for you or a relevant group -- of supervisors, or supervisees and supervisors -- to define the abilities within each competency area that indicate therapists are demonstrating competence. Then, create a statement regarding a description of what is considered to be an expected ability that indicates the competency. Finally, identify the behaviors that indicate an expected and an above expected rating.

You or any relevant group can also tailor the PCD to your or their preferred therapy and supervision ideas. For example, supervisors who prefer family-of-origin models of therapy will probably want to add items assessing supervisees' recognition of the influence of their own family-of-origin experiences on their work. Revise it as often as you like when your ideas change or when you want it to fit a particular situation.

Tomm, K., & Wright, L. (1979). Training in family therapy: Perceptual, conceptual and executive skills. *Family Process, 18,* 227-250.

Note
[1]Associates include Robert Vincent, Teresa McDowell, & Ronald Lewis, all supervisors for Pacific Lutheran University, Tacoma, Washington.

POSTGRADUATE COMPETENCY DOCUMENT

Therapist Name:_____ Supervisor Name:_____ Date:_____

INSTRUCTIONS
This evaluation is designed to assess development in seven competency areas with a number of specific abilities comprising each competency. A rating at "Expected Competency" signifies achievement of an acceptable level of ability for a postgraduate therapist. A rating below the expected competency level signifies additional ability is required in order to obtain a competent rating. A rating above indicates the therapist's ability exceeds competency expectations and is at the advanced level.

KEY
S = Supervisor evaluation   T = Therapist evaluation

GENERAL CASE MANAGEMENT COMPETENCIES
General case management competencies are the abilities to fulfill agency responsibilities and coordinate a caseload.

---

1. Therapist COMPLETES all PAPERWORK requirements adequately.

I------------I------------I------------I------------I------------I------------I------------I
Unacceptable   Below   Expected   Above   Advanced

                                Complies with basic   Paperwork is
                                   paperwork   thorough, complete,
                                requirements on time   & on time

2.   Therapist COMPLIES with work setting POLICIES and PROCEDURES.
I------------I------------I------------I------------I------------I------------I------------I
Unacceptable   Below   Expected   Above   Advanced

                                Adequately familiar,   Very familiar
                                generally follows policies   & assertively
                                   & procedures   participates in setting
                                                         policies & procedures

3.   Therapist USES DSM IVR appropriately.
I------------I------------I------------I------------I------------I------------I------------I
Unacceptable   Below   Expected   Above   Advanced

                                Consistently uses, with   Bridges with
                                a solid interactional   diagnosis &
                                basis for diagnosis   assists others in
                                                              doing so

4. Therapist USES a model of INTERACTIONAL DIAGNOSTICS appropriately.

I-----------I-----------I-----------I-----------I-----------I-----------I-----------I-----------I

Unacceptable   Below   Expected   Above   Advanced

                              Confident & proficient   Assists others in under-
                              at using interactional model   standing interactional model

5. Therapist DEVELOPS working relationships with REFERRAL SOURCES and other PROFESSIONALS.

I-----------I-----------I-----------I-----------I-----------I-----------I-----------I-----------I

Unacceptable   Below   Expected   Above   Advanced

                              Always contacts & is   Is also contacted
                              beginning to establish   by referral sources, has
                              working relationships   established professional
                                                            relationships

6. Therapist able to INTEGRATE and ESTABLISH collegial working relationships.

I-----------I-----------I-----------I-----------I-----------I-----------I-----------I-----------I

Unacceptable   Below   Expected   Above   Advanced

                              Knows relevant staff, relates   Assuming leadership
                              in a professional manner,   role, viewed as an
                              overall is confident &   established clinician
                              secure in role

COMMENTS:

THERAPEUTIC RELATIONSHIP COMPETENCIES
Therapeutic relationship competencies are the abilities to establish and maintain a therapeutic relationship.

---

1. Therapist CONVEYS RESPECT (understanding, acceptance, and warmth; affirms worth, uniqueness, strengths and potential; and belief in problem solving capacity) to clients.

I-----------I-----------I-----------I-----------I-----------I-----------I-----------I-----------I

Unacceptable   Below   Expected   Above   Advanced

                              Consistently   Communicates even when
                              communicates   clients are upset with
                                                            therapist

2.   Therapist USES SELF in establishing and maintaining the therapeutic relationship.

I----------I-----------I-----------I-----------I-----------I-----------I-----------I-----------I
Unacceptable   Below   Expected   Above   Advanced

                              Own style emerging   Comfortable with
                                                                   own style

3.   Therapist MAINTAINS CLIENTS' engagement in therapy.

I----------I-----------I-----------I-----------I-----------I-----------I-----------I-----------I
Unacceptable   Below   Expected   Above   Advanced

                              Able to maintain clients   Can reengage most clients
                              to appropriate termination   who temporarily drop out
                                 of treatment   of therapy for unknown
                                                                      reasons

COMMENTS:

PERCEPTUAL COMPETENCIES
Perceptual competencies are the abilities to observe therapy interaction.

1.   Therapist OBSERVES global system interactional PATTERNS.

I----------I-----------I-----------I-----------I-----------I-----------I-----------I-----------I
Unacceptable   Below   Expected   Above   Advanced

                              Observes how pattern is similar   Articulates & addresses
                              to other patterns & beginning   more general pattern
                              articulation of more general pattern

2.   Therapist DISTINGUISHES between CONTENT and PROCESS.

I----------I-----------I-----------I-----------I-----------I-----------I-----------I-----------I
Unacceptable   Below   Expected   Above   Advanced

                              Relates appropriately to content   In most cases can move
                                 without losing sight   to process level quickly
                              of process when intervening

3.   Therapist ASSESSES SELF as PART of the SYSTEM.

I----------I-----------I-----------I-----------I-----------I-----------I-----------I-----------I
Unacceptable   Below   Expected   Above   Advanced

                              Includes self in assessment   Constantly aware of
                              & uses self to intervene   influence of self in all
                                                                      interactions

COMMENTS:

CONCEPTUAL COMPETENCIES

Conceptual competencies are the abilities to integrate observations with theory, resulting in appropriate interventions and decisions about treatment goals.

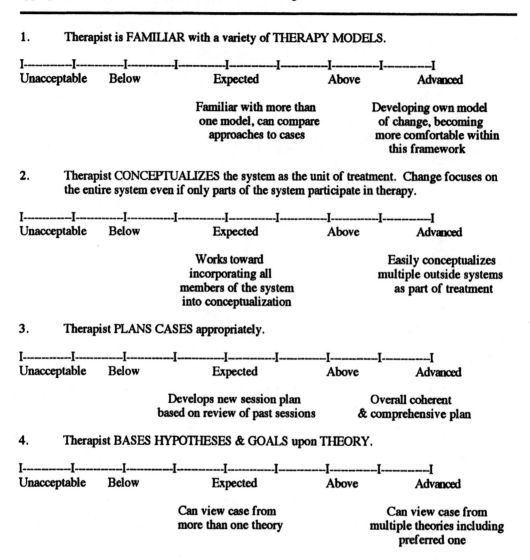

1.   Therapist is FAMILIAR with a variety of THERAPY MODELS.

I-----------I-----------I-----------I-----------I-----------I-----------I-----------I-----------I
Unacceptable   Below   Expected   Above   Advanced

Familiar with more than   Developing own model
one model, can compare   of change, becoming
approaches to cases   more comfortable within
this framework

2.   Therapist CONCEPTUALIZES the system as the unit of treatment. Change focuses on the entire system even if only parts of the system participate in therapy.

I-----------I-----------I-----------I-----------I-----------I-----------I-----------I-----------I
Unacceptable   Below   Expected   Above   Advanced

Works toward   Easily conceptualizes
incorporating all   multiple outside systems
members of the system   as part of treatment
into conceptualization

3.   Therapist PLANS CASES appropriately.

I-----------I-----------I-----------I-----------I-----------I-----------I-----------I-----------I
Unacceptable   Below   Expected   Above   Advanced

Develops new session plan   Overall coherent
based on review of past sessions   & comprehensive plan

4.   Therapist BASES HYPOTHESES & GOALS upon THEORY.

I-----------I-----------I-----------I-----------I-----------I-----------I-----------I-----------I
Unacceptable   Below   Expected   Above   Advanced

Can view case from   Can view case from
more than one theory   multiple theories including
preferred one

5. Therapist ASSESSES EXTRA-FAMILIAL STRESS (i.e., family-of-origin, school or work, other professionals, etc.) upon the system and INTERVENES ACCORDINGLY.

I-----------I-----------I-----------I-----------I-----------I-----------I-----------I
Unacceptable   Below   Expected   Above   Advanced

                          Skilled in assessing impact   Skilled at convening
                            of extra-familial stress,   meetings involving
                              often intervenes by   clients & professionals
                                including others   regarding treatment

6. Therapist ACCOUNTS for MULTICULTURALISM (e.g., race, socioeconomic status, culture, ethnicity, religion, etc.) of self & clients in therapy.

I-----------I-----------I-----------I-----------I-----------I-----------I-----------I
Unacceptable   Below   Expected   Above   Advanced

                            Consistently notes   Consistently notes
                              overt influences   subtle influences

7. Therapist RECOGNIZES how GENDER organizes relationships and therapy.

I-----------I-----------I-----------I-----------I-----------I-----------I-----------I
Unacceptable   Below   Expected   Above   Advanced

                           Recognizes influence of   Recognizes & addresses
                             gender in assessment   subtle influences of gender
                                & intervention   in assessment
                                                             & intervention

COMMENTS:

STRUCTURING COMPETENCIES
Structuring competencies are the abilities to appropriately direct therapy.

1. Therapist RESTRUCTURES client interaction verbally and/or physically.

I-----------I-----------I-----------I-----------I-----------I-----------I-----------I
Unacceptable   Below   Expected   Above   Advanced

                           Consistently intervenes   Consistently intervenes
                         with a variety of theoretically based on own model of
                             based interventions   change

2. Therapist ESTABLISHES and REVIEWS therapy GOALS with clients.

I----------I----------I----------I----------I----------I----------I----------I----------I
Unacceptable   Below   Expected   Above   Advanced

                                Consistently establishes clear,   Bridges client goals with
                                appropriate & realistic goals   those of larger treatment
                                   which guide therapy   context

3. Therapist CONCLUDES TREATMENT in a planned manner.

I----------I----------I----------I----------I----------I----------I----------I----------I
Unacceptable   Below   Expected   Above   Advanced

                                   Determines a mutual   Conclusion of therapy
                                    plan with clients   is ethical as well
                                                                       as cost-effective

COMMENTS:

INTERVENTION COMPETENCIES
Intervention competencies are the abilities to purposely behave in some way to facilitate change.

---

1. Therapist LINKS INTERVENTIONS and THEORY.

I----------I----------I----------I----------I----------I----------I----------I----------I
Unacceptable   Below   Expected   Above   Advanced

                             Theory clearly defined with a   Own theory defined with a
                                variety of alternative   rational for preferred
                                    interventions   interventions

2. Therapist FOLLOWS UP on INTERVENTIONS.

I----------I----------I----------I----------I----------I----------I----------I----------I
Unacceptable   Below   Expected   Above   Advanced

                               Conscientiously follows up   Follows-up & expands on
                                                                        interventions

3. Therapist UTILIZES a wide RANGE of INTERVENTIONS.

I----------I----------I----------I----------I----------I----------I----------I----------I
Unacceptable   Below   Expected   Above   Advanced

                                 Familiar with variety of   Uses a wide range of
                                     interventions   interventions effectively
                                                                       & creatively

COMMENTS:

PROFESSIONAL DEVELOPMENT COMPETENCIES

Professional development competencies are the abilities to use resources to promote growth and present oneself as a marriage and family therapist.

1.   Therapist SEEKS and INCORPORATES FEEDBACK about therapy from supervisor.

I------------I------------I------------I------------I------------I------------I------------I------------I
Unacceptable   Below   Expected   Above   Advanced

A self-directed learner,   Self-supervises &
initiates & pursues   seeks consultation from
constructive feedback   colleagues as normal part
of professional activity

2.   Therapist RECOGNIZES and appropriately DEALS with ETHICAL ISSUES (i.e., recognizes limits of own competency, uses consultation and referral, distinguishes between professional and personal roles, adheres to AAMFT Code of Ethics and practices according to state law, and respects other professionals).

I------------I------------I------------I------------I------------I------------I------------I------------I
Unacceptable   Below   Expected   Above   Advanced

Learning to practice   Highly knowledgeable
according to standards   regarding standards
of practice   of practice

3.   Therapist PRESENTS a PROFESSIONAL IMAGE.

I------------I------------I------------I------------I------------I------------I------------I------------I
Unacceptable   Below   Expected   Above   Advanced

Presents self as a professional who   Has professional identity
is responsible for therapy to clients   of a marriage and family
& other professionals   therapist

4.   Therapist is PREPARED for supervision.

I------------I------------I------------I------------I------------I------------I------------I------------I
Unacceptable   Below   Expected   Above   Advanced

Provides raw data,   Uses opportunity
consistently prepared   for maximum learning
with live, tape, or
case presentation

5.   Therapist is aware of their own PROFESSIONAL DEVELOPMENT process.

I----------I------------I-----------I----------I----------I----------I----------I----------I
Unacceptable   Below   Expected   Above   Advanced

                           Is self-reflective of own work,   General ideas for post-
                           incorporates feedback from self   supervision professional
                              & others to establish   development
                              goals for future growth

COMMENTS:

OVERALL COMPETENCY
This refers to the overall competency of the supervisee.

The therapist's overall competency for this point in his/her career development.

-I----------I-----------I-----------I----------I----------I----------I----------I----------I
Unacceptable   Below   Expected   Above   Advanced

OVERALL COMMENTS:

GOALS FOR FUTURE DEVELOPMENT:

Instrument developed by: Cheryl L. Storm, Charles D. York, Robert Vincent, Teresa
McDowell, & Ronald Lewis.
Copyright © 1997 by Allyn and Bacon

How Are You Doing as a Supervisor? The SFF

Lee Williams

You can use the Supervision Feedback Form (SFF) to obtain information from your supervisees on how well supervision is meeting their needs. In addition, the SFF can help you identify areas of strength and areas for growth in terms of your supervisory skills.

The SFF (Williams, 1994) was designed to be used with supervisees regardless of their theoretical orientation. The top half of the SFF assesses what the supervisory experience is like from a process perspective, while the bottom half assesses how helpful supervision is from an outcome perspective. The SFF illustrated here is only meant to be an example of how a SFF could be designed. In fact, if you design your own SFF you may find the experience helpful in clarifying your thinking about the essential components to supervision. The SFF can also be tailored to you and your supervisees' specific needs. For example, the SFF can be modified to reflect specific skills that are being worked on by either you or your supervisees.

Since the SFF takes less than five minutes to complete, you can have your supervisees routinely fill it out after each supervision experience. The SFF can also be used periodically to provide an overall assessment of supervision. The quantitative data from the SFF makes it easier for you to compare scores across therapists or cases in order to identify possible areas of strength or growth. For example, one supervisor discovered that he was more effective with beginning therapists than more experienced therapists when comparing scores across therapists. Although you can simply rely on the SFF scores for evaluating the supervisory experience, it can also provide an excellent springboard for you and your supervisees to discuss the supervision experience.

Williams, L. M. (1994). A tool for training supervisors: Using the Supervision Feedback Form (SFF). *Journal of Marital and Family Therapy, 20,* 311-315.

SUPERVISION FEEDBACK FORM (SFF)

Using the scale below, please circle the number that best corresponds with how you would describe your supervision experience (this session overall):

0=NOT AT ALL	1=A LITTLE BIT	2=SOMEWHAT
3=A FAIR AMOUNT	4=QUITE A BIT	5=GREAT DEAL

Supervision was relaxed	0	1	2	3	4	5
Supervision was empowering	0	1	2	3	4	5
Supervision was stimulating	0	1	2	3	4	5
Instructions were clear	0	1	2	3	4	5
Supervision was unintrusive	0	1	2	3	4	5
Supervision was collaborative	0	1	2	3	4	5
Supervision was supportive	0	1	2	3	4	5
My supervisor was genuine	0	1	2	3	4	5

Using the scale below, please circle the number that corresponds to how helpful supervision was in each of the following areas:

NA=DID NOT APPLY	0=NOT AT ALL	1=A LITTLE BIT
2=SOMEWHAT	3=A FAIR AMOUNT	4=QUITE A BIT
5=GREAT DEAL		

Developing use-of-self:	NA	0	1	2	3	4	5
Conceptualizing cases:	NA	0	1	2	3	4	5
Developing structuring skills:	NA	0	1	2	3	4	5
Developing interventions:	NA	0	1	2	3	4	5
Developing creativity:	NA	0	1	2	3	4	5
Learning theory:	NA	0	1	2	3	4	5
Developing confidence:	NA	0	1	2	3	4	5
Developing relationship with clients:	NA	0	1	2	3	4	5

Note: Feel free to make any additional comments on the back.

Instrument developed by Lee Williams.

Reprinted from Volume (20), Number (3), of the *Journal of Marital and Family*, Copyright 1994, American Association for Marrriage and Family Therapy. Reprinted with permission.

Bang for Their Buck: Are Supervisees Satisfied?

Cheryl L. Storm, Charles D. York, & Teresa McDowell

Supervisees and their significant others are usually making great personal and financial sacrifices to obtain their supervision. (Remember when you made yours!) In our experience, it is important for supervisees to feel their supervision is worth every dollar spent. When they feel they receive a sound clinical experience with high quality supervision, supervisees believe they have received a lot for their money, since becoming competent in the practice of therapy is why they are making the sacrifices.

On the next page is a quick and easy way to assess if supervisees are satisfied with their supervision. Although the questionnaire is designed to assess supervisee satisfaction with supervision occurring in an educational context, it can easily be revised to fit other ones. For example, the term "practicum" can be replaced with "work setting" and the other items can be changed accordingly for supervisees practicing in agencies or private practices.

The supervisors of the program at Pacific Lutheran University, who developed the instrument, invite you to use it to find out if your supervisees are satisfied! We have used it to obtain group data which has helped us strengthen our supervision practices. Although comments asking for more supervision are predictable, other feedback has helped us become more effective supervisors for our supervisees. For example, when we were told that supervisees wanted more emphasis by supervisors on applying specific therapy approaches, supervisors easily refocused themselves in supervision. It also helps us to evaluate the supervision we provide over time. Although we always ask supervisees for their evaluation of the supervision process and of our work throughout supervision, this instrument provides reticent supervisees another avenue to give constructive input anonymously.

MFT INTERNSHIP EVALUATION FORM

Please circle the response that best represents your opinion: *Strongly Agree (SA) Agree (A) Undecided (U) Disagree (D) Strongly Disagree (SD)*

The following statements pertain to your group supervision:

Group time was structured in a useful way.	SA	A	U	D	SD
Group interaction helped me apply theory & develop interventions.	SA	A	U	D	SD
Group members offered useful feedback in a supportive manner.	SA	A	U	D	SD
My group supervisor helped me discover areas for potential growth & built on my strengths.	SA	A	U	D	SD
My group supervisor offered useful feedback in a supportive manner.	SA	A	U	D	SD
My group supervisor was open to my concerns & problems.	SA	A	U	D	SD
My group supervisor encouraged discussion of gender & multicultural issues.	SA	A	U	D	SD
Overall my group supervision was excellent.	SA	A	U	D	SD
There was a good balance between application & discussion of theory.	SA	A	U	D	SD
Presentations made by other students were helpful to me.	SA	A	U	D	SD
Group interaction supported the development of my own approach.	SA	A	U	D	SD
The supervision atmosphere supported self-reflection.	SA	A	U	D	SD
Group supervision supported my professional development.	SA	A	U	D	SD

The following statements pertain to your individual supervision:

My individual supervisor was open to my concerns and problems.	SA	A	U	D	SD
Given the time limitations of my supervisor, he/she was available to discuss cases.	SA	A	U	D	SD
My individual supervisor offered useful feedback in a supportive manner.	SA	A	U	D	SD
My individual supervisor helped me develop & maintain a clear theoretical direciton in my therapy.	SA	A	U	D	SD
My individual supervisor helped me discover areas for potential growth & built on my strengths.	SA	A	U	D	SD
My individual supervisor encouraged discussion of gender & multicultural issues.	SA	A	U	D	SD
My individual supervisor helped me build confidence in my own competence.	SA	A	U	D	SD
Individual supervision time was structured in a useful way.	SA	A	U	D	SD
My individual supervisor helped me develop my own theory.	SA	A	U	D	SD
Individual supervision supported my professional development.	SA	A	U	D	SD
Overall, my individual supervision was excellent.	SA	A	U	D	SD

The following statements pertain to your internship in general:

I was satisfied with my placement.	SA	A	U	D	SD
I was assigned adequate cases to meet clinical hour requirements.	SA	A	U	D	SD
Supervision and clinical support was adequately available.	SA	A	U	D	SD
My placement setting supported my development as a professional.	SA	A	U	D	SD
Overall, my placement was excellent.	SA	A	U	D	SD

What do you consider to be the strengths of your practicum experience?

What do you consider to be the weaknesses of your practicum experiences?

Resources For Evaluating Supervision

Cleghorn, J., & Levin, S. (1973). Training family therapists by setting learning objectives. *American Journal of Orthopsychiatry, 43*, 439-446.

Flemons, D., Green, S., & Rambo, A. (1996). Evaluating therapists' practices in a postmodern world: A discussion and a scheme. *Family Process, 35*, 43-56.

Piercy, F., Laird, R., & Mohammed, Z. (1983). A family therapist rating scale. *Journal of Marital and Family Therapy, 9*, 49-59.

Liddle, H. (1991). Training and supervision in family therapy: A comprehesive review. In A. Gurman & D. Kniskern (Eds.), *Handbook of family therapy* (vol. 2, pp. 638-697). New York, New York: Brunner/Mazel.

Supervisors who are rated highly by their supervisees track supervisees' concerns while those with low ratings focus almost exclusively on the clients.

Shanfield, S., Mathews, K., & Heatherly, V. (1993). What do excellent psychotherapy supervisors do? *American Journal of Psychiatry, 150*, 1081-1084.

Sharon, D. (1986). The ABCX model: Implications for supervision. In F. Kaslow (Ed.), *Supervision & training: models, dilemmas, and challenges* (pp. 69-94). New York: Haworth Press.

Tomm, K., & Wright, L. (1979). Training in family therapy: Perceptual, conceptual, and executive skills. *Family Process, 18*, 227-250.

Turner, J., & Fine, M. (1995). Postmodern evaluation in family therapy supervision. *Journal of Systemic Therapies, 14*, 57-69.

Wetchler, J. (1989). Supervisors' and supervisees' perceptions of the effectiveness of family therapy supervisor interpersonal skills. *American Journal of Family Therapy, 17*, 244-256.

Wetchler, J., Piercy, F., & Sprenkle, D. (1989). Supervisors' and supervisees' perceptions of the effectiveness of family therapy supervisory techniques. *American Journal of Family Therapy, 19*, 35-47.

Wetchler, J., & Vaughn, K. (1991). Perceptions of primary supervisor interpersonal skills: A critical incident analysis. *Contemporary Family Therapy: An International Journal, 13*, 61-69.

Wetchler, J., & Vaughn, K. (1992). Perceptions of primary family therapy supervisory techniques: A critical incident analysis. *Contemporary Family Therapy: An International Journal, 14*, 127-136.

Williams, L. (1994). A tool for training supervisors: Using the Supervision Feedback Form (SFF). *Journal of Marital and Family Therapy, 20*, 311-315.

V. TRAINING SUPERVISORS:
TEACHING & SUPERVISING

Supervisory Challenge 13: Teaching A Course

A variety of reasons may prompt a therapist to take a course on marriage and family therapy supervision before beginning to supervise. While everyone - supervisors, supervisors-in-training, and the American Association for Marriage and Family Therapy who stipulates training requirements - recognizes that this situation is not ideal from a learning standpoint, nevertheless it is permissible to take a supervision course while still in a doctoral program or before embarking on supervisory practice.

How can you help such a novice supervisor acquire the perceptual, conceptual, and executive skills necessary to become an adequate supervisor? Conceptual skills are easiest to teach; how can teaching be structured to allow the consensual validation needed to ground perceptual skills? Can executive skills be taught through modeling, videotaped examples and role plays? What about the longer-term relationship skills needed for successful supervision?

Most beginning supervisors report a dramatic shift in levels when they stop focusing on the supervisee's case and focus on the larger system of supervisor/supervisee/clients. How can such a shift be facilitated in the absence of supervisees and client families seen under supervision? To the extent that it is impossible to fully achieve such shifts or other important learning, how can you plant the seeds for later learning and identify important resources for later use?

Add Variety to Your Professional Life: Teach a Supervision Course

You can use any or all of the following ideas to design a supervision course for marriage and family therapists in your area who are either interested in diversifying their practices by becoming supervisors or in improving the supervision they already do. Supervisors-in-training are prepared to become supervisors by focusing on the important theories and requisite skills for supervising in today's changing mental health environment. The learning objectives (next page) are consistent with those required by the American Association for Marriage and Family Therapy (AAMFT) for individuals interested in pursuing designation as an Approved Supervisor. The course can be designed for individuals with no supervision experience, but it is typically a better experience for participants if they are currently practicing supervision. You can also design the course to include a supervision-of-supervision component.

A Course That Satisfies the AAMFT Course Requirement

Courses can be approved by the AAMFT which has advantages. When a course is approved, supervisors-in-training only have to verify they took the course rather than completing a course report document describing how they met the required learning objectives. Supervisors offering courses receive free advertising by being on the list of approved courses distributed by AAMFT. See the *AAMFT Approved Supervisor Designation: Standards and Responsibilities* (1991) for details regarding the approval process.

Comprehensive Courses

Comprehensive courses address the topics below via content and learning activities.

Isomorphism Between Therapy & Supervision	Major Models
Supervisory Skills	Record keeping
Supervision Contracts	Methods & Formats
Personal Issues & Supervision	Evaluation
Legal & Ethical Issues	Contextual Issues
Supervisory Relationships	Critical Incidents
Supervisor's Responsibilities	Empirical Findings
Multilevel Supervisory System	Supervision Stages
Supervision-of-Supervision	Supervision Styles
Learning Styles	

PARTICIPANTS LEARN TO

- Be sensitive to the influence of contextual variables (e.g. race, culture, gender, ethnicity, and economics) on supervision.

- Understand ethical and legal issues in supervision. In particular, ethical responsibilities for supervisors are addressed as described in the *American Association for Marriage and Family Therapy (AMFT) Code of Ethical Principles for Marriage and Family Therapists.*

- Distinguish between training, supervision, and consultation.

- Describe several major models of MFT supervision and contrast them in terms of their philosophical assumptions and pragmatic implications.

- Understand the individual, co-therapy, group, and team structures of supervision.

- Observe and describe the co-evolving therapist-client and supervisor-therapist-client relationships.

- Structure supervision, solve problems, and implement supervisory interventions in a range of supervision modalities (i.e., case presentation, audiotape, videotape, and live supervision).

- Monitor, evaluate, and resolve problems in therapist-client and supervisor-therapist-client relationships.

- Articulate a personal model of supervision, drawing from existing models of supervision and from a preferred style of therapy.

- Outline the distinctive issues that arise in supervision-of-supervision.

- If participants are interested in becoming designated an Approved Supervisor by AAMFT, they will understand the requirements and procedures for supervising applicants for AAMFT Clinical Membership and the Approved Supervisor designation as described in the *AAMFT Membership Requirements* and the *AAMFT Approved Supervisor Designation: Standards and Responsibilities.*[1]

---

[1] See page 10 regarding how to obtain these documents.

Suggested Learning Activities and Assignments

STRUCTURE SUPERVISION TO FIT YOU

Create a Supervision Contract

Supervisors-in-training develop a written supervision contract, consistent with their ideas about supervision, by addressing the following: fees, hours, structure, evaluation procedures, case responsibility, caseload review, and procedures for the handling of emergencies. Other items supervisors-in-training may wish to include are: a cancellation policy, guidelines for supervisee presentation of cases, malpractice insurance, policies if supervision terminates prematurely, and ways supervisors-in-training can receive feedback about supervisees' satisfaction with supervision.

Critique Methods of Supervision

Supervisors-in-training can experiment with various methods of supervision (e.g., audiotape, video, live, and so on) or with various formats of supervision (co-therapy, team, group, and so on) then discuss the advantages, disadvantages, and challenges of each. For those supervisors-in-training with no experience as a supervisor, they can describe their own reactions when they experienced the methods or formats as supervisees and discuss their tentative conclusions about using these methods and formats as supervisors.

Practice Videotaped Supervision

Ask supervisors-in-training to supervise a videotaped session of therapy while you play the supervisee. Their assumptions about supervision surface quickly as differences in when they would stop the tape, in information they feel they need, and in the interventions they would make become evident.

Design a Supervisory Form

Supervisors-in-training develop a supervisory form, or revise an existing one. The form should in some way function to structure the supervisory process. For example, it could be a form supervisees use when they present cases or a form supervisors-in-training use to organize observations and ideas during live supervision.

Develop A Process for Evaluation

Supervisors-in-training develop a process for the evaluation of their supervisees. Then, they write a paper describing their method. This paper should address: ongoing evaluation, an end of supervision evaluation, and specific steps they will take when difficulties occur in supervision.

LEARN ABOUT CONTEXTUAL INFLUENCES

Assess the Larger Professional Context
Supervisors-in-training assess how the individual supervisor fits within the structure, both administratively and politically; philosophy, etc. of the organization where they supervise or an organization of their choosing.

Highlight a Contextual Influence
Supervisors -in-training describe in detail an example from their supervision experience (preferably as a supervisor-in-training, but could be as a supervisee) the impact of contextual variables on supervision and therapy, describing appropriate supervisory and therapeutic responsibility for handling instances of contextual "fit" or incongruence, with particular regard for the influence of power and hierarchical imbalances.

Analyze an Ethical or Legal Issue
Supervisors-in-training write a brief synopsis of an ethical or legal issue concerning supervision which has surfaced in their work. If they do not have a suitable issue, they can use one that has been stimulated by the course material. The synopsis includes the nature of the dilemma, why it was a problem, the thought process used in assessing possible responses, and ways the issue could be (was) handled.

Compare Ethical Decision-making
Supervisors-in-training listen to experienced supervisors' responses to ethical scenarios presented to them on the *Where to Draw the Line* videotape (see page 26 for information about obtaining the tape). Initially they hear the scenario presented. The tape is stopped while they formulate their supervisory response. Then they compare their ethical decision-making with the experienced supervisors. Supervisors-in-training determine if their thinking is consistent with others in the field.

Understand the Influence of Work Setting
Supervisors-in-training from different work settings (i.e., agencies, universities, institutes, and private practices) comprise a panel. They compare their approach to contracting and evaluation, their access to supervision structures and formats, and their context specific supervisory challenges.

213

DEVELOP YOUR PHILOSOPHY

Discuss Purist or Eclectic Supervision Philosophies
Supervisors-in-training summarize the relationship between their preferred theory of therapy and their theory of supervision. What are the implications of operating from a specific theoretical framework versus an eclectic orientation?

Simulate The Supervision Experience
Supervisors-in-training provide supervision to another classmate over a number of weeks. This process includes sessions devoted to at least two of the following supervisory methods: audiotape, videotape, and case presentation. A session devoted to live supervision is optional, but encouraged. One of these sessions is videotaped and shown in class. Class members provide peer consultation and feedback regarding the presenter's evolving perceptual, conceptual, executive, and relational skills. Supervisors-in-training write a critique of the supervision and their developing supervisory abilities. Supervisees also critique the supervisory process and the developing skills of supervisors-in-training.
-Sandra A. Rigazio-DiGilio

Write a Philosophy Statement
Supervisors-in-training outline their initial ideas about their philosophy of supervision including their theoretical assumptions, preferred methods and interventions, and evaluation procedures. For those interested in becoming an Approved Supervisor, guidelines are used in preparing the paper from the Standards Committee of AAMFT. If supervisors-in-training have experience supervising, they are encouraged to illustrate their approach with examples.

APPLY YOUR IDEAS

Illustrate Your Supervision Philosophy Via A Case Study
Supervisors-in-training present a videotape of their supervision which illustrates the basic assumptions of their approach to supervision. If supervisors-in-training are not currently supervising, a role play can be substituted. A brief written overview accompanies the presentation which describes the supervisory context, the supervisee, and the goals of the supervision session.

Testing Your Ideas Against the Masters

Thomas C. Todd

I use a tape of a panel I moderated featuring Liddle, Berg, and Freidman (available on video -- see below) in training supervisors for two reasons: 1.) It is difficult to find standard situations where supervisors can compare their responses with other supervisors, especially experienced ones; and 2.) It is useful to have prototypical situations to highlight the importance of theoretical assumptions in supervision. The tape presents three purposely sketchy supervisory vignettes. After the vignettes are presented on the tape, I stop the tape and ask supervisors-in-training to address the same questions the supervisors on the panel will be answering:

- What additional information would you need in order to proceed with supervision?

- What kinds of general assumptions would you make about the case? About the therapist's relation to the case? About your role and relationship as supervisor?

- What would be the focus of your supervision? What kinds of supervisory interventions would you be making?

- How would you judge your effectiveness as a supervisor? What kinds of feedback would you be looking for?

- What would you not do as a supervisor? What would you avoid doing as a supervisor that a supervisor with a different theoretical orientation might do?

We then watch the responses the three panelists have to the cases. We pay particular attention to the theoretical differences that account for differences between panelists and with them.

Using the video in this way can be particularly stimulating in a course because class members can clarify their own perspectives and compare them. It can also be useful when working only with one supervisor, to counteract the absence of other supervisors for consensual validation.

Berg, I., Freidman, E., Liddle, H., & Todd, T. *Fielding supervision impasses.* (Video #531). Norcross, VA: The Resource Link.

A Personal Examination of Assumptions & Practices

Sandra A. Rigazio-DiGilio

You can use this four part exercise to assist supervisors-in-training to review their own supervision experiences and examine their supervisory assumptions. The exercise, derived from the systemic cognitive-developmental model (see chapter 14) helps supervisors-in-training explore the experiences they have had from the unique vantage point of each cognitive-developmental orientation. When you bring supervisors-in-training through this process, you encourage them to learn about each of the four orientations and to experience how working within each one extends and enhances their way of experiencing, understanding, and operating as supervisors.

PART ONE: Primary Experiences in Supervision

This part of the exercise provides a structured framework for supervisors-in-training to review their own supervision experiences by gathering sensimotor/elemental data without actually working to frame the information. This enables supervisors-in-training to begin a journey wherein they construct multiple perspectives and feelings regarding their memory search on this topic.

PART TWO: Narrative Recollection of These Experiences

This part of the exercise provides a structured set of concrete/situational questions that supervisors-in-training can use to recollect their primary supervision experiences. It serves to provide a template to organize their thoughts and feelings as these are recollected for each supervisory experience. As they answer these questions, experiences, thoughts, and feelings may begin to resonate into themes about supervision.

PART THREE: Primary Themes Across Experiences

This part of the exercise provides a structured set of formal/reflective questions that supervisors-in-training can use to develop an awareness of their emerging themes regarding how to frame the process of supervision. Additionally, they can begin to examine ways to enhance and modify their emerging themes.

PART FOUR: Basic Assumptions About Supervisorn

This final aspect of the exercise draws on the information gathered in the first three parts. It includes a set of dialectic/systemic questions that supervisors-in-training can use to identify their perspectives regarding supervision and then requests that they try to understand the underlying assumptions inherent in their evolving perspectives. Supervisors-in-training begin to examine and refine the constructions they have evolved during their supervisory journey as well as the ramifications of these constructions.

PART ONE: AN ACCOUNTING OF SUPERVISORY EXPERIENCE(S)

Complete the following graph by listing, in chronological order, the supervisory relationships you have experienced to date.

Starting Date	Length of Experience	Frequency of Meetings	Modalities Used	Supervisor: *Discipline, Age, Gender, Race, Years of Experience*	Super-visory Setting	Clinical Setting	Significance 1 to 5/Why

This exercise is reproduced here by permisssion of S. Rigazio-DiGilio, copyright 1995.

PART TWO: NARRATIVE RECOLLECTIONS OF PRIMARY SUPERVISORY EXPERIENCE(S)

Provide narrative recollections of your primary supervisory relationships.

- How would you describe your stage of development at the time this supervision took place?

- How would you describe the supervisor's relational style?

- How would you define the supervisor's theoretical perspective and therapeutic approach?

- How would you describe the supervisor's supervisory perspective and supervisory approach?

- What were the supervisor's expectations of you and what were your expectations of the supervisor?

- What was the most salient aspect of this supervisory relationship?

- What was the most significant obstacle to your development in this relationship?

PART THREE: THEMES ACROSS SUPERVISORY ENCOUNTERS

Looking back on each of these experiences, reflect upon each of the following:

- Your learning style and how it has changed over time. How will this affect your supervision style?

- Your relational style and how it has changed over time. How will this affect your supervision style?

- Your supervisory expectations and how these have changed over time. How will this knowledge affect your perspective of the supervisory process as it develops over time?

- Your personal barriers to learning and development, and how these were handled in each supervisory relationship. How will this knowledge influence the process of your supervision?

- Your reaction to male and female supervisors. How will this influence your work with male and female supervisees?

- Your reaction to other contextual variables (e.g., ethnicity, socio-economic status, career status, educational degree, age).

- How will this influence your supervision style? What are the personal qualities you want to enhance or avoid in your role as supervisor? What are the skills you want to learn or avoid in your development as a supervisor?

This exercise is reproduced here by permisssion of S. Rigazio-DiGilio, copyright 1995.

218

PART FOUR: BASIC ASSUMPTIONS UNDERLYING THE SUPERVISORY PROCESS

Using parts one tothree as a base, respond to each of the following questions.

- What are the goals and objectives of supervision?

- How is movement toward these goals and objectives facilitated in supervision?

- How is movement toward these goals and objectives impeded in supervision?

- What is the responsibility and role of the supervisor?

- What is the responsibility and role of the supervisee?

- After completing this exercise, what awareness have you gained about the basic assumptions underlying your perspective of the supervisory process?

- What are the potential strengths of these assumptions?

- What are the potential limitations of these assumptions? How does your own developmental and contextual history influence these assumptions?

- How does your current context influence these assumptions?

Resources for Teaching Supervision

Bruenlin, D., Liddle, H., & Schwartz, R. (1988). Concurrent training of supervisors and therapists. In H. Liddle, D. Breunlin, & R. Schwartz (Eds.), *Handbook of family therapy training and supervision* (pp. 207-224). New York: Guilford Press.

Caldwell, K., & Diamond, D. (1996). In the cauldron: A case study of training for clinical supervisors. *Supervision Bulletin, 9, 6 & 7.*

Clarkson, P., & Gilbert, M. (1991). The training of counselor trainers and supervisors. In W. Dryden, & B. Thorne (Eds.), *Training and supervision for counseling in action* (pp. 143-169). London: Sage.

Heath, A., & Storm, C. (1985). From the ivory tower to the institute: The live supervision stage approach for teaching supervision in academic settings. *American Journal of Family Therapy, 13,* 27-36.

A qualitative study of supervisors taking a supervsion course found they experience tension and change around coping with complexity, integrating theory into practice, taking on the evaluative role, and increasing awareness of liability and ethical concerns in their supervision.

Caldwell, K., Diamond, D., & Furrow, J. (1995). *In the cauldron: A case study of training for clinical supervisors.* Unpublished paper.

Liddle, H., Breunlin, D., Schwartz, R., & Constantine, J. (1984). Training family therapy supervisors: Issues of content, form, and context. *Journal of Marital and Family Therapy, 14,* 293-303.

Storm, C. *Marketing supervision tutorials* (Video #533). Washington, DC: The American Association for Marriage and Famiy Therapy.

220

Supervisory Challenge 14: Supervising Supervisors

We both know of therapists who are outstanding clinicians (in large part due to the excellent supervision they received), but have been fired from agencies because they could not adequately manage the paperwork aspects of their jobs and became expensive cogs in their organizations. Out of work and seen as a kiss of death for public agencies and needing similar skills to survive in private practice, these clinicians are in serious danger of remaining permanently unemployed. It is hard to believe any supervisors would want this to be the result of their labor.

When we supervise supervisors, we spend increasing amounts of time focusing on how they are preparing their supervisees for today's work world. Helping supervisors-in-training to manage the multiple levels of the supervisory system, deal with increased gatekeeping responsibilities, and develop philosophies of supervision are some of the ways supervising supervisors is distinctive from supervising therapists (see chapter 27). We ecourage our supervisors-in-training to expand their views of the supervision system even further to include the larger health care context. For example, how are they helping their supervisees develop treatment plans which reflect family therapy goals and fulfill organizations' requirements for funding? We encourage our supervisors-in-training to expand their gatekeeping function beyond the idea of evaluating their supervisees' clinical competency (and only casually evaluating their case management abilities) to evaluating their supervisees' overall professional competency. And finally, we also encourage our supervisors-in-training to enlarge their philosophies of supervision to encompass the whole professional.

What competencies do supervisors-in-training believe novice therapists need to have to survive in todays professional climate? How do they help supervisees clinically deal with limitations on resources with therapeutic integrity? How do they assist their supervisees to learn to balance their love of clinical work with the other type of work requirements that exist? How do you supervise supervision so supervisors-in-training consider the wider professional context, expand their gatekeeping role, and develop theories of supervision that prevent us from having a generation of unemployed clinicians like those cited above?

A Spin-Off of Your Supervision Contract

Your supervision of supervision contract will in all likelihood be a spin-off of your supervision contract and include similar components (see chapter 19). However, there are certain aspects that receive special attention (see chart below), since this contract is the agreement reached regarding supervision-of-supervision. Certain components must be revised to highlight the development of supervisors-in-training and their ability to supervisee. For example, evaluation procedures are changed to assess supervisors'-in-training rather than supervisees' competencies, raw data refers to the supervision sessions not the therapy sessions, and the contract addresses how you and your supervisors-in-training are creating an effective *supervision learning context* for them that has some breadth.

Although you are more removed from the actual clinical work of supervisees, you are however ultimately responsible for the clinical services they provide. Because you are responsible as well as privy to the therapy being done by

---

SPECIFIC ASPECTS RECEIVING SPECIAL ATTENTION

- **Evaluation**
- **Use of Raw Data**
- **Learning Context**
- **Supervisory Disclosure to Supervisees & Clients**
- **Emergencies**
- **Documentation of Supervisees' Therapy**

---

supervisees and their supervision, you must address with supervisors-in-training disclosure to clients and supervisees of your involvement. Most supervisors request that their name be given to clients and supervisees with a description of their role. It is also important to be included in the information loop regarding emergencies and risky situations since you will be looked to ethically and legally as the person at the top of the pyramid of responsibility. Similarly, because you verify the clinical and supervision hours being done by supervisees, you must develop a method for keeping accurate records via your supervisor-in-training. (Remember you have no direct contact with the supervisees!)

Supervisor-In-Training Evaluation Form

Susan H. McDaniel, Susan H. Horwitz, Pieter le Roux

The supervisor-in-training evaluation form is an assessment tool to help supervisors and supervisors-in-training in the overall appraisal of the progress of supervision. We have found it to be a versatile supervision and educational aid. Supervision is a complex and multi-faceted process. It is therefore often difficult to consistently keep track of all the aspects involved. The form provides an organized and systematic review format.

Although originally designed for the supervisor-in-training working in group supervision, the form can be modified for individual supervision as well as for the needs within different supervisory settings such as community agencies, hospital based clinics, or academic institutions. The form covers areas such as the overall process of supervision, the quality of conceptual, perceptual, and executive skills (Tomm & Wright, 1979); case management, group process, the ability of the supervisor-in-training to evaluate the progress of supervision, family-of-origin issues (McDaniel & Landau-Stanton, 1991), and issues related to professional growth.

Completion of the form can take 10-15 minutes. In our context, supervisors and supervisors-in-training complete the form separately and then compare and discuss their evaluations during subsequent supervision meetings.

Thorough planning will enhance the different ways in which the evaluation instrument can be used to:

1.) Address contractual arrangements. During the planning phase of supervision, supervisors and supervisors-in-training use the form to discuss how they plan to work, and how they plan to assess and review the progress of supervision. It can help to define and set exceptions, and it can help to describe the scope of what will be involved in supervision.

2.) Develop a focus. The form can be used during any stage of supervision to develop a focus (e.g., focusing on executive skills, case management, and so on). It provides a systematic way to negotiate and renegotiate specific points of focus during the different phases of supervision.

3.) Set goals. The form is specifically well suited to help specify short and long term goals. Different goals for different supervisory situations can also be formulated, for example focusing on specific family-of-origin issues in one situation versus concentrating on facilitating group process more effectively in another situation.

4.) Assess progress. The form can be used to assess the overall progress of supervision during different developmental stages, such as during the beginning and during the end phase of supervision; or it can be used during regular intervals.

5.) Conduct self-evaluation. Self-evaluation is an important part of supervision. Supervisors as well as supervisors-in-training use the form to evaluate their own progress. They can also explore their own questions at different times during their development or during their work with a specific supervisee by using the form.

6.) Use as a checklist. The form can also be used as a checklist to make sure that the important aspects are covered during supervision.

McDaniel, S., & Landau-Stanton, J. (1991). Family-of-origin work and family therapy skills training: Both-and. *Family Process, 30,* 459-471.

Tomm K., & Wright L. (1979). Training in family therapy: Perceptual, conceptual, and executive skills. *Family Process, 8,* 227-250.

UNIVERSITY OF ROCHESTER
SUPERVISOR-IN-TRAINING EVALUATION FORM

Supervisor-in-training:_____   Date: _____

Supervision Setting/Format:_____

Supervisees:_____   _____

                _____   _____

                _____   _____

Key To Skill Development

1=Underdeveloped   2=Just Beginning   3=Acceptable   4=Good
                5=Advanced & Creative

Overall Approach to Supervisory Process:	1	2	3	4	5
Open to supervision					
Sets appropriate goals for professional growth					
Fosters own growth through:					
Reading					
Workshops					
Presentations					
Role model for supervisees					
Respects time boundaries					
Establishes appropriate leadership role					
Handles disagreements with supervisor constructively					

Conceptual & Perceptual Skills:	1	2	3	4	5
Clarifies theoretical issues					
Links theory to cases					
Assigns appropriate readings					
Discusses readings					
Helps supervisees track process in cases on video & behind the mirror					
Uses video to teach specific points					

Executive Skills:	1	2	3	4	5
Addresses with supervisees:					
Goal-setting for cases					
Goal-setting for sessions					
Intake skills					
Helping family to adjust to team approach & video					
Genograms					
Time boundaries					
Extra-sessions boundaries					
Balancing alliances					
Networking					
Homework assignments					

Executive Skills (continued):

	1	2	3	4	5
Homework follow-up					
Terminating					
Appropriately firm with supervisees					
Appropriately empathic with supervisees					
Pitches interventions appropriate to level of supervisees					
Uses humor appropriately					
Creative supervisory interventions					
Phone calls are clear, appropriate & concise during live supervision					

Management of Cases:

	1	2	3	4	5
Cases successfully treated					
Tracks supervisees' casework responsibilities					
Tracks supervisees' paperwork responsibilities					
Aware & up-to-date on homework assignments					

Group Process:

	1	2	3	4	5
Has supervisees set appropriate individual goals for training					
Elicits & uses each supervisees' strengths					
Appropriate use of self-discipline					
Involves supervisees' from behind the mirror					
Fosters group collaboration on cases					
Channels competition constructively					
Utilizes intragroup gender issues to facilitate treatment & training					
Uses group members for interventions when appropriate					
Organizes session breaks effectively & efficiently during live supervision					
Polls each member for ideas before final interventions during live supervision					

Family-of-Origin Issues:

	1	2	3	4	5
Progress on own family-of-origin issues					
Has each supervisee present family of origin					
Links family-of-origin issues to supervisee's role as therapist					
Links family-of-origin issues to case materials					
Sensitive to supervisee's current family issues & their influence on supervision & treatment					

Evaluation:

Gives direct feedback

Formulates strategies to resolve supervisee
stuckness

Each supervisee receives verbal & written feedback
at the end of the year

Facilitates group evaluation

	1	2	3	4	5

Encourages Professional Growth:

Encourages long-term planning for professional
growth

Encourages relevant workshops

Attends national family therapy meetings

Presents at national family therapy meetings

Attends local workshops/seminars

Presents at local workshops/seminars

Publishes papers or books

Creates own teaching/supervision tapes

	1	2	3	4	5

Comments:

Instrument developed by S. McDaniel, S. Horwitz, & P. le Roux.

Resources For Supervising Supervisors

Constantine, J., Piercy, F., & Sprenkle, D. (1984). Live supervision-of-supervision in family therapy. *Journal of Marital and Family Therapy, 10*, 95-97.

Edwards, J. (1989). On being supervised as a supervisor. *Illinois Association for Counseling and Development Quarterly, 112*, 11-22.

Fine, M., & Fennell, D. (1985). Supervising the supervisor-of-supervision: A supervision of supervision technique or a hierarchical blurring? *Journal of Strategic and Systemic Therapies, 4*, 55-59.

Supervisors reported their criteria for accepting a prospective supervisor-in-training as having good clinical skills, exhibiting personal maturity, and demonstrating interest.

Wilcoxen, S. (1992). Criteria for selection and retention of supervisees: A survey of Approved Supervisors. *Family Therapy, 19*, 17-24.

MacKinnon, L. (1986). Supervision and supervision-of-supervision, one perspective. *Australian and New Zealand Journal of Family Therapy, 7*, 133-139.

Westheafer, C. (1990). Intervening in a rigid supervisory system: A Bowen/structural view of neutrality. *Australian and New Zealand Journal of Family Therapy, 11*, 148-153.

Wilcoxen, S. (1992). Criteria for selection and retention of supervisees: A survey of Approved Supervisors. *Family Therapy, 19*, 17-24.

Wright, L., & Coppersmith, E. (1983). Supervision-of-supervision: How to be meta to a metaposition. *Journal of Strategic and Systemic Therapies, 2*, 40-50.

Printed in the United States
1207500001B/99-103